CHURCH AND STATE IN CONTEMPORARY EUROPE

BOOKS OF RELATED INTEREST

The Enlarged European Union: Diversity and Adaptation
edited by Peter Mair and Jan Zielonka

The Swiss Labyrinth: Institutions, Outcomes and Redesign
edited by Jan-Erik Lane

Europeanised Politics? European Integration and National Political Systems
edited by Klaus H. Goetz and Simon Hix

Recasting European Welfare States
edited by Maurizio Ferrera and Martin Rhodes

The Changing French Political System
edited by Robert Elgie

Compounded Representation in West European Federations
edited by Joanne B. Brzinski, Thomas D. Lancaster and Christian Tuschhoff

Politics and Policy in Democratic Spain: No Longer Different?
edited by Paul Heywood

Britain in the Nineties: The Politics of Paradox
edited by Hugh Berrington

Crisis and Transition in Italian Politics
edited by Martin Bull and Martin Rhodes

Southern European Welfare States: Between Crisis and Reform
edited by Martin Rhodes

The Euro-Mediterranean Partnership: Political and Economic Perspectives
edited by Richard Gillespie

The State in Western Europe: Retreat or Redefinition?
edited by Wolfgang C. Müller and Vincent Wright

The Regions and the European Community
edited by Robert Leonardi

The Regional Dimension of the European Union
edited by Charlie Jeffery

National Parliaments and the European Union
edited by Philip Norton (new in paperback)

CHURCH AND STATE IN CONTEMPORARY EUROPE

The Chimera of Neutrality

Editors

JOHN T.S. MADELEY
ZSOLT ENYEDI

Routledge
Taylor & Francis Group

LONDON AND NEW YORK

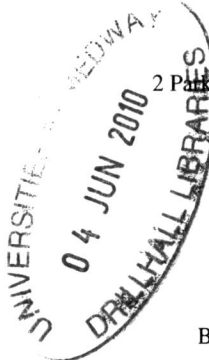

First Published in 2003 in Great Britain by
Routledge
2 Park Square, Milton Park, Abingdon, Oxon, OX14 4RN
270 Madison Ave, New York NY 10016

Transferred to Digital Printing 2010

Website: www.routledge.com

Copyright © 2003 Routledge Publishers

British Library Cataloguing in Publication Data

Church and state in contemporary Europe: the chimera of neutrality
1. Church and state – Europe 2. Religion and state – Europe
I. Madeley, John T.S. II. Enyedi, Zsolt
322.1′094

ISBN 0 7146 5394 2 (hb)
ISBN 0 7146 8329 9 (pb)

Library of Congress Cataloging-in-Publication Data

Church and state in contemporary Europe: the chimera of neutrality /
editors, John T.S. Madeley, Zsolt Enyedi.
    p. cm.
Includes bibliographical references and index.
    ISBN 0-7146-5394-2 (cloth) – ISBN 0-7146-8329-9 (paper)
    1. Church and state – Europe. I. Madeley, John T.S., 1944–
Enyedi, Zsolt.
    BR735 .C485 2003
    322′.1′094–dc21   2002153289

This group of studies first appeared in a Special Issue of
West European Politics (ISSN 0140-2382) Vol.26, No.1 (January 2003),
[Church and State in Contemporary Europe: The Chimera of Neutrality].

Publisher's Note
The publisher has gone to great lengths to ensure the quality of this reprint
but points out that some imperfections in the original may be apparent.

Contents

European Liberal Democracy and the Principle
of State Religious Neutrality   **John T.S. Madeley**   1

A Framework for the Comparative Analysis of
Church–State Relations in Europe   **John T.S. Madeley**   23

Church–State Separation Swedish-Style   **Göran Gustafsson**   51

The Illusion of State Neutrality in a
Secularising Ireland   **Bill Kissane**   73

The Italian State: No Longer Catholic,
no Longer Christian   **Mark Donovan**   95

Orthodoxy and Nationalism in the
Greek Case   **George Th. Mavrogordatos**   117

Catholicism and Democratic Consolidation
in Spain and Poland   **John Anderson**   137

The Contested Politics of Positive Neutrality
in Hungary   **Zsolt Enyedi**   157

The Catholic Church and Civil Society:
Democratic Options in the Post-Communist
Czech Republic   **Joan O' Mahony**   177

The Policy Impact of Church–State Relations:
Family Policy and Abortion in Britain, France,
and Germany   **Michael Minkenberg** 195

Conclusion: Emerging Issues in the Study
of Church–State Relations   **Zsolt Enyedi** 218

Abstracts   233

Notes on Contributors   238

Index   241

European Liberal Democracy and the Principle of State Religious Neutrality

JOHN T.S. MADELEY

Far from being a subject of interest only to antiquarians or canon lawyers, the field of church–state relations in Europe represents an interconnected series of issues, institutional arrangements and processes, which collectively present something of a challenge to political science. Towards the close of the twentieth century a number of live issues served as a reminder that the subject was neither dead nor sleeping, even in the relatively secular environment of Western Europe where the more direct impact of the collapse of communism further east was not felt. Instances of religio-political controversy included the renegotiation of concordats, for example in the 1980s in Italy, the recognition (or otherwise) by public authorities in a number of countries of Scientology as a religion, French state support for private, in the main Catholic, schools, or, in Britain, the problems arising over Islamic religious sensibilities (the Rushdie case, religious schools and so on). Nor did the opening of the twenty-first century fulfil millennial hopes of peace and harmony on this front; instead, the cataclysmic events of 11 September 2001 in America and their continuing aftermath across the world have threatened to aggravate tensions between Muslims, Christians and secular liberals across Europe as elsewhere. Continuing international conflicts in the Middle East and South Asia have also served to raise questions about the contribution religion makes to their causes or their course, while Cassandras like Samuel Huntington have painted doom-laden scenarios of a coming clash of civilisations.[1] Seen in a world context, Europe, the principal theatre of the now extinct Cold War, might appear to be 'The Quiet Continent', but it too is reverberating to new religio-political challenges which in a number of cases have served only to resurrect some of the old.[2] Among the 'new–old' challenges are the perennial questions of how to accommodate refugees, asylum seekers and economic migrants, often of quite alien cultural-religious backgrounds; how to settle disputes over the restitution of church property or religious freedom issues in the transitional societies of the former communist bloc countries; and, not least, how to purge the poison of ethno-religious conflicts on Europe's several peripheries such as Northern Ireland, Cyprus, Nagorno Karabakh and the former Yugoslavia, a distinctive internal or 'interface' periphery.

Casanova, Kepel and others have argued that the latter-day emergence or re-emergence of troublesome issues such as these represents a significant cultural shift towards the deprivatisation, and repoliticisation, of religion.[3] Numerous authors have used the term 'resurgence' to describe either a widespread revival of religion itself or a developing context in which religion-related issues have become newly controversial in politics.[4] In the case of Western Europe there is little evidence of a resurgence of religion as such, except at the margins; rather, as Crouch points out, in terms of the conventional indicators of religious activity and attitudes there is plenty of evidence of continuing and, in some cases, steepening decline.[5] The overall picture in Europe is, however, more ambiguous and varies widely from place to place; since approximately 1990 there is evidence both of religious revival (for example in Russia) and of religious decline (for example in Poland, a part of eastern Europe where the Catholic Church is no longer able to act as a vehicle for anti-regime sentiment). And there are few parts of the Continent where the presence of 'non-traditional' sects, cults and other unconventional religious movements has not been controversial; here the old arguments for religious liberty and tolerance have once more had to be deployed in support of the requirements of the UN Universal Declaration of Human Rights with its requirement for respecting freedom of thought, conscience and religion.[6] It is probably no exaggeration to say that almost nowhere in Europe's 50-odd sovereign territories are significant issues of the relationship between religious organisations, society and the state completely absent from the political agenda. Their salience and significance, as well as their precise content, varies enormously as between different religious, cultural and political contexts, however, and one of the first presenting questions is how these variations may be identified and accounted for.

In most cases, the hand of history is all too visible. Take, for example, the case of the United Kingdom, which is otherwise not much considered in the contributions to this volume; it may have avoided revolutionary upheaval since the late seventeenth century but, in a manner which seems increasingly bizarre, it still parades the stigmata of that age of open religious conflict. At the end of May 2002, just before the main celebration of Queen Elizabeth II's Golden Jubilee, Britain's leading liberal daily newspaper, *The*

Guardian, launched a campaign for the repeal or amendment of the 1701 Act of Settlement.[7] This Act had legislated that only Protestant heirs of Princess Sophia of Hanover, granddaughter of James I of England (VI of Scotland) could succeed to the throne, thereby ruling out of consideration any 'who are or shall be reconciled to or shall hold communion with the see of Rome or shall profess the popish religion or shall marry a papist'. *The Guardian*'s campaign was only one of a number of reminders in 2002 that almost all the central political institutions of the United Kingdom continue to be marked by arrangements inherited from the age of the confessional state. The forthcoming retirement of the Archbishop of Canterbury had also brought into action the machinery for appointing a successor, which involved the final choice (between two candidates submitted by the Crown Appointments Commission) being made by the prime minister. The actual appointment itself is made, of course, by the Queen in her capacity as 'supreme governor' of the Church of England, bound as she is by her coronation oath of 50 years ago to maintain the established Protestant religion in the United Kingdom. Once appointed, the new Archbishop will as a matter of course join 25 other senior bishops of the established church as 'Lords Spiritual' in the upper chamber of the legislature, the House of Lords. Recent government proposals to reform the House, which would *inter alia* have reduced the bishops' representation in favour of a more proportional representation (by appointment, not election) of the principal 'faith communities' to be found in the UK, have been shelved for lack of consensus. In the elected House of Commons, meantime, only at the 2001 election was the ban on the election of priests lifted after the repeal of restrictive provisions in no fewer than nine pieces of legislation.[8] The difficulty of reforming such arcane provisions was indicated during a 'ten-minute rule' House of Commons debate in February 2002 on the repeal of the Act of Succession during which it was objected that such a move 'would be daunting, requiring the amendment of at least eight other pieces of legislation ... and needing identical legislation in at least 15 Commonwealth countries'.[9]

The *Guardian* called the Act of Settlement 'the last blatantly anti-Catholic piece of legislation left on the statute book', a raft of other such legislation discriminating against religious minorities having been progressively repealed since the abolition of the Test and Corporation Acts in 1827 and the passing two years later of the Catholic Relief Act, which first removed the general prohibition against any Catholic holding public office. In 1998 the European Convention of Human Rights had finally been incorporated into the law of the United Kingdom, thereby outlawing discrimination on grounds of sex, race and religion and making the provisions of the 1701 Act anomalous, if not unenforceable. It was conceded that it was 'part of the complex web of arcane legislation that binds our monarch and government with the Church of England' and that 'repealing it could well lead to the disestablishment of the church'.[10] This prospect had evidently served as no deterrent however – rather, probably as a further incentive – to the 150 members of the Houses of Commons and Lords who, along with a number of religious leaders, had signed up to the campaign. While a number of bishops and other leaders of opinion in the Anglican church had recently spoken out in favour of disestablishment, the soon-to-retire Archbishop, George Carey, argued in a speech delivered on St George's day that church establishment was an essential bulwark of British society.[11] Significantly, it remains the position of the Labour government that it 'would not contemplate disestablishment of the Church of England unless the Church itself wished it'.[12]

The occasionally bizarre and anomalous sets of arrangements which are conventionally referred to under the label 'church–state relations' can of course be dismissed as much less important than they are colourful. Alternatively, it can be argued that, in a period where religion-related controversies seem to have a rising profile, such anomalies deserve serious attention, not least from political scientists, who have tended collectively to ignore the subject. The fact of this neglect is perhaps all the more surprising because of the great stress given by normative political theorists of a liberal persuasion to the principle of the neutrality in matters of religion of the liberal democratic state and its arrangements. With this in mind one might have expected greater attention to be paid to the many different ways in which actual arrangements in Europe have deviated – and continue to deviate, some more, some less – from any feasible notion of neutrality. To examine why, and in what ways, this has been – and continues to be – the case requires the development of an approach to the subject, which facilitates comparative understanding. One place to start is with liberal political philosophy itself.

NORMATIVE PRINCIPLES OF STATE RELIGIOUS NEUTRALITY

Since the mid-1970s a number of distinguished political philosophers have developed a doctrine of state neutrality, which, while far from uncontested, has come to constitute a central plank of liberal thinking about the state and its ethical dimensions. At its simplest, a neutral state is seen as 'one that deals impartially with its citizens and which remains neutral on the issue of what sort of lives they should lead'.[13] Neutrality in this sense is not seen as merely one of a number of desirable features a liberal political system should exhibit; for many it is to be regarded as 'the defining feature of liberalism: a liberal state *is* a state which imposes no conception of the good upon its citizens but which allows individuals to pursue their own good in their own way'.[14] While of relatively recent date, the doctrine is not intrinsically novel, however; rather, it represents the latest statement of a position which liberals have occupied for centuries, its ancestry traceable directly through John Stuart Mill and Emmanuel Kant at least as far as John Locke.[15]

Kymlicka presents the doctrine as a corollary of the liberty principle which John Rawls laid out in his influential treatise *A Theory of Justice* in 1972; attachment to this principle 'should lead us to endorse a "neutral state" – i.e. a state which does not justify its actions on the basis of the intrinsic superiority or inferiority of conceptions of the good life, and which does not deliberately attempt to influence people's judgements of the value of these different conceptions'.[16] Locke's earlier arguments for the toleration of various forms of religious faith (other than those of Catholics, anti-Trinitarians and atheists!) and Mill's for freedom of individual choice in lifestyle matters are thus generalised to a demand for state neutrality when it comes to citizens choosing between 'conceptions of the good life'. Attention to citizens' moral autonomy and to considerations of justice requires that the state neither favour nor disfavour any particular conception of the good life, any more than neutrality in time of war can allow a state to involve itself on behalf of any belligerent.

Even in the study of international relations, where the term neutrality has long been at home, it is not by any means an uncomplicated or uncontroversial concept; nor does its metaphorical transfer to the sphere of the proper relations between states and citizens make it any less so. The debates between Nozick, Dworkin, Ackerman, Barry and others have led to the development of rival conceptual analyses which have spawned a number of subsidiary distinctions, for example between positive and negative, consequential and intentional (or justificatory), formal, substantive and disaggregated, neutrality, and between non-interventionist, equal promotionist, Benthamite (or utilitarian) and proceduralist versions.[17] Thus, for example, Raz distinguishes two distinct neutrality principles, which he labels 'neutral political concern' and 'exclusion of ideals', before going on to criticise both and advocate his own, perfectionist, viewpoint.[18] The first of these principles requires that government action should not help or hinder any life-plan or way of life more than any other and that the consequences of government action should therefore be neutral. The 'exclusion of ideals' principle, on the other hand, requires only that the state be precluded from justifying its actions on the basis of a preference for any particular way of life, even though the consequences of government action for different life-plans may be unequal. Kymlicka argues that consequential neutrality is inconsistent with Rawls' two fundamental components of liberal justice: respect for liberty and fairness in the distribution of material resources.[19] Simply by upholding respect for civil liberties, government action is bound to have non-neutral consequences insofar as free competition for adherents will almost always lead to some ways of life prevailing over others. Justificatory neutrality involving 'exclusion of ideals', on the other hand, is quite compatible with Rawls' conception of justice as fairness. Here the government expresses no preference for any way of life, and individuals or groups are precluded from using 'the coercive apparatus of the state to win for themselves a greater liberty or larger distributive share on the grounds that their activities are of more intrinsic value'.[20]

Liberal political philosophers have not had the field entirely to themselves, of course, even in the liberal democracies. As Eric Mack noted in 1988: 'In recent years the increased strength and assertiveness of socially conservative movements have heightened public debate about the legitimate role of the state in enforcing moral prescriptions that are arguably the product of particular, sectarian, religious or moral perspectives.'[21] In particular, the political resurgence starting in the 1970s of the religious right in the USA and of movements in many countries opposed to the liberalisation of the abortion laws has underlined the perennial character of the issues at stake.[22] For early liberals such as Locke, the leading questions of the day revolved around the appropriate relations between church and state and freedom of religious belief and practice rather than the content of social legislation. The cultural-conservative resurgence has brought these issues back into prominence, however, and thus led directly to the 'reassertion of the liberal doctrines that political institutions must be neutral between competing moral and religious ideals, between competing conceptions of the good and that political neutrality precludes state enforcement of anyone's religious or moral program'.[23] Third- and fourth-wave democratisation at the end of the twentieth century has further helped to increase the salience and topicality of the issues, as liberal democracy attempts to secure its advances in what for it are relatively new and unfamiliar parts of Europe and the world.

In the USA the abortion issue was not alone in rekindling the debate over state religious neutrality, although the Supreme Court judgment in

1973 on *Roe v. Wade* is often taken as a turning point. Other issues such as homosexuality law reform, prayer in the public schools, genetic engineering and the control of pornography have also provoked intense debate in which religion-related themes have been to the fore. For religious conservatives, American public life is seen as having been progressively stripped of all but the most perfunctory reference to religion: 'Without ever having put them to a vote, without even subjecting them to democratic debate, some of the key arguments of what is properly called secular*ism* have prevailed. ... One idea that has been insinuated and legally rooted is a peculiar reading of what the First Amendment means for 'the separation of church and state'. It is not, as some fundamentalists claim, that God has been taken out of our public schools or out of our public life. ... It is the case that truth claims and normative ethics that have specific reference to God or religion have been, in theory at least, excluded'.[24] This statement accurately reflects the centrality in American jurisprudence, at least at Supreme Court level, of the justificatory principle of neutrality; as the implicit complaint makes clear, however, the consequence has been anything but neutral in its impact on the public face of religion in America.[25]

In their 1997 comparative study of church–state relations in the USA and four other liberal democracies, Stephen Monsma and Christopher Soper identified some form of governmental neutrality in matters of religion as a basic ideal or goal.[26] In defining neutrality, however, they adopted the consequentialist version as requiring that government 'neither favour nor burden' any particular religion, or religion as a whole, or secular belief systems as a whole. 'Governmental religious neutrality is attained when government does not influence its citizens' choices for or against certain religious or secular systems of belief, either by imposing burdens on them or by granting advantages to them. Instead, government is neutral when it is evenhanded toward people of all faiths and of none.'[27] This conception of religious neutrality was presented as contrasting in important respects with 'the assumptions and beliefs of Enlightenment liberalism' which would seem to support and require the justificatory conception. Enlightenment liberalism is presented as relying on three interrelated assumptions:

> that particularistic religion could be safely assigned to the purely private sphere without infringing on the religious beliefs and practices of its adherents, that a public realm stripped of all its religious elements would be a neutral zone among the various religious faith and between faith and non-belief, and that religious freedom would flourish in the absence of governmental restraints and with no need

for positive governmental actions to equalize the advantages enjoyed by religious and nonreligious groups.[28]

The authors' argument is that arrangements based on Enlightenment liberal assumptions actually offend against the principle of governmental religious neutrality because they privilege secular beliefs over religious ones and consign religion to the margins of social life. This means that in areas such as the provision of education, health care and other social services, where churches have traditionally maintained a strong interest, they receive little or no encouragement from the state, which instead provides secular alternatives out of the public purse. Monsma and Soper portray Enlightenment liberalism, with its attachment to a particular idea of the separation of church and state, as much more strongly entrenched in the USA (despite its vigorous religious culture) than in 'secular Europe'. They did not examine the case of France, where a strong and distinctive tradition of *laïcite* also continues to uphold Enlightenment liberal assumptions, directing their attention instead to the Netherlands and Germany, where they identified arrangements which on their analysis better approximated governmental religious neutrality or even-handedness. Even England (the only other European case examined), with its pattern of 'partial establishment' and other significant elements of unequal treatment of different religious traditions, was found in certain respects to achieve a higher measure of religious neutrality than the USA.[29] Whatever view is taken of the merits of their argument, it nicely illustrates the ambiguity of the concept of governmental religious neutrality. Taking this cue, some understandably take the view that it is a chimera, an illusory goal, particularly in the context of church–state relations in Europe.[30]

CHRISTIANITY AND THE STATE IN EUROPE

Europe's historic association with Christianity is itself unambiguous and strong; indeed, it is the only part of the old world which has ever been integrated on the basis of adherence to a single world religion, although, as will shortly be argued, the level of integration is often exaggerated.[31] As the birthplace of the modern nation-state and the cradle of both liberal democracy and capitalism, its political and economic legacy to the rest of the world has also carried a massive secular – and secularising – charge. However, at no time has secularisation become so comprehensive as to obliterate the Christian stripe in European culture, as this has been carried around the world and implanted in other continents.[32] In sixteenth-century allegorical representations of the continents, Europe alone was crowned; but if its symbolic crown is taken to represent its domination of the other continents, it should perhaps be shown as a triple crown, since its precedence derives from the development within its borders of at least three separate sources of power, each with institutional and ideological underpinnings – church, state and nation.[33] The relationship between these three has been contested throughout. Tension rather than harmony has from the first characterised church–state relations; and nationalism, with its in-built particularism, has always tended to undermine both the universalist claims of the Christian church and the sovereign demands of states whose boundaries have only rarely coincided with those of supposed nations. In terms of their historical origin, the three form a series: first, the church inherited part of its claim to universal dominion from the Roman Empire; then, after centuries of strain between religious *sacerdotium* and secular *regnum*, this claim was successfully contested and set aside by ever more powerful dynastic states and empires in the early-modern period; and, finally, from approximately 1800, the claim of the nation to be the unique font of sovereignty and political authority has progressively been pressed.

In this series, the contribution of the religious institution, the church, is sometimes overlooked or assumed to have been completely superseded by the more forceful impact of modern state-formation and nation-building, especially from the sixteenth century on. It can be argued, however, that the contemporary nations and states of modern Europe have been profoundly affected by the religious legacy of Christianity, as this was taken up and adapted to different local conditions in the age of the confessional state from approximately 1550 to 1800.[34] If the birth of the modern state can reasonably be dated to the end, in 1648, of more than a century of religious wars, it is wrong to assume that the state, which then was born, had no religious mission. Instead, the process of the confessionalisation of different European societies under different confessional labels was greatly accelerated as, territory by territory, confessional conformity became a badge of political loyalty and belonging.[35] Since then, at each stage in the development of most European societies up to and including the most recent, religion has been deeply implicated in the moulding and structuring of both states and nations, sometimes as a force for internal unity and sometimes as a factor of conflict and opposition. It is, of course, an open question how much of the role it has performed results from any internal religious dynamic and how much it has, on the other hand, been a vector of other, secular, forces and interests. This question is all the more open because of the protean nature of Christianity's relations with secular authority since its first foundation.

More than any other of the world religions, Christianity has from the first been plagued by the problem of how to relate to the powers that be; 'no other religion ... had to go through quite such a long and complicated process of defining its relations with political authority'.[36] Its eventual, intimate connection with secular power in Europe was surely no foregone conclusion. Having begun as a Jewish millennarian sect in a West Asian province of the Roman Empire, the Christian church only emerged as a significant medium of power and influence at all early in the fourth century of the Common Era, shortly after Diocletian had failed in the last and most violent of a series of imperial attempts to crush it. In 313 the Edict of Milan marked the great change in Christian fortunes by abrogating all laws prejudicial to the church, restoring its confiscated property and permitting it to become a legal entity, so enjoying the same toleration as other religions. In addition, Emperor Constantine, one of the supposed authors of the Edict, made other symbolic concessions and considerable gifts of property to the church. From this point on, the church's worldly future was assured as the so-called Constantinian Alliance took form.[37] Though he is thought to have remained unbaptised until the very end of his life, Constantine took his pagan imperial title *pontifex maximus* (high priest) seriously and involved himself directly in the internal affairs of the church.[38] Despite this seeming takeover of presiding authority within the church, the imperial embrace clearly brought great advantages and, not unnaturally, these were regarded at the time by most orthodox Christians as being of providential origin. However, it was left to Theodosius in 380 to make the final, decisive move, declaring Christianity the official religion of the Empire, and decreeing the general prohibition, never to be revoked, of all pagan cults and sacrificial rites. It was thus Theodosius, rather than Constantine, who 'made Christianity a state religion, the Catholic church a state church and heresy a state crime. ... It [had taken] less than a century for the persecuted church to become a persecuting church'.[39] The fateful shift from toleration to compulsion was thus made, although it would take a further 1,000 years before the process of the, in large part, forcible conversion of Europe was finally completed, with the acceptance of Christianity by Grand Duke Jogaila of Lithuania in 1385.[40]

David Martin claimed that 'Europe is a unity by virtue of having possessed one Caesar and one God i.e. by virtue of Rome. It is a diversity by virtue of the existence of nations. The patterns of European religion derive from the tension and the partnership between Caesar and God, and from the relationship between religion and the search for national integrity and identity'.[41] It might be objected that the history of European Christianity could equally be characterised as one of disunity and conflict. Nor, arguably, was this just a matter of the subversion of Christian unity by particularistic forces embodied in empires, nations and states: within Christianity itself, riven as it has been by major schisms approximately every 500 years since its beginning, there have famously been at least three 'Romes' claiming precedence within the church, in addition to other geographical centres of confessional allegiance within Europe.[42] Whatever view one takes of the 'scandal of disunity' among Christians, as a point of fact at no time during the last two millennia has Christianity provided a religious basis for the unity of all parts of Europe. As the next contribution to this volume argues, even though the Constantinian (or Theodosian) Alliance in one form or another has been a commonplace until relatively recently across the continent, in the context of church–state relations it makes more sense to speak of several different and conflicting Europes. Nor has the recent unpicking of that alliance – where it has been carried through more or less thoroughly – obliterated the legacy of the different patterns of church–state arrangements, which have characterised these contrasting Europes.[43]

THE RELIGIOUS PARTIALITY OF THE EUROPEAN STATE

However much it might have been internally divided over time, Christianity is still very much the dominant religious tradition in contemporary Europe. As Table 1 indicates, Christian adherents vastly outnumbered the adherents of all other world religions in 1900 and continued to do so, if slightly less overwhelmingly, a century later. The decline in overall levels between 1900 and 1970 is significant, if comparatively modest, given the widely shared assumptions and expectations of social theorists and others, for whom secularisation was a natural and inevitable concomitant of modernisation. Since 1970 there has been a slight recovery of these losses, principally because of the decline and collapse of communism in Eastern Europe and the re-emergence there of both the traditional churches and other religious movements. It has been objected that these figures vastly overestimate levels of genuine religious attachment by relying on the most nominal of nominal criteria for religious identity. On the other hand, there is no reason to suppose that atheists and the determinedly non-religious (that is, those who refuse to acknowledge any confessional identity or link) are greatly underrepresented unless one takes the view that atheism and non-religiosity should be defined in a different way, for example, in practical terms of behaviour (church non-attendance) and attitude or belief (anti-clericalism or dissent from core doctrines). Barrett et al. do not, of course, claim that all

TABLE 1

EUROPE: PERCENTAGE BREAKDOWN BY CONFESSIONAL ADHERENCE

	1900	1970	2000
Christians	94.5	75.1	76.8
crypto-Christians	0.0	5.4	0.0
professing Christians	94.5	69.6	76.8
unaffiliated Christians	3.1	3.7	3.1
Affiliated:	91.5	71.4	73.7
Roman Catholics	44.9	39.1	39.2
Orthodox	25.8	16.3	21.7
Protestants	14.8	12.5	10.6
Anglicans	6.2	4.5	3.7
Others	0.0	1.8	4.0
Nonreligious	0.4	13.1	14.7
Jews	2.5	0.7	0.4
Muslims	2.3	2.7	4.3
Atheists	0.1	8.2	3.1
POPULATION 100%	402.6m	656.4m	728.9m

Note: summary, as presented, does not include discounting for double affiliation or disaffiliation (1900: 0.2%; 1970: 2.9%; 2000: 5.6%).

Source: D. Barrett, G. Kurian and T. Johnson, *World Christian Encyclopedia: A Comparative Survey of Churches and Religions AD30–AD2200* (New York: Oxford University Press 2001), Tables 1–4.

adherents are practising believers and provides scaling of the figures, which suggest that only just over half of adherents should be seen as in any way committed Christians.[44]

Given the predominance in the Continent's population of Christian adherents, it is perhaps not surprising that almost all individual territories should have highly skewed religious population distributions. More surprising at the start of the new millennium is the fact that a large majority of the states which rule these territories should be marked with religious labels. On a simple view, this may seem to follow from a core notion of democracy understood as the decision rule that the preferences of as little as 51 per cent should prevail over those of 49 per cent, however constituted. In fact, of course, as the following contribution to this volume illustrates, very few European societies are divided on criteria of religious adherence anywhere near as closely as 51:49. The great majority are either overwhelmingly of one confession or divided in such a way that no religious group enjoys a majority.

In 1982 Barrett first published data which among other things provided the basis for a *de jure* classification of all the world's territories, including those of Europe, in terms of their formal stances relative to religion.[45] States were coded as either Religious (most often also with commitment to a particular confession), Secular, or Atheistic. The criteria used for determining the 'state religion or philosophy' of a particular case indicate that this was not just a matter of consulting constitution documents and provisions. Unpacking the criteria used for classification they can be seen to be based:

- on how sovereign or non-sovereign states ... officially see themselves in their formal relation to religion, religions and the churches (as defined in their state constitutions, party constitutions, manifestoes and other definitive legal declarations),
- to what extent they are formally, officially or explicitly concerned with religion or claim the right to intervene in religious affairs, and
- to what extent they formally acknowledge or recognise or approve of religions and churches.

TABLE 2

CHURCH–STATE RELATIONS IN EUROPE, c. 1980

	Religious	Secular	Atheistic	
1. State exists solely to promote Christianity	Vatican			1
2. Large state subsidies	Bel, Dk, Fin, FRG, Gr, Ice, Liecht, Lux, Mon, Nor, Sp, Swe, Switz	Austria		14
3. Indirect state aid, no control	*Andorra*, Port, UK, It, Malta	Netherlands, *San Marino*		7
4. State subsidises religious schools, hospitals		France		1
5. State non-interference	Ireland			1
6. State imposes limits (e.g. on political activity)			Yugoslavia	1
7. State obstructs some churches	Cyprus		GDR	2
8. State obstructs all churches		Turkey	Bulg, Hun, Pol, Rom	5
9. Active state hostility to religion			Cze, USSR	2
10. State suppression of religion			Albania	1
Number of cases:	21	5	9	35

Note: Ministates in italics.

Source: Constructed from data in D. Barrett, *Christian World Encylopaedia* (Oxford: Oxford University Press 1982).

As Table 2 indicates along its horizontal dimension, according to the attributions based on these criteria, in 1980, out of 35 European territories listed, only five could be coded as secular in the sense that the 'State is secular, promoting neither religion nor irreligion' and nine were deemed Atheistic. On the other hand, 21 states or governments were found to be committed in one way or another to the support of religion and/or religious institutions.[46] Of these, 14 were associated with single confessional traditions, while Finland, unusually, supported two (in the form of both the Lutheran and Russian Orthodox state churches). The other six were committed to the support of a plurality of religious organisations; thus, Belgium is presumably classified as religious because there the state recognises and supports (not least by paying the salaries and pensions of their ministers) six denominations: Catholicism, Protestantism, Judaism, Anglicanism, Islam and the (Greek and Russian) Orthodox church.[47] It hardly needs saying that in the USA all of these commitments, including those, which make no mention of any particular religion, would be deemed contrary to the First Amendment ban on establishment. This despite the fact that a number of these commitments are not understood locally to amount to establishment. This was the case, for example, in Ireland, despite the fact that the 1937 Constitution invokes 'the Name of the Most Holy Trinity, from Whom is all authority and to Whom, as our final end, all actions of both men and States must be referred', and (until 1972) also recognised 'the special position of the Holy Catholic Apostolic and Roman Church as the guardian of the Faith professed by the great majority of the citizens'.[48] Even the arrangements in some of Europe's states classified by Barrett as Secular would offend against the American ban on establishment. This might not be unexpected in the anomalous cases, for instance the existence in France of special arrangements in Alsace-Lorraine where the terms of the old Napoleonic system of support for the Catholic church still obtain, these territories having not been part of France at the time of the 1905 Law of Separation. The fact that the 1905 law, where it does apply (that is, in the rest of France), took all existing church buildings into state hands where they still reside, would be regarded as doubly offensive, going against both the establishment and free exercise clauses of the First Amendment. Even the states listed as Atheist have, paradoxically, often recognised the special standing of particular religious traditions; thus, in Bulgaria the 1949 Religious Denominations Act, which still remains on the statute book, declared 'The Bulgarian Orthodox Church is the traditional faith of the Bulgarian people. It is bound up with their history and, as such, its nature and its spirit can be considered a church of the popular democracy'.[49] And in all of the Atheist states, including the only one – Albania – which in 1980 was still officially committed to repressing all religion, religious affairs were closely monitored and controlled by agencies of the state and Communist party.

These classifications primarily relate only to formal, or *de jure*, rules and commitments. When other evidence relating to the actual, *de facto*, relations of support and/or control between governments and religious organisations is added and cross-tabulated, as in Table 2, a fuller picture emerges, which demonstrates the religious partiality of the state in Europe *circa* 1980 even more completely. In this more detailed picture, no cases of full state neutrality are found; the cell which combines a Secular state with state non-interference in the affairs of the church is empty. The most populated cell by far is that occupied by the 13 territories where the state is *de jure* supportive and *de facto* provides religious organisations with large subsidies. Nine East European states are located in the opposite quarter of the table, all deemed Atheistic but varying in the degree of control exercised over religion, with Yugoslavia effectively policing only the politicisation of religion, while Albania remained committed to a campaign of eradication of both the majority Islamic faith and a number of Christian denominations. On these measures, then, in none of the 35 territories included in Barrett's survey can the state authorities be adjudged neutral.

Since 1980 there have been a number of remarkable changes, which have affected the distributions just identified. The collapse of communism and the disintegration of the Soviet Union, Yugoslavia and Czechoslovakia led to an increase in the number of relevant cases from 35 to 47 (a number which would have been higher by one had East and West Germany, against the trend, not re-unified). Communism, with its animus against organised religion, had been responsible for the classification of the East European states as Atheist in 1980 when the Cold War was still ongoing. Table 3 indicates by the number and direction of the arrows the effect of the removal of communist political hegemony across the region; the arrows indicate that almost none of the former communist territories remained where they had been only 20 years before. The exception is the rump of Yugoslavia (Serbia and Montenegro with Kosovo), where the embargo on religious groups engaging in political activity continued in 2000 to be policed by the Milosevic regime, albeit with extreme variations as between the Serbian Orthodox church, which was favoured, and others, such as the breakaway Montenegrin Orthodox Church and Islam generally in Kosovo. All the other successor states moved from the Atheistic to the Secular (ten cases) or Religious column (11 cases), although some of these attributions can be contested.[50]

TABLE 3
CHANGES IN CHURCH–STATE RELATIONS, EUROPE, 1980–2000

	Religious	Secular	Atheistic
1. State propagates Christianity	Vatican*		
2. Massive state subsidies to churches	Monaco Bel, Dk, Fin, Greece, Ice, Liecht, Lux, Norway, Spain, Swtz, [Swe] ----▶ *FedRepGer*	Austria Sweden	
3. Limited state subsidies to churches	Andorra Portugal, Britain, Italy, Malta, **Armenia** **Poland**	San Marino Netherlands **Russia** **Hungary** **Romania**	
4. State subsidies only to schools, hospitals etc		France	
5. Complete state non-interference	Ireland, **Macedonia** **Croatia** **Slovenia** **Ukraine, Mold.,** **Georgia**	**Germany,** ◀— **Estonia** **Lithuania** **Slovakia** **Czech Rep**	
6. Limited political restrictions		**Latvia**	*Yugoslavia*
7. Minorities discriminated against	**Bulgaria** Cyprus, **Belarus**	**Albania**	*GerDemRep* [>1991]
8. State interference and obstruction	**Bosnia**	Turkey	Bulgaria, Hungary, Poland, Romania
9. State hostility and prohibition	**Azerbaijan** ◀—		*Czechoslovakia* *USSR*
10. State suppression or eradication			**Albania** 1967–91
TOTALS (2000)	**30**	**17**	**1**

Note: Bold type indicates countries, which have changed their classification. Italics indicates states that have ceased to exist since 1980.

Source: Constructed on the basis of attributions in D. Barrett (ed.), *World Christian Encyclopaedia: A Comparative Study of Churches and Religions in the Modern World AD 1900–2000* (New York: Oxford University Press 1982??) (1982 and 2001 – no reference for 2001), supplemented by *2000 Annual Report on International Religious Freedom: Europe and the New Independent States* (US Dept of State, Sept. 2000), and K. Boyle and J. Sheen (eds.), *Freedom of Religion and Belief: A World Report* (London: Routledge 1997).

The other direction of change between 1980 and 2000 is reflected by the overwhelmingly upward direction of the arrows. In all but two cases change has been in the direction of dismantling controls on religion and increasing the availability of state assistance, whether in the form of funds for the rebuilding of cathedrals, as in Russia, or the widespread use of national taxation systems to funnel resources to recognised denominations. The two exceptions are Bosnia, where the Barrett classification appears to indicate that political interference with religion was greater in 2000 than was the case for Yugoslavia as a whole in 1980, and Germany. German reunification is seen as producing a convergence of its two parts, which had previously contrasted strongly in their church–state relations, in the maximally neutral central cell of the table. One of the most notable features of the table is a convergence towards this cell, which in 2000 is no longer empty as in 1980 but occupied by five newly independent (or in Germany's case newly reunified) states. This trend is only a modest one, however; as already noted, more territories moved from the Atheist column to the Religious than to the Secular and in the case of the one significant shift among the West European states, that of Sweden from the Religious to the Secular column, the degree of *de facto* separation introduced was relatively modest.[51] While Sweden was moving towards a form of disestablishment, in Romania, serious attempts were being made to have the Romanian Orthodox Church declared the national church. Shortly before, in 1997, furthermore, new Russian legislation, which had been prepared in consultation with the leadership of the Orthodox church, cut back on the religious freedoms which an exemplary Freedom of Conscience law had introduced in 1990.[52]

STATE RELIGIOUS NEUTRALITY: A CHIMERA?

Antidisestablishmentarianism, for long believed to be the longest word – and maybe one of the most obscure – in the English language, can now be seen as a more robust phenomenon than is usually appreciated. It is not of course the same thing as pro-Establishment sentiment, although, as the last reference to Romania indicates, such a thing is not unheard-of at the start of the third Christian millennium. Rather, it is a matter of opposing, or at least not supporting, the destruction of an existing establishment.[53] This means it tends to be restricted to those societies which actually have a church establishment to be defended, whether the term 'by law established' is used or not. It tends not to be a doctrinal or ideological 'ism', more a cover for a particular brand of conservatism which does not like to see old landmarks unnecessarily done away with. If formal or actual establishment was directly associated with the systematic disadvantaging or 'burdening' of alternative creeds and traditions then antidisestablishmentarianism would be weaker. Since the European Council and its legal organs stand guarantee for the protection of religious freedoms throughout Europe, the basis for this objection would seem to be have been removed. Furthermore, the European Union declares matters relating to church establishment as outside its remit.[54]

There is, however, another view of the matter, which ranges secular liberals and religious radicals on the same side and in favour of disestablishment. The argument is not, as with other advocates of disestablishment, that it would be good, even salutary, for the church affected. It is rather that, particularly in an age when religious pluralism is growing as a result of increased migration flows and the growth of 'new religious movements' of different kinds, religious-cultural differences can resonate and aggravate other, more threatening conflicts. A sense of marginality or exclusion on the part of religious-cultural groups should on this view be taken seriously and addressed.

Brian Barry has argued persuasively that 'the principle of neutrality [is not itself] neutral between different belief systems and conceptions of the good', 'it suits liberals better than it suits nonliberals' and 'there is no way in which nonliberals can be sold the principle of neutrality without first injecting a large dose of liberalism into their outlook'.[55] This does not mean that the neutrality principle cannot be operationalised and could not then in principle be institutionalised; indeed, American jurisprudence at its highest reaches was long committed to doing just this, with the result, noted earlier, that many alternative understandings of what neutrality requires have been developed and deployed. But it does mean that, until underlying liberal principles become the object of consensus, then liberals will just have to fight their corner and argue their case. State religious neutrality is still far from realisation in Europe and whichever side one stands on – including that of the 'plague on both your houses' neutrals – it still clearly matters.

NOTES

1. Huntington's article of this title appeared in the journal *Foreign Affairs* in the summer of 1993. It was followed three years later, after it had raised a storm of controversy, by an extended if somewhat revised statement of the same thesis: S.P. Huntington, *The Clash of Civilizations and the Remaking of World Order* (New York: Simon and Schuster 1996)

2. The term appears in the title of Colin Crouch's chapter: 'The Quiet Continent: Religion and Politics in Europe', in D. Marquand and C. Crouch (eds.), *Religion and Democracy* (Oxford: Blackwell 2000). It is noteworthy that Crouch only refers to Western Europe, however; as so often, Eastern (and parts of Central) Europe are treated implicitly as though it belonged to 'another Continent' – or even, as Huntington would have it, another civilisation.

3. J. Casanova, *Public Religions in the Modern World* (London: University of Chicago Press 1994); G. Kepel, *The Revenge of God: The Resurgence of Islam, Christianity and Judaism in the Modern World* (Cambridge: Polity Press 1994).

4. See for instance Kepel, *The Revenge of God*; R. Antoun and M. Hegland (eds.), *Religious Resurgence: Contemporary Cases in Islam, Christianity and Judaism* (Syracuse: Syracuse University Press 1987); E. Sahliyeh (ed.), *Religious Resurgence and Politics in the Modern World* (Albany: State University of New York Press 1990); D. Westerlund (ed.), *Questioning the Secular State: The Worldwide Resurgence of Religion in Politics* (London: Hurst & Co. 1996).

5. He argues in fact that the decline in 'basic beliefs about God' has nowhere been quite so precipitate. Crouch, 'The Quiet Continent', p.90.

6. In 1986 the UN appointed a 'Special Rapporteur on the Implementation of the Declaration on the Elimination of All Forms of Intolerance and of Discrimination Based on Religion or Belief'. See K. Boyle and J. Sheen (eds.), *Freedom of Religion and Belief: A World Report* (London: Routledge 1997).

7. *The Guardian*, 31 May 2002.

8. The ludicrously complex and anomalous nature of this ban ('a mass of archaic anomalies') is briefly indicated in S. de Smith and R. Brazier, *Constitutional and Administrative Law* (London: Penguin, 6th edn. 1989), pp.250–51: 'Ministers of the Church of England, the Episcopalian Church of Scotland and all other Protestant clergymen (including ministers of the [disestablished] Church of Ireland) ordained by bishops, except ministers of the disestablished Church of Wales, are disqualified; so are Roman Catholic priests, and ministers of the Established (Presbyterian) Church of Scotland; but nonconformist ministers, and ministers of non-Christian denominations, are not disqualified.' Gilbert and Sullivan could not have done better.

9. *The Guardian*, 11 Feb. 2002.

10. Ibid., p.12.

11. In a veiled rebuke to those campaigning for church disestablishment, outgoing Archbishop George Carey was quoted as saying, 'The Church of England will still be established in 25 years' time. Establishment is a contract between nation and church, and the church is an essential part of the fabric of the constitution of this country'. *Sunday Times*, 7 July 2002, p.A:10.

12. Hansard, House of Lords, 27/7/2000; col.571.

13. P. Jones, 'The Ideal of the Neutral State', in R. Goodin and A. Reeve (eds.), *Liberal Neutrality* (London: Routledge 1989), p.9.

14. P. Jones, 'The Ideal of the Neutral State', p.11 (emphasis in original). In a footnote Jones adds that this view is taken by all three of the neutralists on whom he concentrates: Rawls, Dworkin and Ackerman.

15. Waldron claims that the image of neutrality is relatively new to the liberal tradition and dates its importation from a 1974 essay of Ronald Dworkin. Waldron, 'Legislation and Moral Neutrality', in Goodin and Reeve (eds.), *Liberal Neutrality*, p.62. Curiously, both Frederick II (the Great) and Benjamin Franklin are credited in the same year (1740) with almost identical sayings about religious toleration in a neutralist vein: 'All religion must be tolerated, for this way everyone may get to heaven in his own way' (Cabinet order of

Frederick II, 22 June 1740). The Franklin source is *In re the Catholic Schools*, 1740. See L.D. Eigen and J.P. Siegel, *Dictionary of Political Quotations* (London: Hale 1993), p.609.
16. W. Kymlicka, *Contemporary Political Philosophy: An Introduction* (Oxford: Clarendon Press 1990), p.205.
17. E. Mack, 'Liberalism, Neutralism and Rights', in J.R. Pennock and J.W. Chapman (eds.), *Religion, Morality and the Law* (London: New York University Press, 1988); D. Laycock, 'Formal, Substantive, and Disaggregated Neutrality Toward Religion', *De Paul Review* 39 (1990), pp.993–1018.
18. J. Raz, *The Morality of Freedom* (London: Oxford University Press 1986), chapters 5 and 6.
19. W. Kymlicka, 'Liberal Individualism and Liberal Neutrality, *Ethics* 99 (July 1989), p.885.
20. J. Rawls, *A Theory of Justice* (London: Oxford University Press 1971), p.329.
21. Mack, 'Liberalism, Neutralism and Rights', p.47.
22. 'In American public life today, abortion law is the single most fevered and volatile question that inescapably joins religion and politics. ... No other dispute so clearly and painfully illustrates the problematic of the naked public square.' R.J. Neuhaus, *The Naked Public Square: Religion and Democracy in America* (Grand Rapids: Eerdmans 1984), p.27.
23. Mack, 'Liberalism, Neutralism and Rights', p.47
24. Neuhaus, *The Naked Public Square*, p.25 As Neuhaus points out 'There are remnants in public oaths, prayers in legislatures, and the like. Determined secularists view these as residual inconsistencies that they have not yet got around to extirpating and that may not be worth bothering about. ... Residual religion in public poses no threat. Something of this reasoning is reflected in a recent state court ruling that tolerated even some prayer in a public classroom The prayer, said the court in effect should be seen as a morale-boosting folk custom and not significantly religious in nature. When religion has been tamed and its triumph no longer threatens, it can be tolerated as cultural trivia.' (ibid.).
25. See J. Witte, *Religion and the American Constitutional Experiment: Essential Rights and Liberties* (Boulder, CO: Westview Press 2000).
26. S. Monsma and C. Soper, *The Challenge of Pluralism; Church and State in Five Democracies* (Oxford: Rowman & Littlefield 1997).
27. Ibid., p.6.
28. Ibid., p.9.
29. 'The current educational system [in England] treats religions unequally, but it still expands choice for Jewish or Christian parents who want a school permeated by religious ideas. In this way, the system is more neutral between a religious and nonreligious educational perspective than in the United States. This is even more true for nonprofit social service organizations.' Ibid., p.149.
30. The *Shorter Oxford English Dictionary* gives as the ordinary modern use: 'A mere wild fancy; an unfounded conception.' *Chambers 20th Century Dictionary* also lists 'an organism made up of two genetically distinct tissues', nicely rhyming with the old notion that church and state are totally distinct entities.
31. 'In the matter of religion, of all the continents Europe presents one original feature which is a point of major importance: it is the only one to have been totally christianised, although it was not the first to be evangelised.' R. Rémond, *Religion and Society in Modern Europe* (Oxford: Blackwell 1999), p.17. See also K. Wilson and J. van der Dussen, *The History of the Idea of Europe* (London: Routledge 1995)
32. A view, which can be traced to Weber, is that Christianity has an inherent tendency towards rationalisation and secularisation.
33. See Wilson and van der Dussen, *The History of the Idea of Europe*, pp.48–58. The papal tiara or triple crown became symbolic of the papacy in the fourteenth century. Its wearing was abandoned by Pope Paul VI (1963–78).
34. See A. Hastings, *The Construction of Nationhood: Ethnicity, Religion and Nationalism* (Cambridge: Cambridge University Press 1997).
35. See H. Schilling, 'Confession and Political Identity in Europe at the Beginning of Modern Times', in J. Coleman and M. Tomka (eds.), *Religion and Nationalism* (London: SCM Press

1995/96), pp.3–13. Also D. Nicholas, *The Transformation of Europe 1300–1600* (London, Arnold 1999), ch 10: 'Antiquity and Modernity: the Religious Division of Europe in the Sixteenth Century'.

36. J.R. Strayer, 'The State and Religion: An Exploratory Comparison in Different Cultures (Greece and Rome, the West and Islam)', *Comparative Studies in Society and History* 1 (1958–59), p.39.

37. M. Reuver, *Requiem for Constantine; A Vision of the Future of Church and State in the West* (Kampen: Kok Publishing 1996).

38. Thus he presided in person over the Councils of Arle (314) and Nicea (325), which saw major attempts to settle, respectively, the Donatist and Arian disputes, the pope being only represented by junior priests.

39. H. Küng, *Christianity: The Religious Situation of Our Time* (London: SCM Press 1994) p.183. The edict establishing Catholicism as the state religion also attempted to finally end controversy about the doctrine of the Trinity: 'We order those who follow this doctrine to receive the title of Catholic Christians, but others we judge to be mad and raving and worthy of incurring the disgrace of heretical teaching, nor are their assemblies to receive the name of churches. They are to be punished not only by Divine retribution but also by our own measures, which we have decided in accordance with Divine inspiration.' S. Ehler and J.B. Morrall (eds.), *Church and State Through the Centuries: A Collection of Historic Documents with Commentaries* (London: Burns & Oates 1954), p.7.

40. See R. Fletcher, *The Conversion of Europe from Paganism to Christianity 371–1386AD* (London: Fontana 1998)

41. D. Martin, *A General Theory of Secularization* (Oxford: Blackwell 1978), p.100.

42. See P. Duncan, *Russian Messianism: Third Rome, Holy Revolution, Communism and After* (London: Routledge 2000). Examples of other European centres are Geneva for international Calvinism and Canterbury for the worldwide Anglican communion.

43. See the next contribution in this volume

44. See the brief discussion in J. Taylor, 'The Future of Christianity', in J. McManners (ed.), *The Oxford History of Christianity* (Oxford: Oxford Universtiy Press 1993), pp.650–51. This is not the place to review the relevant debates among religious sociologists. Suffice to note Grace Davie's argument that in parts of Europe (e.g. Britain) 'believing without belonging' forms a pattern, while elsewhere (e.g. Scandinavia) 'belonging without believing' is not uncommon. G. Davie, *Religion in Modern Europe: A Memory Mutates* (Oxford: Oxford University Press 2000), ch.1.

45. D. Barrett (ed.), *World Christian Encylopaedia: A Comparative Study of Churches and Religions in the Modern World AD 1900–2000* (New York: Oxford University Press 1982).

46. Unpacking Barrett's coding it appears that a state is deemed Religious if it is a: **State** (identified/formally linked/heavily involved/joined in law) **with** (a religion or religions or churches) **and its/their promotion.**

47. See R. Torfs, 'State and Church in Belgium', in G. Robbers (ed.), *State and Church in the European Union* (Baden-Baden: Nomos 1996), pp.18–19.

48. J. Casey, 'State and Church in Ireland', in ibid., pp.147–68. See also Kissane's contribution to this volume.

49. *2000 Annual Report on International Religious Freedom: Europe and the New Independent States* (US Department of State, Sept. 2000).

50. In fact Barrett *et al.* coded Russia, Bulgaria, Hungary, Romania and Czechoslovakia as still Atheist in 2000. The other sources consulted clearly support the case for reclassification however. The classification of Sweden, where church–state separation came into force from 1 January 2000, has also been changed.

51. See Goran Gustafsson's contribution to this volume.

52. See J. Anderson, *The Politics of Religion in Transitional Politics* (forthcoming).

53. Evidence for the prevalence of this view in Scandinavia is reviewed in S. Sundback, 'Medlemskapet i de lutherska kyrkorna i Norden', in G. Gustafsson and T. Pettersson (eds.), *Folkyrkor och religiös Pluralism – den Nordiska Religiösa Modellen* (Stockholm: Verbum 2000)

54. Declaration 11 'on the status of churches and non-confessional organisations' appended to

the Treaty of Amsterdam reads: 'The European Union respects and does not prejudice the status under national law of churches and religious associations or communities in the Member States. The European Union equally respects the status of philosophical and non-confessional organisations.' 'Declarations annexed to final act of Amsterdam', *Eur-Lex: Selected Instruments taken from the Treaties*.

55. B. Barry, 'How Not to Defend Liberal Institutions', in R.B. Douglas, G.M. Mara and H.S. Richardson (eds.), *Liberalism and the Good* (London: Routledge 1990), pp.50, 54, 55. For a full, extended working out of this argument, see B. Barry, *Culture and Equality: An Egalitarian Critique of Multiculturalism* (Cambridge: Polity Press 2000).

A Framework for the Comparative Analysis of Church–State Relations in Europe

JOHN T.S. MADELEY

Even a cursory overview of church–state relations in contemporary Europe reveals what Grace Davie calls 'a bewildering variety'.[1] And if closer attention is paid to the details of different local patterns in respect of the legal status of religious bodies, churches' internal organisation, the impact of labour law, church financing and the legal status of priests, the overall picture becomes even more bewildering.[2] David Martin's *Toward a General Theory of Secularization* represents a heroic attempt to identify the key elements which have combined in different historical contexts in Europe to produce the complex mosaic as it stood at the end of the 1970s.[3] However, since then much has happened to change the picture in a number of key respects; for example, the collapse of communism around 1989 represented the end of an ice age for religious institutions in Central and Eastern Europe, while in the West large-scale immigration has led to the mushroom-like growth of multicultural settings. This article takes a step back in an attempt to gain perspective on the new picture as it presents itself at the start of the third millennium. It attempts to do this by both narrowing the focus and broadening the scope of inquiry: the focus is restricted to the institutional aspects of what is conventionally called church–state relations and the scope is broadened and deepened by extending it both spatially and temporally.[4]

Stein Rokkan's path-breaking work on nation building, cleavage formation and the structuring of mass politics in Western Europe provides a useful starting point for any attempt to develop a framework for analysing church–state relations in Europe. He was concerned to identify and explain a much broader range of phenomena, namely, the principal contrasts in political structures and processes which were observable in Western Europe after World War II. Coming from the north of Norway, he was always acutely aware of political variations across geographical space; for him, patterns of politics in the widely dispersed parts of Europe varied greatly in terms of inherited systems of territorial control, the impact of cultural and economic forces, and the mechanisms of representation, including both the electoral and party systems. Faced with such a broad range of variations across such a wide space he did not restrict himself to a synchronic approach, however. Instead, he availed himself of the work of a number of important historical sociologists and pioneered a historical-developmental approach within European political science which has been widely influential.[5] What follows is a modest attempt to follow his lead 25 years after his untimely death and establish a framework with sufficient geographical breadth and historical depth to serve the purposes of comparing and contrasting patterns of church–state relations across the whole of Europe.

Although, particularly in his later work, he followed the path of (almost) infinite regress via the *Völkerwanderungen* of Europe's so-called Dark Ages back to the Roman Empire, his most influential writings were based on an ordered analysis of so-called critical junctures and their consequences, starting with the momentous conflicts of the Reformation period. The choice of starting-point was quite deliberate and explicit:

> The developmental model to be explored posits clear-cut time limits to its operation:
>
> its *terminus a quo* is the conflict over the cultural-religious identity of the emerging nation-state in the sixteenth century;
>
> its *terminus ad quem* is the establishment of universal and equal electoral democracy and the "freezing" of party alternatives, in most countries during the 1920s and the 1930s, at any rate before World War II.[6]

It was his view that critical junctures, which occurred in the case of the Reformation and French Revolution centuries ago, had generated contrasting systems of power and opposition which continued to shape and inform the politics in the post-Second World War era. Thus the Reformation–Counter-Reformation conflicts were seen to have generated the first of two dimensions of opposition, which he referred to under the common heading of the National Revolution. The second of these, which also related in part to church–state conflicts and tensions, he saw as arising out of the French Revolution, as its influence was spread across Continental Europe in the French Revolutionary and Napoleonic Wars. Other, more material interest-based dimensions of conflict generated through the Industrial Revolution – between opposing interests in the commodity and labour markets – were also presented as being of great significance, of course, in the fixing of the decisive cleavage patterns which underlay patterns of modern mass politics. These more materialistic cleavages based on class and market position, in addition to dominating the political landscape, also added a distinctive twist to issues affecting church–state relations. In Rokkan's sequential analysis they did so within the context of, and under the constraints given by, pre-existing patterns of conflict deriving from the National Revolution cleavage structures. Thus, the sharp division in Latin Europe between revisionist social democracy on the one hand and 'revolutionary anarchists, anarcho-syndicalists and Marxist factions' on the other were seen as developing within a force-field where culture wars between the Roman Catholic church (and its allies) and radical anti-clericals (and their allies) were already ongoing. The distinctiveness of the Latin pattern of what Martin dubbed 'reactive organicism', then, was seen to derive as much if not more from the distortive impact of the earlier, rather than otherwise relatively straightforward impact of the later, cleavage base.[7] Rokkan argued that the activation of the owner–worker cleavage, which generated mass working class parties in all countries of Western Europe before World War I, was the one feature which made for similarity across party systems, while the impact of the cleavages rooted in the National Revolution made for the 'decisive contrasts' which it was his particular concern to identify and explain.[8] The distinctive ideologies, movements and organisations which made politics so different in different parts of Europe were in his analysis all seen as implicated in particular approaches to issues related to, if not solely concerned with, church–state–society relations.

As Rokkan clearly explained, the limitations of time (sixteenth century to the 1920s) were suggested by the geographical focus of his model on the competitive political systems of Western Europe; it only applied 'to the territories and the polities which were immediately affected by the clashes between Reformers and the Roman Catholic Church and the consequent strains between secular and religious powers'.[9] By the same logic, in order to develop a necessarily more extended model for the analysis of church–state relationships across the whole of Europe, 'from the Atlantic to the Urals', it is necessary not only to move eastwards in spatial terms but also further backwards and forwards in temporal terms. The natural *terminus a quo* for an all-Europe model would then be 1054, the conventional date for the decisive schism between Latin Catholic, and Greek – or Eastern – Orthodox, Christianity. And the natural *terminus ad quem* would be the reopening of Central and Eastern Europe to competitive democratic politics since 1989.

As Rokkan's 'intellectual executors' point out in their comprehensively annotated commentary on his core works, extending his model geographically is not an easy task:

The fundamentally different historical development of the Eastern European 'nation-states' would have complicated his already complex model even further. In order to be able to arrive at general conclusions despite this complexity, Rokkan always advocated developing region-specific models. The end of the division of Europe that resulted from World War II would have forced him to think more about how to delimit the "region" Europe, i.e. about the long-term effects of its historical boundary-building: the division of the Roman Empire into an eastern and a western empire, the confrontation between the Roman Catholic and Greek Orthodox Churches, the long isolation of the emerging Muscovite empire from the West, the carving-up of the East under the despotic Ottoman Empire, the autocratic Russian Empire, and the absolutist Austrian Empire, and finally the totalitarian Soviet Empire.[10]

Since the focus here is restricted to identifying the institutional aspects of church–state relations, however, the task can be made less daunting by removing one of the sources of complexity which is not directly relevant and substituting a confessional one.[11] The latter is, hypothetically at least, both relevant and, arguably, of wider significance in identifying and defining differences between East and West in Europe.[12] Church–state relations in the world of Eastern Orthodoxy are collectively quite distinctive, relative to both Catholic and Protestant patterns, and can therefore be expected to have direct implications and consequences for patterns of political conflict in the successor states of the former empires of Eastern and Central Europe. The map 'Religious Europe 1900' illustrates the spatial distribution of the major confessions as they existed in the last days of the established empires. As will be seen, the broad lines of this confessional map of Europe have survived the violence and destruction of the great wars of the twentieth century and can still be detected today despite large-scale alterations in state boundaries. Figure 1 represents an attempt to clarify the overall picture by presenting an adaptation of Rokkan's conceptual map of Western (and, in part, Central) Europe, as established by Flora *et al.* in its most complete form, and extending it so as to embrace Eastern Europe. It indicates schematically the significance of both the principal mono-confessional blocs and the intervening multi-confessional belts, which have provided the context for widely differing patterns of church–state relations. Identifying the nature of the connections between these structures and their contexts would require a major research effort, however; all that can be attempted here is to identify some of the principal features such an effort would have to address.

THE LONG SHADOW OF THE PAST: CONTEMPORARY EUROPE'S CONFESSIONAL STRUCTURE

From the sixteenth to the eighteenth century Europe knew three mono-confessional culture areas of major size located severally across the eastern, southern and northern margins of the Continent: the Orthodox, Catholic and Lutheran. One can even say that there were, and are, several religious Europes, each with its own range of variation attaching to local or regional religious traditions.[13] In each the confessional state pattern was institutionalised for most if not all of this period so as to make membership of the political community coincident with submission to the locally dominant creed. This rule was typically adhered to even in adjacent subject territories which contained populations of mixed confessional loyalties; here the adherents of dissident or minority traditions were typically excluded from holding public office and sometimes even effectively denied the right to hold land or have their marriages officially recognised. Nowadays almost all the punitive sanctions which underwrote church establishment in the age of the confessional state have been removed. Article 9 of the European Convention on Human Rights of 1951 guaranteed to everyone 'the right to freedom of thought, conscience and religion; this right includes freedom to change his religion or belief and freedom, either alone or in community with others and in public or private, to manifest his religion or belief, in worship, teaching, practice and observance'. The only limitations on these freedoms should be such 'as are prescribed by law and are necessary in a democratic society in the interests of public order, health or morals, or for the protection of the rights and freedoms of others'. Despite the almost completely successful abolition of discriminatory legislation and controls in this area, however, the heritage of the European confessional state is still around for all to see. Geographical patterns of adherence to particular confessional traditions, which were once created and/or reinforced by these now discarded means, are still very much in evidence.

The second edition of Barrett's *World Christian Encyclopaedia* provides figures for adherence to different religious traditions in all the 50 or so territories which make up Europe as of 2000.[14] A brief analysis of the

MAP 1

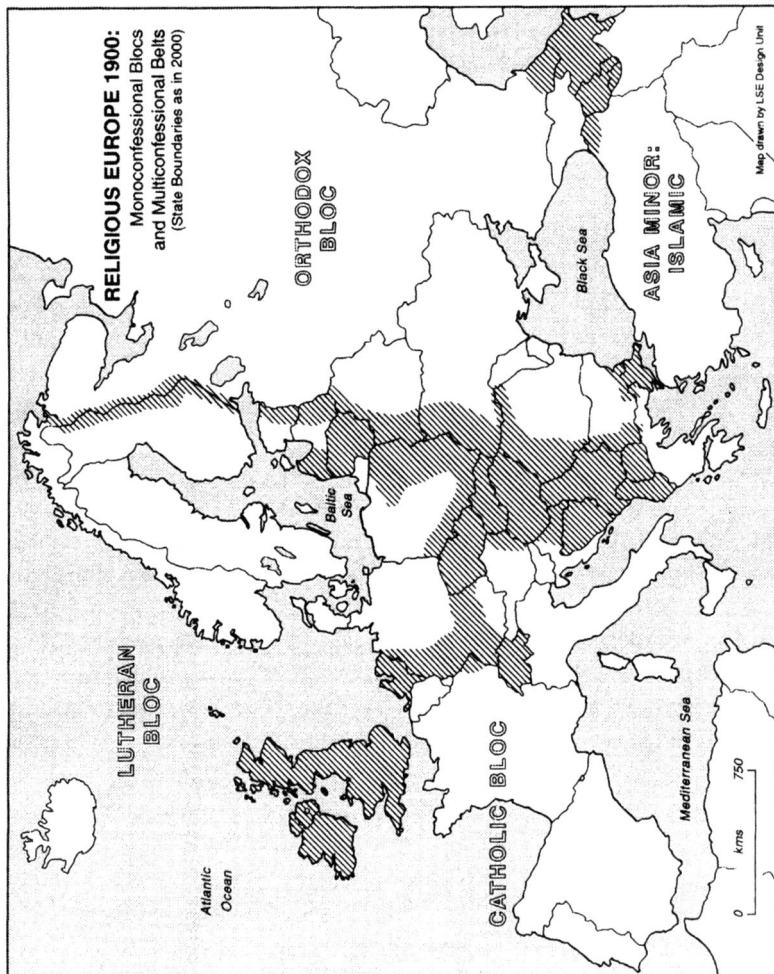

RELIGIOUS EUROPE 1900:
Monoconfessional Blocs
and Multiconfessional Belts
(State Boundaries as in 2000)

LUTHERAN
BLOC

ORTHODOX
BLOC

CATHOLIC BLOC

ASIA MINOR:
ISLAMIC

Atlantic
Ocean

Baltic
Sea

Black Sea

Mediterranean Sea

0   kms   750

Map drawn by LSE Design Unit

FIGURE I

AN ADAPTATION OF ROKKAN'S CONCEPTUAL MAP OF EUROPE INCORPORATING THE TERRITORIES ONCE COVERED BY THE RUSSIAN AND OTTOMAN EMPIRES

Geopolitical type>>	Seaward peripheries	Seaward empire nations	City-state Europe	Landward empire-nations	Landward buffers	Landward Empires	Geopolitical <<type
Beyond reach of Rome: *Protestant>>*	Iceland: from 13C under Norway; from 16C, Denmark	← Norway Denmark →		Sweden: state-building 16C, major empire 17C	Finland: under Sweden> 1809: under Russia; Estonia, Latvia, E. Prussia	RUSSIA: Hegemony established from 16C, empire extended from early 18C, wars against Ottomans	Beyond reach of Rome: *<<Orthodox*
Territories once under Roman Empire &/or influenced by Roman law: *Protestant*	Scotland: united with England 1707; Wales: subjected 15C	ENGLAND: consolidated 11C, major overseas empire 17–20C	Hanseatic League: loose federation of cities around the Baltic and North Seas 13–16C	PRUSSIA: state-building 17C, empire 18C, nucleus for unification of German Reich, 1870: *GERMANY*	Lithuania Poland	Belarus Ukraine	Territories contested between *Orthodox and Catholic*
Religiously Mixed: *Protestant & Catholic*	Ireland: subjected 16-17C		Neths: Provinces united agst Habsburgs, indep. 1648 Switz: confedn 1291, indep 1648		Bohemia: Moravia subjected by Austria 1620 Hungary	Romania	Territories once under the Eastern Roman Empire/Byzantium: *Predominantly Orthodox*

FIGURE 1 (Cont'd)

Geopolitical type>>	Seaward peripheries	Seaward empire nations	City-state Europe	Landward empire-nations	Landward buffers	Landward Empires	Geopolitical <<type
Catholic	Brittany: subjected 16C	**FRANCE:** consolidated 16C, empire-building frustrated except in Indo-China, Africa	**Belgium:** indep 1830 Savoy-Piedmont: indep nucleus for unific'n of *ITALY*	Bavaria	**Slovenia Croatia**		
					Serbia-Montenegro	**Bulgaria Macedonia Greece Cyprus**	*Religiously Mixed* Catholic. Orthodox, Islamic
					Bosnia-Hercegavina		
Counter-Reformation Territories: *Catholic*		*Crusading Empires:* built up in fight against Moslems, major overeas empires: **PORTUGAL SPAIN**	**Aragon-Catalonia:** with Spain 1474	*Crusading Empire:* Built-up on dynastic claims and wars against Ottomans: **AUSTRIA**	Albania Eur-Turkey	*From 1699 on the defensive:* **OTTOMAN EMPIRE**	**Beyond reach of Rome:** *Islamic*

Notes: This is more a confessional than a conceptual map of Europe, although the East–West dimension is still described, following Rokkan, in terms of geo-political type.

The vertical broken line which cross-cuts the 'Landward buffers' column represents the East–West fault-line, here defined partially by confessional type (especially Catholic v. Orthodox) and partially by imperial spheres of influence.

TABLE 1

THE HISTORIC MONO-CONFESSIONAL CULTURE BLOCS
Populations and Confessional Breakdowns by State in 2000

Lutheran North	Catholic South	Orthodox East
Iceland: 0.28 [96] Sweden: 8.91 [94] Norway: 4.46 [94]	Italy: 57.30 [97] Spain: 39.63 [96] Malta 0.39 [95]	Greece: 10.64 [93]
Denmark: 5.29[90] Finland: 5.18 [89]	Portugal: 9.87 [91]	
		Romania: 22.33 [O85;C14;P11] Belarus: 10.24 [O49;C13]
	France: 58.08 [82] Belgium:10.16 [80] Austria: 8.31 [75]	Ukraine: 50.46 [O54:Ind17;C 11;P3] Russia: ca.110.00 [O75:M15;Oth 10]* Moldova: 4.38 [O44;Ind15;M5] Bulgaria: 8.23 [72: M12]
	Slovenia: 1.99 [83]	
Tot popn: 24.12 m	Tot popn: 165.99 m Grand Total: 406.39m	Tot popn: 216.28 m

Notes: Figures in square brackets indicate percentage of population belonging to dominant (and, where relevant, principal minority) confession.
Codes: Arm = ; Ath = Atheist; C = Roman Catholic; Cv = Calvinist; M = Muslim; O =Orthodox; P= Protestant.

Sources: * Figures from K. Boyle and J. Sheen, *Freedom of Religion and Belief: A World Report* (London: Routledge 1997), p.373. Population estimates and confessional breakdowns from D. Barrett, G Kurian and T. Johnson, *World Christian Encyclopedia: A Comparative Survey of Churches and Religions AD 30–AD 2200* (New York: Oxford University Press 2001).

resultant patterns indicates the contemporary extent of the deposits left by the early-modern confessional state system. This is seen most strikingly in the case of the historically mono-confessional territories, which, as the maps have already indicated, form Lutheran, Catholic and Orthodox blocs by virtue of being contiguous (see Table 1). The survival of these patterns might appear all the more striking because the baseline is the territorial division as existing in 2000, not those existing in the heyday of the confessional state. On the other hand, most of the territorial changes which have occurred over the twentieth century – and not least in its last decade –

have involved the division of the former imperial domains in Eastern Europe and greatly increased the degree of confessional concentration. Thus, the twentieth century re-creation of the Polish and Irish states actually led to historically unprecedented levels of religious homogeneity, in the Polish case accentuated by the demographic effects of the holocaust and mass population transfers of mid-century. The re-emergence as separate states in the 1990s of the constituent parts of the former Yugoslavia also made for the coincidence of confessional and territorial lines of differentiation by the most violent means.

In Western Europe, as Rokkan pointed out, the boundary between the Counter-Reformation south and the mono-confessional Lutheran north, centred on Scandinavia, was historically marked by a belt of territories of mixed confession (see Table 2) . Most of these territories were prey to rulers in adjacent mono-confessional territories and in the age of religious wars up to 1648 few were unaffected by attempts to impose single-confession settlements on them. The distinctiveness of this belt of territories is that these attempts failed despite the threat and use of force and penal laws; in each of them significant groups of the population resisted such attempts. Some barely survived, for example in Bohemia where the Hapsburgs almost managed to eliminate the old Hussite tradition. Others maintained impressive levels of resistance, emerging triumphant despite the attempts of larger and more powerful neighbours to impose obeisance to other confessions; this was the case with Irish Catholicism. Despite repeated efforts over a long time in the British Isles, Anglicanism never succeeded in establishing itself as the dominant tradition in Scotland, Ireland and Wales; these resisted and developed instead an alternative, in the case of Scotland Presbyterian establishment, and, in the other two, complete Anglican disestablishment in, respectively 1869 and 1914 (effective 1920). Even within England, where Anglicanism had been re-established in 1660 after a brief flirtation with religious toleration during the Civil War period, religious dissent could only be marginalised, never eradicated. By the mid-eighteenth century, when new forms of non-conformity began to emerge, religious pluralism was becoming a distinctive feature and early in the nineteenth century a successful campaign got under way to remove discriminatory religious legislation. With their moderate to high levels of both inter- and intra-confessional pluralism, then, the British Isles should then be seen as the north-western pole of the NW-SE multi-confessional belt.

The intervening belt of territories does not, as might be supposed, simply represent the juxtaposition of groups otherwise attached to the confessions which dominated the adjacent blocs. As in the case of Britain, these societies were fertile sources of new religious traditions right from the time of the Reformation. Rokkan emphasised the partial coincidence of this band of territory with the 'city belt', for long 'the stronghold of the Roman Church, with a high density of cathedrals, monasteries and ecclesiastical principalities'.[15] Here, in the turmoil of the Reformation period, the sects of the Radical Reformation were able to emerge and, despite vigorous persecution, eventually survive. Early experiments in religious toleration occurred, as for example with the freedom granted the Hutterites on the Liechtenstein estate in Moravia in 1529 and the settlement of Dutch Mennonites around the estuary of the Vistula, at the encouragement of the council of Danzig.[16] In the 1570s a large number of such experiments were even attempted on the wider stage, for example with the Pacification of Ghent and the Edict of Beaulieu (France) both in 1576. Most of these experiments were to fail, however; instead, the multi-confessional belt became a patchwork of small territories with established confessions and more or less marginalised religious minorities. Symbolic of this pattern are the two Swiss Landfrieden treaties of 1529 and 1531, which established the principal of confessional parity between the core cantons of the Confederation. It was this same principal which lay at the heart of the 1555

TABLE 2

THE HISTORIC NW-SE MULTI – CONFESSIONAL CULTURE BELT
Populations and Confessional Breakdowns by State in 2000

Ang-Cath-Calv-Sectn	Calv-Cath-Other	Luth-Calv-Cath	Cath-Calv-Luth
United Kingdom: 58.83 [An55:C9:P9:M2]	Netherlands: 15.76 [C34:P27:M4]	Germany: 82.22 [P37:C35:Other38]	Hungary: 10.04 [C63:P35]
Cath-Ang-Prot	*Switzerland*: 7.39 [C44:P41]	*Czech*: 10.24 [C40:P6:Ath37]	
Ireland: 3.73 [C85:Ang3.5]			
Total: 62.56 m	Total: 23.15 m	Total: 92.46m	Total: 10.04 m
	Grand Total 188.21m		

Notes: Figures in square brackets indicate percentage of population belonging to dominant (and, where relevant, principal minority) confession.
Codes: An = Anglican; Ath = Atheist; C = Roman Catholic; Cv = Calvinist; M = Muslim; O =Orthodox; P= Protestant.

Sources: Population estimates and confessional breakdowns from D. Barrett, G. Kurian and T. Johnson, *World Christian Encyclopedia: A Comparative Survey of Churches and Religions AD 30–AD 2200* (New York: Oxford University Press 2001).

Augsburg and 1648 Westphalian settlements which generalised it to the whole of the territory of the Holy Roman Empire until its dissolution in 1803.

A second, more easterly and narrower band of mixed-confession territories running north–south has also separated the Orthodox east from the two other mono-confessional culture areas from Estonia and Latvia (Lutheran–Orthodox mix)[17] in the north to Bosnia-Herzegovina (Catholic–Orthodox–Islamic mix) (see Table 3). More than was the case with the other multi-confessional belt, these are all classic buffer territories, constituting historically contested peripheries of the great landward empires of early-modern Eastern Europe, such as the Russian and the Ottoman. In the north Lutheranism is a legacy of Swedish overlordship, while the division between Uniates and Orthodox in the Ukraine stands as a reminder of the time when Poland–Lithuania was locally hegemonic. The scattered Islamic populations of the Balkans represent a deposit from the period of Ottoman rule when significant proportions of Slavs in some areas converted to the religion of their imperial masters. The presence throughout this band of territories of as many as six major confessional types (including the Armenian Orthodox, descending from the first of Christianity's great schisms, approximately 500 AD) makes for considerable complexity particularly at the southern end in the former Yugoslavia, where in the 1990s bitter ethno-religious struggles have occurred.

The implicit assumption of this Rokkanian exercise in mapping Europe is that it makes a difference which confession, if any, is dominant in a particular society or group of societies. In the present context, the lead hypothesis is that the pattern of church–state relations in society X can, in part at least, be explained by the fact that it is a mono-confessional Orthodox or Catholic or Lutheran society; alternatively, in the case of society Y, that it is a multi-confessional society with a particular range and balance of confessions represented. To make sense of these patterns, two factors must be examined in each case: the character of the different confessional traditions, particularly as this relates to church–state relations, and how strongly they are represented relative to other traditions. Spatial location as such is irrelevant except insofar as it is related to whether or not a society forms part of a mono-confessional bloc or, alternatively, of an intervening, multi-confessional belt of territories.[18] Of course, as is already clear, the patterns which have been identified are themselves in large part the product of a particular set of church–state relations in the early-modern period of the confessional state and it might be objected that the analysis is circular. This would only be so, however, if other contextual factors are left

TABLE 3
THE HISTORIC NE-SE MULTI-CONFESSIONAL CULTURE BELT
Populations and Confessional Breakdowns by State in 2000

Lutheran-Orthodox
Estonia: 1.40
[P17;O17]

Luth-Orthodox-Catholic
Latvia: 2.36
[P24;O24;C21]

Catholic-Other

Lithuania: 3.67
[C85;O3]
Poland: 38.77 [C92;O3]
Croatia: 4.47 [C88:O6;M3]

Muslim-Orthodox-Catholic	**Orthodox-Muslim-Catholic**	**Orthodox-Muslim**
Bosnia-Herzegovina: 3.97	Yugoslavia: 10.64	Georgia 4.97
[M60:O17:C17]	[O57:M16:C5]	[O58:M19]
Albania 3.11	**Orthodox-Muslim**	**Peripheral Dominance**
[M39:O16:C17]	Macedonia: 2.02	Armenia 3.52
	[O59:M28;C3]	[Arm78;C5]
	Cyprus: 0.60	Azerbaijan 7.73
	[O87:M18]	[M84:O4]

Grand Total: 87.23m

Notes: Figures in square brackets indicate percentage of population belonging to dominant (and, where relevant, principal minority) confession.
Codes: Arm = Armenian; C = Roman Catholic; M = Muslim; O =Orthodox.

Sources: Population estimates and confessional breakdowns from D.Barrett, G. Kurian and T. Johnson, *World Christian Encyclopedia: A Comparative Survey of Churches and Religions AD 30–AD 2200* (New York: Oxford University Press 2001).

out of account in such a way that the characteristic responses of the different confessional traditions to, say, urbanisation or anticlericalism, do not enter the analysis. For the purpose of developing a framework of analysis it is sufficient here to restrict attention to the core elements.

THE PHENOMENON OF MONO-CONFESSIONALISM

Use of the term mono-confessionalism points up the idea that there are features common to all settings characterised by the dominance of a single confession, regardless of any differences that may exist between the major confessions. Where it exists in three of Europe's corners, it is the outcome of histories of successful monopolistic regulation by either church or state authorities – and, most commonly, by both in combination. Prior to the great schisms of 1054 and 1517, 'the unity of the faith' was a more or less distant ideal throughout Christendom, despite the actual existence of much local variety and occasional 'subterranean' heretical movements of a more or less mystical or magical stripe. In the mono-confessional territories which emerged in the early-modern period, it was effectually underwritten by the legal apparatus of the confessional state, whereby conformity with the locally established religion was rewarded and nonconformity punished. In West and East the dominant rule was in effect, if not in always in law, *cuius regio, eius religio* (to whom the territory, to him the religion – that is, the rule that it was for rulers alone to decide which creed should be established within their territory). Thus, in Russia, which was not a party to the peace of Westphalia, the Tsars from the time of Peter the Great until the Revolutions of 1917 controlled the Russian Orthodox Church through the so-called Holy Synod. Even – and perhaps particularly – where elements of ecclesiastical independence survived the established religion and its officials enjoyed a range of privileges associated with their status. In each case, the precedence accorded to bishops in church and state reflected the honour attaching to established religion and encouraged attitudes of submission in the population at large for as long, at least, as religious observance and orthodox belief – shored up by legal protections and incentives – retained some hold. In early-modern Europe, the confessional state was the norm, varying little in substance, if greatly in outward form, between the different confessional culture areas; everywhere by the mid-eighteenth century the state authorities were in the ascendant.[19]

Orthodoxy, Catholicism and Lutheranism were all emphatically church, as opposed to sectarian, traditions.[20] As such they had a common prejudice in favour of 'comprehension', the principle that all members of society should be included. The corollary of this prejudice was that those who for whatever reason resisted inclusion in the church and submission to its demands were typically excluded from society and subjected to numerous indignities and punishments. As church traditions, the three principal confessions all made their own accommodations with the world, developing bodies of social teaching which typically promoted the legitimacy of state authority under certain conditions and elaborated a social ethic not based on excessive demands. Whereas sectarian traditions by contrast maintained strict boundaries between themselves and the surrounding society and attempted to keep themselves 'unspotted from the world', church traditions typically embraced worldly institutions and attempted to guide them.

Undeniably, an aspect of these church traditions was a tendency towards social and cultural conservatism, and a tendency to support the status quo, although the mission to embrace all sorts and conditions within society occasionally led them to take up certain issues of inequality and social justice which less comprehensive organisations tended by the nature of things to be less troubled by.

Where historic uniformity of religion could only be achieved and maintained by the actual use of coercive means, there often remained a heritage of resentment, and a tendency to attack the enforcers of religious uniformity when occasion offered. Where the coercive imposition of a particular religion on a society was, or is, *merely* a historical fact (that is, its dominance was so successfully established as virtually to eliminate deviant alternatives, as in the cases of Catholicism in Scandinavia, Protestantism in Austria, or Judaism, Islam and Protestantism in the Iberian peninsular) it is less likely to have any continuing impact in more recent times.[21] In a number of historically mono-confessional societies, however, remnants of long-suppressed minorities survived as living monuments to the repressive practices of the past. Thus, in the case of French Protestantism, a leftist political orientation is clearly a legacy of the repression which followed the Revocation, in 1685, of the Edict of Nantes, which had previously protected them. The consequences of the *dragonnades* of the late seventeenth and early eighteenth centuries is seemingly still reflected in levels of left-secular strength in the Cevennes and elsewhere.

Long-established mono-confessionalism also has its own pathologies, regardless of confession. Insofar as a virtual confessional monopoly in a particular territory has been maintained by positive state support on the one hand and the repression of challenges on the other, established churches might be expected to become less vital as organisations. They no longer depended for their sustenance on mobilising support within society, looking instead to those in authority within the state to provide, pursuant to the bargain of mutual support between 'Crown and Altar'. Finke, Iannacone and others trace to this circumstance the 'hollowing out' of the established churches of much of Europe.[22] Protected from the challenges of competition in an open religious 'market' of the sort which patently exists in the USA, many, if not most, of Europe's established churches are seen progressively to have lost the ability to maintain levels of commitment and loyalty, without which they have tended to go into institutional decline. A second pathology arises from the likelihood that over time state-guaranteed mono-confessionalism engenders secularist counter-reactions which are all the more vigorous because of the absence of alternative channels of religious expression of the sort that are provided in multi-confessional settings. In this case, the intolerance of the established religion is mirrored in the intolerance of its opposition. Eighteenth- and nineteenth-century France provides the classic illustration:

> The Baroque autocracies eliminate substantial religious dissent and forces build up within the system towards a revolution with an explicit secular ideology. Such revolutionary explosions become endemic, and religion as such is frequently a political issue. Coherent and massive secularism confronts coherent and massive religiosity.[23]

This indicates a generic feature of mono-confessionalism which has only been mitigated, for example in the Lutheran case, by the virtual relaxation of religious monopoly regulations and the effective toleration over time of intra-confessional differences and indifferentism.

Outside its core territories effective mono-confessionalism has occasionally been the product not of long histories of church establishment, but rather of successful resistance to neighbouring, alternative power centres which have attempted to impose other, alien creeds. The cases of Ireland, Poland and Belgium attest to the powerful mobilising effect of such predicaments. In each case, attachment to Catholicism was associated with the successful assertion of claims to national autonomy against powerful neighbours: respectively, England with its Anglican establishment, Prussia with its Protestant and Russia with its Orthodox establishments, and the Netherlands with its Calvinist establishment. The relative vibrancy of the Catholic tradition in each case, at least until recently, can be taken to reflect the fact that in such circumstances religion can operate powerfully as a vector of ethnic mobilisation and come out of the struggle greatly strengthened. Similarly, the strength of Bulgarian or Romanian Orthodoxy or of the Armenian Apostolic Church can be taken to reflect the importance of religion in maintaining an independent ethnic identity vis-à-vis the Ottoman Turks.

Whatever the historical background, where there is a strong tradition of religious uniformity within a particular society one would not expect confessional conflict to become politically contentious simply because the basis for such a conflict is not to hand. This does not mean that religion need be politically irrelevant; rather, it can as often as not be associated with the political entrenchment – to the point of virtual unchallengeability – of a particular religious tradition. On one view this is the case in the Irish Republic, where it has often been argued that, until recently at least, the position of the Catholic Church has been so strong that no party (and very few individual politicians) dare to challenge it.[24] This is a limiting case, however, since Catholicism has, as just noted, for long been as much a matter of loyalty to country as to church. In core mono-confessional countries, on the other hand, religion-related conflicts tend to run between orthodox believers and observants ('true believers') on the one hand and those who resist the pressures towards religious conformity on the other, often to the point of becoming militant unbelievers. In all the mono-confessional blocs, significant groups of unbelievers developed cultures of anti-clerical protest and secular dissent in the nineteenth century, if not earlier. It was among these that secularist liberalism and radicalism found their devotees and militants. Even in Scandinavia, where the weight of ecclesiastical establishment was moderated by the relative lukewarmness of the political elites, social democracy in its early days took on a secularist anticlerical bias.

Mono-confessional societies might be expected to be less tolerant than multi-confessional societies, where pluralism and difference has for long been part of common experience, and civility is held to require mutual non-interference, if not respect. They might be expected to be particularly sensitive to the multicultural challenges posed by recent increases in immigration and the emergence of more or less exotic new religious movements and cults. Such an association might, on the other hand, be moderated by a contrary tendency that some traditionally mono-confessional societies would appear to provide a natural context for the development of a broad moral consensus which embraces even the religiously indifferent. Which of these tendencies actually prevail in which contexts can only be established by further research.

THE DISTINCTIVENESS OF THE CONFESSIONS

However much the societies and cultures of the mono-confessional blocs resemble each other by virtue of a common mono-confessionalism, they also differ from each other because the confessions which dominate each of them are distinct. Even though they each represent 'churchly' forms of Christianity, the Orthodox, Lutheran and Catholic traditions each have their particularities. Some of the points of difference and distinction derive from the doctrinal and other conflicts occurring at the time of schism when they divided from each other. These arise in such different areas as central doctrines and beliefs, attitudes to authority, and traditions of social teaching. Once fixed in the initial conditions of conflict and incorporated into the shibboleths of each faith, such characteristics are not easily or lightly

40   CHURCH AND STATE IN CONTEMPORARY EUROPE

abandoned. Almost all versions of Christianity, whether churchly or not, share with the other monotheistic religions a commitment to preserving an original deposit of faith and practice, however much changing conditions in the world call for interpretative responses. While the commitment might be common, the nature of the responses varies and these have a tendency to take institutional form.

Hans Küng provides a useful shorthand for identifying how what he calls the principal paradigms still extant within present-day Christianity were initially generated and fixed.[25] His text also provides a useful summary of the principal differences between these paradigms; for example, on the basis of his account it is possible to generate a table illustrating contrasts between the Eastern Orthodox (or Byzantine) and the Western Catholic church traditions (see Figure 2).

An additional aspect of the contrast between Eastern and Western traditions, not mentioned by Küng, concerns the important connections

FIGURE 2

(BYZANTINE) ORTHODOX AND (ROMAN) CATHOLIC PARADIGMS COMPARED

Byzantine Paradigm	Roman Catholic Paradigm
I. Church forms a fellowship (koinonia) of churches without centralised authority. Ecumenical Patriarch has only primacy of honour	I. Church completely focussed on the Pope in faith, law, discipline and organisation: highly centralised absolute monarchy.
II. Church law incorporated into imperial state law under the authority of the imperial authorities	II. Own church law totally oriented on Pope as absolute ruler, lawgiver and judge – even over secular rulers..
III. Church incorporated into imperial system in which secular power dominated spiritual.	III. Church presented itself as a completely independent ruling institution, which at times succeeded in getting almost complete control over secular power.
IV. Entangled in most of the political and military conflicts of the secular power, the church often gave theological legitimation to wars, even inspired them.	IV. Augustinian doctrine of the legitimate use of force to achieve spiritual ends approved wars of conversion, wars against pagans, wars against heretics, even crusades against fellow Christians.
V. Clergy, apart from bishops, remained married and so closer to the people and more assimilated into structure of society.	V. Celibate clergy, set apart by celibacy. Dominant social status, superior to the lay state and totally subordinate to the Pope, who was thus supported by an omnipresent, centrally organised and mobile troop of auxiliaries inc. the mendicant orders.

between confessional traditions, language and ethnicity. As Flora *et al.* point out, the Catholic Church using Latin as its official language for the liturgy as well as internal communication hindered the development of vernacular literatures in its core regions: 'In the East, the situation was rather different: Greek was never as dominant as Latin in the West, and the rise of Church Slavonic paved the way for vernacular literatures; in the Greek Orthodox realm it was much easier to establish autocephalic churches.'[26]

The subjugation at different times by outside powers of most, if not all, of the Orthodox territories in Eastern Europe, from the Mongol destruction of Kievan Rus in the twelfth century until the final stages of liberation from Ottoman rule in the early twentieth, made for a close identification between the autocephalic churches of the East and the communities they served. The Ottoman 'millet' system, which allowed the Orthodox churches to subsist with relative autonomy and provide a central cultic focus for their communities, had the effect of further strengthening this bond. The continuing close connection between religious and ethnic identity reflects an important feature of Eastern Orthodoxy.

With his focus on Western Europe, Rokkan laid great emphasis on the religious-cultural contrasts between the mono-confessional Protestant north and the mono-confessional Catholic south; indeed, he placed these contrasts at the forefront of his analysis. It was partly a matter of the contrasts generated at the time of the Reformation and the ensuing Wars of Religion and partly a matter of how nineteenth-century elites responded to the challenges arising out to the French Revolution and its ensuing wars. His understanding of the consequences of decisions taken at the time of these two critical junctures highlighted a contrast between the weight of the different cleavages in the formation of the national party systems as between the Protestant and Catholic (mono-confessional) culture areas. In each case, the distinctive amalgams of values, institutional patterns and traditions of social doctrine associated with the different religious traditions are clearly associated with different outcomes in terms of the nature, depth and political 'translatability' of different cleavages. In each case, the cast of elite actors who were involved in making the critical decisions, and the nature of the strategic choices they made, varied in ways which were partly constitutive of, and partly derivative from, distinctive confessional traditions.

Clearly the three-way comparisons involving East–West and North–South contrasts cannot be addressed here except in the most summary way. Rémond, in his recent survey of church–state–society relations across Europe since 1789, refers to a number of the more salient points: in the Orthodox East the heritage of Byzantium was taken up by the Russian tsars who developed their own form of Caesaro-papism. The tradition of the Eastern churches' submission to the will of the sovereign would appear to be partly explained by this tradition; in none of the nations in which Orthodoxy was established did the churches ever enjoy more than a minimum of independence. This corresponded with the development within Orthodoxy of a spiritual tradition turned more towards union with God than to sustaining the body of society, so encouraging a passive acceptance of fate and/or providence. By contrast, not only did the Roman Catholic church 'expect the secular powers to recognize it as the perfect society, but it also made it their duty to support the faith in the exercise of its spiritual mission ... for the catholic church relations between religion and society were especially close, and ran counter to the idea of a total separation between the two ... catholicism is always characterized in its relation with society by its attitude of maintaining an active presence'.[27] So far as the Protestant north was concerned, the churches of the Reformation were more willing to accept the virtual privatisation of religion, thus restricting its purview to matters of personal conscience and social morality.

THE PHENOMENON OF MULTICONFESSIONALISM

Most empires from the Roman to the Russian/Soviet have spanned wide territories where the coexistence of different religious traditions was generally an accepted fact of life.[28] Imperial religious policies have typically had two aspects: on the one hand, there was the insistence that certain central symbols of political authority be acknowledged and deferred to, and, on the other, that adherents of the different religious traditions should not offend each other and so disturb the imperial peace. The Ottoman Empire was exemplary in this respect: under the 'millet' system, Jews and Christians as 'peoples of the book' were allowed to maintain their own communities and perform their own religious rites so long as they acknowledged Ottoman overlordship and paid their taxes.

By contrast, in the early modern period, the Spanish realm, born of the *reconquista* of the Iberian peninsular, was rather untypical in its religious intolerance. The expulsion, persecution and forcible conversion of the Moors, Jews and heretics represented a legacy of the anti-Islamic crusade which had culminated in the re-establishment of Christianity by the end of the fifteenth century. The policy of ruthless repression symbolised by the Spanish Inquisition also presented an omen of a new, rising religious intolerance, which established the repressive monopoly structures of the confessional state across Europe. In the other Habsburg territories, on the other hand, and in particular in the Holy Roman Empire after the first wave of religious wars in the sixteenth century, a tradition of mutual tolerance more typical of imperial regimes was first pioneered through the *cuius regio eius religio* rule of the 1555 Peace of Augsburg. A further century of religious wars followed before this rule was finally accepted and expanded in the scope of its application in 1648. The limits of imperial toleration were also clear, however; in 1555 only Lutherans and Catholics were to benefit and in 1648 its application was extended only so far as to include recognised Calvinist communities. At no time were adherents of the Anabaptist and other sectarian traditions officially allowed the benefits of toleration anywhere in Europe before approximately 1700, except for short periods in the mixed-religion territories of England (during the Interregnum), the Netherlands, Hungary and Poland.[29] For most of the early modern period even in the mixed-religion territories established churches were upheld as the only officially recognised cult and adherents of deviant traditions – even where they constituted large majorities of the population, as for example in Ireland – suffered the consequences of more or less draconian systems of legal persecution.

The other, eastern belt of mixed-confession territories had a much longer history of confessional oppositions and rivalries. As one author points out, popes and Byzantine emperors competed for authority in the Balkans as early as the eighth century.

> As relations grew more strained, the disputes took on a sharper tone. The conversion of Bohemia and Moravia in the ninth century had seen the clash of the two brothers, Constantine and Methodius, natives of Thessalonica and inventors of the Slav script with "the cohorts of Latins", Bavarian priests from Regensburg and Salzburg. Even today one of the sharpest cultural divisions in the Slavic world is between those peoples who were converted by Germans and those converted by Greeks.[30]

Despite this, Eastern Europe in the early modern period experienced a greater degree of mutual confessional tolerance than was the case in the West; nor was this simply a reflection of the existence of the millet system in the Ottoman territories. In late sixteenth century Poland and Transylvania remarkable experiments in religious toleration were the product more of a balance between the sponsors of alternative traditions.

In both cases the territorial belts of mixed confessional allegiance suffered the fate of buffer territories, dominated alternately by stronger neighbours with less ambiguous confessional commitments. Few suffered the fate of Poland (partition) but all, including Switzerland, bore the marks of proximity to rivalrous imperial neighbours. Nor did many succeed, as Poland finally did, in moving to a vigorous mono-confessional identity. Instead, the historic pattern of religious pluralism within society tended over time to be reflected in the structure of the state, typically through the recognition of the dominance in different areas of alternative religious traditions. In the Swiss case, the cantonal structure first developed in the old Catholic core of the Uri, Schwyz and Unterwalden allowed for the establishment of a range of different arrangements in different areas. In the Holy Roman Empire until its demise in the first years of the nineteenth century, a tradition of parity between the principal confessions was observed on the basis of the lines established in 1648. In the patrimonial territories of the Habsburgs religious toleration was finally introduced in 1781. Although this was too late for the last Protestants of Austria who had been expelled 60 years earlier from the Salzburg area, it allowed for the survival in Bohemia and Hungary of Protestant minorities which had long been hard pressed. Unsurprisingly, practical and permanent measures of religious toleration were first established in the mixed-confession territories, principally in the eighteenth century. This achievement nowhere took the form of full religious liberty and equality, however, let alone of a religiously neutral state.

As Rokkan demonstrated, in the countries of mixed confession in Western Europe, 'Church vs. Secular State' cleavages were translated into the party system with the same regularity and strength as in the mono-confessional Catholic territories.[31] This was partly because of the existence of large Catholic minorities, which had survived periods of Protestant ascendancy.[32] In the Netherlands it was also translated into the existence of the (Calvinist) Anti-Revolutionary Party, which rivalled, and in some respects excelled, the Catholic party in its opposition to liberal secularism. In the end, during the First World War, Calvinist, Catholic and secular parties agreed on a consociational bargain by which the state would remain officially neutral vis-à-vis the religious bodies. In Switzerland the bargain was a different one, building as it did on a confederal structure which accorded to the cantons wide discretion in the matter of church support. The German solution lay in between. In the Eastern band of mixed confession territories, the inter-war period saw a number of different experiments to accommodate religious differences. One of the most novel was that undertaken in Finland where, uniquely in Europe, two state churches were established for the same territory, one to serve the large Lutheran majority, the other the very small Russian Orthodox minority.

Arend Lijphart argued that in the two mixed-confession territories where Catholics and Calvinists had historically faced off against each other, the Netherlands and Switzerland, distinctive consociational arrangements had eventually been negotiated in order to avoid destabilising conflict. Both were traditionally Protestant-dominated states where Catholic rights had been (largely) secured only in the nineteenth century. The elements of the consociational bargain have included Grand Coalitions, *Proporz* arrangements, mutual veto, and different mixes of pillarisation and federalism sufficient for the purpose of underwriting the religious autonomy of the different confessional groups. In neither state, significantly, does either of the two major confessions enjoy a majority position, the once-dominant Protestants indeed having become a minority among the religiously observant section of the population. In Germany, where confessional competition has involved an opposition between Lutherans and Catholics, with the Calvinists embracing a considerably smaller element, a weaker version of the same pattern is in evidence. The existence within German Christian Democracy of a cross-confessional axis, reminiscent of the parity arrangements of the old Holy Roman Empire, has further strengthened what amounts at party level to a consociational bargain. In the UK a more variegated pattern developed: separate state churches for England and Scotland (respectively Anglican and Presbyterian), with no establishment in Wales and Northern Ireland, made for an uneven disposition of symbolic authority, while the existence on the left of religious nonconformity has undercut the development of anticlerical secularism as a political force. Only in Northern Ireland, where Protestants (Anglican, Calvinist and other) face Catholics across both psychological and physical barricades, do the cleavages between the different confessions continue to add to, rather than take away from, the depth of political cleavages. In this respect, and because of the connection between ethnicity and the uses of religion as a mobiliser of ethnic identity, conditions of conflict in Northern Ireland continue to resemble, if in somewhat less sanguinary form, the ethno-religious conflicts of the Balkans. The conditions under which confessional competition or mere coexistence translates into conflict or consociational compact therefore remains an unresolved question, but one in which the contribution of the inherited religious factor remains ambiguous and contested.

CONCLUSION

From the fourth to the nineteenth centuries the holders of secular authority throughout Europe, with few exceptions, tended to support or maintain systems of monopoly religious control, which were based on the premise that true Christianity – especially in the form favoured in their own jurisdiction – alone could provide for the ultimate interests of themselves and their subjects. As an incidental, but for long not inconsiderable, extra, religious uniformity and conformity was also without doubt seen as providing a valuable extra support of internal order and stability. In this judgement they were, not unnaturally, seconded by church authorities, which had their own reasons, both theological and prudential, for maintaining religious discipline and cohesion.

When faced with populations dividing, or divided, into groups or communities characterised by religious differences, however, secular authorities for almost 1,000 years tended to regard themselves as faced with the necessity of choosing between two principal options:

1. They could undertake to suppress or eliminate what the ecclesiastical authorities deemed to be heresy, so uniting the whole population on the basis of a continuing single, authoritative tradition. Historically, this was the dominant strategy of governments east and west, north and south from the ancient to the early-modern period, indeed for as long as the *ancien regime* remained in place – that is, in much of Western Continental Europe until approximately 1800 and in Russia until after 1900. Throughout the early modern period, after the wars of religion had by 1648 virtually finalised the religious borders of Europe, confessional state regimes shored up conformity to the locally dominant religious tradition and suppressed heretical or treasonous deviations. In 1685 the earlier 'error' of providing a measure of toleration for Huguenot deviations in France was rescinded. In 1817 the Prussian king forced Lutheran and Calvinist subjects to sink their differences in a United Protestant state church, while in the Russian home of the so-called Holy Alliance itself, the Tsar continued for another century to impose his government's will on the Church and on the population at large.

2. Or they could take sides with one of the groups committed to change or reform, granting it recognition and support, and promoting it in preference to all others. Positive support for one such group or community would typically be buttressed by discrimination against the others through the use of penal laws and other measures. This was the option chosen by the Elector of Saxony in his support and protection of Luther, as it was elsewhere throughout what became Protestant Europe. It was also practised in the other mixed-religion territories of Europe,

where the first option of suppression or elimination was found to present extreme practical difficulties. The predominant pattern here also involved state support for an established church underwritten by discrimination against non-conformists through the use of penal laws. In Britain the system involved the incorporation of two established churches, the Presbyterian and the Anglican in, respectively, Scotland and the rest of Britain, with those who refused to conform being excluded from public office, the suffrage and the other amenities of public life.[33]

There were of course two other logical options. The first of these was rarely taken seriously by governmental elites until during the twentieth century international standards of religious freedom and tolerance were finally set in place across most of the continent.

3. They could choose to tolerate all groups equally, holding the ring between them in case of conflict, either arbitrating their differences without prejudice or refusing to have any involvement except occasionally through the judicial settlement of disputes. This stance was attractive where divided loyalties were deeply entrenched and the difficulty of eliminating them correspondingly great. As Chadwick points out, however, in the Reformation period '[n]owhere in Europe was religious toleration thought compatible with civil stability, and the few lone Erasmian voices who advocated it were drowned in the general call for religious uniformity, whether Protestant or Catholic'.[34] The case for toleration, which was pushed by the *politiques* in France in the late sixteenth century and by Enlightenment thinkers in the eighteenth, by and large went by default until the nineteenth century, early experiments in Poland and Transylvania remaining for long merely exotic failures.

4. Or they could logically also choose to attempt the suppression of all existing religions, or religion as such. There are cases where the first of these was attempted, for example during what should have been the Year Zero of the French Revolution, when Catholicism was declared replaced by a Cult of the Supreme Being. Other attempts in the same heroic vein were made only in the twentieth century by the Bolsheviks after 1917 and by the Albanian regime of Enver Hoxha between 1967 and 1990. These two experiments were in the end comprehensive failures insofar as in neither case could it be said that religion was remotely destroyed.

In fact, the choice of options actually made by state elites has always been a mixture of more than one of these four. In the multi-confessional territories of Europe, in particular, elements of all four could sometimes be found – including the last in respect of radical sectarian traditions deemed dangerous or subversive. It is noteworthy that the one (No 3) that would seem most to recommend itself to liberal philosophers, namely neutrality of state orientation *de jure* and state non-interference *de facto*, only finally began to come into its own across Europe in the 1990s, when under the impact of the collapse of communism some five of the Continent's 50 or so territories opted for it.[35] In none of these five, on the other hand, would the church–state arrangements, which have been instituted in recent years, pass muster in the US Supreme Court, but then, as Walzer has pointed out, nation states such as most European states either are or still aspire to be provide very different contexts to those of immigrant societies such as the USA.[36]

NOTES

1. G. Davie, *Religion in Modern Europe: A Memory Mutates* (Oxford: Oxford University Press 2000), p.15.
2. The aspects listed are among the stock headings to be found in the 15 country entries in G. Robbers (ed.), *Church and State in the European Union* (Baden-Baden: Nomos 1996).
3. D. Martin, *A General Theory of Secularization* (Oxford: Blackwell 1978).
4. The term 'church–state relations' includes, of course, attention to denominations, sects and cults, as well as churches, and has an important bearing on many questions of individual human rights.
5. See H. Daalder. 'Europe's Comparativist from the Norwegian Periphery: Stein Rokkan 1921–1979', in H. Daalder (ed.), *Comparative European Politics: The Story of a Profession* (London: Pinter 1997).
6. S. Rokkan, *Citizens, Elections, Parties: Approaches to the Comparative Study of Processes of Development* (Oslo: Universitetsforlaget 1970) p.75.
7. Martin, *A General Theory of Secularization*, p.41.
8. 'The decisive contrasts among the systems had emerged before the entry of the working-class parties into the political arena, and the character of these mass parties was heavily influenced by the constellations of ideologies, movements, and organizations they had to confront in that arena'. Rokkan, *Citizens, Elections, Parties*, p.113 .
9. Ibid, p.75.
10. P. Flora, S. Kuhnle and D. Urwin (eds.), *State Formation, Nation-Building, and Mass Politics in Europe: The Theory of Stein Rokkan* (Oxford: Oxford University Press 1999), p.88.
11. The West–East axis/dimension/gradient in Rokkan's conceptual map was derived from his re-analysis of the work of Barrington-Moore, Perry Anderson, Immanuel Wallerstein and William McNeill and refers in different versions to political-structural, economic and even military factors.
12. See E. Prodromou, 'Paradigms, Power and Identity: Rediscovering Orthodoxy and Regionalizing Europe', *European Journal of Political Research* 30 (1996), pp.125–54.
13. See R. Rémond, *Religion and Society in Modern Europe* (Oxford: Blackwell 1999), pp.20–23.
14. D. Barrett, G. Kurian and T. Johnson, *World Christian Encyclopedia: A Comparative Survey of Churches and Religions AD 30–AD 2200* (New York: Oxford University Press 2001).

15. S. Rokkan and D. Urwin, *Economy, Territory, Identity: The Politics of West European Peripheries* (London: Sage 1993), p.27.
16. H. Guggisberg, 'The Secular State of the Reformation Period and the Beginnings of the Debate on Religious Toleration', in J. Coleman (ed.), *The Individual in Political Theory and Practice* (Oxford: Clevedon 1996), p.93.
17. Finland is not included here as the Orthodox community, although it is still represented in the country's second established church, is – and almost always has been, extremely small in size.
18. A further spatial distinction could be added between those mono-confessional territories which are at the relatively unthreatened core of the blocs, and, those which are close to the frontiers, that is, adjacent to multi-confessional areas or even historically close to an adjacent rival confessional bloc. For the importance of boundary location for the linkage between religion and ethnicity, see A. Hastings, *The Construction of Nationhood: Ethnicity, Religion and Nationalism* (Cambridge: Cambridge University Press 1997).
19. J. Casanova, *Public Religions in the Modern World* (London: University of Chicago Press, 1994); Rémond, *Religion and Society*.
20. A pithy summary of the analysis deriving from Weber, Troeltsch, Yinger and others is provided by Beckford: 'The sect-type of religious collectivity stood for social exclusiveness, doctrinal purity and rigorous ethical consistency. The church-type, by contrast, stood for social inclusiveness, doctrinal latitude and a degree of ethical relativism. In other words, the sect-type tried consistently to maintain distance from the world, whereas the church-type sought to influence the world from within.' J. Beckford, *Religion and Advanced Industrial Society* (London: Routledge 1989), p.34.
21. 'The prisoners of Montaillou were the last of the Cathars. But it was not the absolute end. For the brave fight put up by the peasants of Ariege to preserve the remains of their heterodox beliefs after 1300 foreshadowed the great Protestant revolt of two centuries later.' E. Ladurie, *Montaillou: Cathars and Catholics in a French Village 1294–1324* (London: Penguin 1978), p.xi.
22. See L. Young (ed.), *Religion and Rational Choice* (London: Routledge 1997); and M. Chaves and D. Cann, 'Regulation, Pluralism and Religious Market Structure', *Rationality and Society* 4/3 (July 1992), pp.272–90. For a vigorous critique of this approach, see S. Bruce, *Choice and Religion: A Critique of Rational Choice Theory* (Oxford: Oxford University Press 1999)
23. Martin, *General Theory of Secularization*, p.6.
24. See B. Kissane, 'The Illusion of State Neutrality in a Secularising Ireland', in this volume.
25. H. Küng, *Christianity: The Religious Situation of Our Time* (London: SCM Press 1994).
26. Flora *et al.* (eds.), *State Formation, Nation-Building, and Mass Politics in Europe*, p.87. Autocephalic means having its own head, independent.
27. Rémond, *Religion and Society in Modern Europe*, pp.24–6.
28. See M. Walzer, 'The Politics of Difference: Statehood and Toleration in a Multicultural World', in R. McKim and J. McMahan (eds.), *The Morality of Nationalism* (New York: Oxford University Press 1997), pp.247–8
29. Poland in the sixteenth century was a pioneer in the area of religious toleration. In the seventeeth century, however, religious toleration was snuffed out and Catholicism became a defining feature of Polishness, threatened to the West by Protestant Prussia and to the East by a resurgent Orthodox Russia.
30. R. Bartlett, *The Making of Europe: Conquest, Civilization and Cultural Change, 950–1350* (London: Penguin Books 1993), p.8.
31. See J. Madeley, 'Politics and the Pulpit: The Case of Protestant Europe', in S. Berger (ed.), *Religion in West European Politics* (London: Cass 1982), pp.150–53.
32. It was also true in the case of Ireland prior to independence. The Irish Nationalist party (and before it the Catholic Emancipation movement), although it was not officially only for Catholics, represented the Catholic interest vis-à-vis Unionism.
33. In the case of Britain, the 1689 Toleration Act did not match up to earlier promises. Not a single old law against religious liberty was repealed or suspended; instead Protestant dissenters were granted relief by being exempted 'from the Penalties of certaine Lawes'. Catholics and Unitarians, on the other hand, received no relief. Baptists and Quakers were to

be tolerated only if they made a declaration in place of the required oath against the Catholic doctrine of transubstantiation. Dissenters continued to be excluded from public office.

34. H. Chadwick and G. Evans (eds.), *Atlas of the Christian Church* (London: Macmillan 1987) p.111.
35. See J. Madeley, 'Liberal Democracy and the Principle of State Religious Neutrality' in this volume, above.
36. Walzer, 'The Politics of Difference', p.249: 'Homogeneity is rare, if not non-existent, in the world today. It means only that a single dominant group organizes the common life in a way that reflects its own history and culture. It is these intentions that determine the character of public education, the symbols and ceremonies of public life, the state calendar, and the holidays it enjoins. Among histories and cultures, the nation-state is not neutral; its state apparatus is an engine for national reproduction.'

Church–State Separation Swedish-Style

GÖRAN GUSTAFSSON

At the turn of the millennium, a change took place in relations between the Church of Sweden and the state. Thus, an issue that had been on the political agenda for almost 50 years had reached its solution. For a long time there had been talk of a 'separation between the church and the state', but when the point of decision was reached, the outcome instead was a 'change of relations between the church and the state'. This contribution describes primarily the drawn-out process which finally led to a change of status for the Church of Sweden in relation to the state. However, in order to make the description meaningful, it is necessary to start considerably earlier.[1]

300 YEARS OF A CONFESSIONAL STATE: 1593–1900

The transition from Roman Catholic to Evangelical-Lutheran Christianity that had gradually taken place in Sweden in the sixteenth century was confirmed in 1593 at the Uppsala convocation, one of the milestones in Swedish history: the national church in Sweden should be Evangelical-Lutheran. The following century is usually described as 'the century of the Lutheran orthodoxy'. It is characterised by strict confessional adherence. The priests were civil servants as well as ecclesiastical ones, and their duties included a number of non-religious tasks. The situation may be summarised as the absence of any form of religious liberty and the total identification between the state and the church, at the national as well as at the local level.

The strict integration was upheld throughout the eighteenth and a large part of the nineteenth century, although there were some weak attempts at loosening this bond. For a long time it was a criminal offence for a Swedish citizen to dissent from the Lutheran Church and its doctrine. The early Baptists were frequently imprisoned because they had gathered for worship, and their children were forcibly christened. The leader of the Baptists was exiled from the country in 1850. Exile was also the punishment for conversions to Catholicism and that law was last applied as late as in 1858. During the nineteenth century, Swedish society began a slow process of change which from the 1850s onwards also influenced Lutheran attitudes. In 1858 permission was granted for people to meet to pray without the presence of a priest. This was important, not least for the Baptists. In 1860 the presence of other churches – primarily the Roman Catholic Church and the Methodist-Episcopal Church – alongside the Church of Sweden was officially acknowledged. Members of other churches were known as 'confessors of foreign faiths' and although considered 'apostasy from the pure Evangelical doctrine', conversions were permitted. The procedure was somewhat simplified in 1873, but the right to leave the Church of Sweden was only available for those who had some sense of belonging to another Christian tradition. To place oneself completely outside any form of religious life was impossible. In 1863 the regulations stipulating the requirement for everyone to receive communion at least once a year were abolished.

Local administration in Sweden was reformed in 1862 in a way which, in the long-term perspective, proved significant for church–state relations. Prior to that date, the limited groups who had voting rights within a local area had taken almost every decision on virtually every issue, religious or otherwise. The new legislation stipulated that decisions should be taken in the parish on matters concerning the church and in the secular local authority on other matters. Thus every individual was a member of two distinctive but geographically identical units: the parish and the secular borough. These two units each had their own distinctive area of competence, and it was only in the former that the local parish priest had a legally confirmed influence. The finances of the parish were separate from those of the secular borough, and parish finance was founded on the right for the parish to levy taxes on anyone living within its boundaries. Matters handled by the parish were not only purely ecclesiastical ones, but also matters concerning education and public child-care. In the 1860s important constitutional changes also took place at the national level. When the Swedish Diet of the Four Estates was replaced by a two-chamber Riksdag (parliament), and the House of Clergy was thus abolished, the Church Assembly was introduced for the purpose of consultation on ecclesiastical matters and given the right to veto government propositions. The Church Assembly consisted of all the bishops, elected representatives of the clergy and lay representatives elected by the parishes.

THE FIRST REFORMS: 1900–1952

The late nineteenth century is marked not only by industrialisation and urbanisation, but also by the emergence of a number of popular movements. It is particularly the Free Churches and the Labour Movement that are of interest here. The Free Churches comprised international movements, such as the Baptists and the Methodists, as well as national Swedish Covenant Church. The Labour Movement included a trade union as well as a party-political branch, of which the latter, in the form of the Social Democratic Party, is of particular interest here. Unsurprisingly the Free Churches appealed for greater religious liberty and for equality between various religious organisations as well as for an end to the strong position accorded to the Church of Sweden in education. In its early stages, the Social Democratic Party was not only anti-church, but also anti-religious.

Free Church members of the Riksdag, who were usually Liberals, and the Social Democrats were often in agreement on certain issues. Between them they supported legislation permitting civil marriage as an alternative to the regulation that every marriage had to be contracted by a Church of Sweden wedding ceremony. The option of civil marriage became a possibility by a law adopted in 1908. Legislation about funerals was altered in 1927, abolishing the obligation to be buried according to the Church of Sweden rite.

However, when the Social Democrats first entered power at the end of the First World War, it was not the issues of religious liberty and the abolition of the state-church system that were given priority. A new party programme was adopted in 1920, which in its introduction certainly demanded 'religious liberty' among other liberties and in special points underlined the intention to strive for 'a non-confessional educational system' and 'the abolition of the state-church. Properties currently under the disposal of the church should remain in public ownership'. The point made about Christian education in schools was at the time in the process of being applied. In 1919 an alliance between the Social Democrats and the Liberals forced the adoption of a new syllabus for statutory education, which meant that the subject of Christian education should no longer be based on Luther's Small Catechism, but on the Bible. With hindsight, it may seem surprising that this move was considered radical and became the object of fierce debate. In practice the alteration implied the principle that statutory religious education should no longer focus on the interpretation of the Christian faith as embraced by the Church of Sweden, but should be turned into a more general education about the Christian faith. At the end of the 1920s a major step was taken towards transferring education from the area of responsibility of the parishes to that of the local secular authorities.

The demands for religious liberty were not left to rest in Sweden. After 50 years, in 1920, only 0.4 per cent of the population had left the Church of Sweden.[2] This meant that only a minority – for example about a third of the Methodists – of those who had the right to leave the Church of Sweden had actually made use of that opportunity. The 1911 Riksdag had requested an investigation of the issues of religious liberty, but this was not carried out until 1925. The report suggesting that it should be possible to leave the Church of Sweden without stating any particular reason was published in 1927, but no subsequent government proposition was ever put forward. It is worth noting that the investigators took as their starting point the view that church and state were in principle united, so that the church was primarily 'the public agency for moral and religious nurture' rather than a community of believers.

As the process of secularisation continued, the Church of Sweden sought a theologically grounded identity. In the early twentieth century, such an identity was found through attempts to present the church as 'a folk-church'. This phrase reflected an understanding of the church and the parish, which, with its offer of grace, addressed itself to everyone within Sweden or within the local area. The ideology was primarily directed against the Free Churches and their confessional demands. In 1929 the bishops made a proposal to the Church Assembly: the church, while retaining its position as an established state-church, should become less dependent on the state, and the right to withdraw from personal membership should be unlimited. The Church Assembly, whose lay members were by and large politically conservative, united behind the proposals from the bishops and requested a government investigation of the possibilities of carrying out this programme of reforms. This investigation was never undertaken.

The motive behind this initiative from the bishops was at least partly an awareness of the risk that the church might lose its identity as a Christian denomination and become merely an agency of the state. Throughout the 1920s individual Social Democrats expressed their view that 'the care of religion' should not be left entirely outside the control of the state. They found no need to weaken the influence of the state on the affairs of the church. It ought rather to be strengthened, so that the state-church system would be ever more refined. However, the party programme commitment to abolish the state-church system was not altered.

In the 1930s a government dominated by the Conservatives made a proposal for a reform of decision-making structures in the parishes. As mentioned above, legislation from the 1860s had separated the ecclesiastical parish from secular local government. The process of democratisation of Swedish society in the early twentieth century had soon altered the structure of the secular authority but it had had no effect on the parishes, where decisions about work as well as taxation were taken by direct democracy. In many places public gatherings of this sort became too large as urbanisation continued. In 1930 the Riksdag decided that in the larger parishes a representative body, the church council, should be elected using a system of proportional representation. This change implied an opening for the political parties into the ecclesiastical decision-making structures that they were all keen to make use of, and which proved significant 40 years later, when the issue of church–state relations came on the agenda. The position of the parish as a parallel structure for matters of religion, alongside the secular local authority, thus became yet more clearly marked, and representative democracy was later applied also to smaller parishes.

About the same time (in 1932) room for manoeuvre for the parishes was increased by a decision taken by the Riksdag permitting them to use the revenues from the properties the church had accumulated over the centuries. Who the rightful owner of such properties actually was remained unclear, but an initiative from a bishop who for a short while was a member of the government resulted in the right for the local parish rather than for the state to dispose of, and to receive revenue from, them. The parishes thus became the stewards of considerable financial resources. In 1945 they set up a national organisation for the purpose of looking after their common interests, which in time became a significant agency, both externally and internally, in raising issues regarding church organisation and finances.

Religious liberty was finally achieved in Sweden by legislation gaining force on 1 January 1952 without much tension between particular groups or interests. Nobody was henceforth forced to belong to the Church of Sweden against his or her own free will, and withdrawal from membership was made free and uncomplicated. However, only very few people made use of this new freedom. Although the number of people who were not members of the Church of Sweden almost doubled in 1952, those who did belong continued to make up almost 99 per cent of the population. Nor did a great number of withdrawals from the Church of Sweden take place during the following few years.[3] This would seem to indicate that there was no widespread dissatisfaction with the Church of Sweden. The demand in the Social Democrat party programme for 'The abolition of the state-church' remained in place until 1960 and was then replaced by the rather more 'woolly' wording: 'Relations between church and state should be regulated in accordance with the principles of religious liberty.'

THE OPTIMISTIC PHASE: 1956–72

Once main religious liberty issue had been resolved, other matters affecting church–state relations could be brought forward. In 1956 four members of the Riksdag – three Social Democrats and one Liberal – proposed that an investigation should be set up for the purpose of clarifying how a separation of church and state could take place and what effects might be expected from a decision in that direction.[4] They claimed that the Swedish state-church system was incompatible with religious liberty; it is noteworthy that the philosophical legitimation of this proposal did not come from Karl Marx so much as from Immanuel Kant. During the subsequent debate in the Riksdag, the proposal received support from the Social Democrats and from the Liberals, but the Conservatives and the Agrarians took a negative view.

An investigatory commission was set up in 1958, but it did not include any members of the Riksdag. A leading lawyer was appointed to chair it and the membership included representatives from the Church of Sweden and a leading Free Church member, as well as one person with connections to the Labour Movement. The commission's remit stated that its task was 'to present material for a continued discussion and as a basis for a future decision' on the matter in hand. The minister in charge foresaw that this investigation would take time and that many experts would have to be consulted on legal, theological and practical issues. He underlined especially the request that the investigation should highlight the possibilities and suitable methods for 'the clarification of the significance of religion as a social factor'.[5] The request indicates that the government approached church–state matters in the same way as any other. Government-sponsored investigations in Sweden frequently begin by commissioning research, which applies social scientific methods to the field of enquiry. It is worth noting that the remit came close to what is usually considered a basic issue of sociology of religion, and the group was asked to provide a clarification on this matter. And that was not all. Members of the investigation also expressed the desire that the results of this research 'should serve as guidance for the determination of the future relationship between the state and the church' and 'how these relations might be shaped in case of a more complete dissolution of the historic bonds'. This is an instance of the trust in the art of social engineering that partly governed Swedish society during the decades following the Second World War. The social scientists were expected to be able to provide answers as to how circumstances in various fields might best be ordered and then, by referring to these findings, the politicians could arrive at decisions.

The 1958 Church and State Commission produced about ten volumes of studies of ecclesiology, religious liberty, public registration, financial issues and other such issues. The first volume sought to clarify the possibilities for undertaking a study in the field of sociology of religion along the lines requested. Such a clarification of 'the significance of religion as a social factor' was, however, never achieved.

The investigation had completed its various tasks by 1968, that is, after ten years, and its final report drew up four different models for the future relationship between the Church of Sweden and the state:[6]

• The A-model envisaged no alteration of any major significance.
• The B-model envisaged a church organised independently of the state but retaining its property, and which would be aided by the state in the collection of a tax-like membership fee from its members.
• The C-model envisaged the same as the B-model, but with the exception that the state would have no part in the collection of membership fees.
• The D-model envisaged a church organisation entirely independent of the state and the transfer of all church-owned property – apart from the church buildings – to public ownership.

With this inventory of possible models for how this matter might be taken further, the first phase of the inquiry into the future relationship of the Church of Sweden to the state had reached its goal. The initiative returned to the then minister in charge of Church Affairs, Olof Palme. He quickly commissioned a new investigation, but this time with parliamentary membership. An internationally renowned Social Democrat, Alva Myrdal, took the chair and besides her, the group was made up of three Social Democrats and one representative each from the Conservatives, from the liberal Peoples' Party and from the agrarian Centre Party. Of the three Social Democrats, one was an active member of a Free Church, another had a clear orientation towards the Church of Sweden and the third represented the younger generation. Of the other members, two had obvious links with the Church of Sweden and another had a background in the Free Church Movement. The remit for this investigation, which would become known as the 1968 Preparatory Committee on State and Church, stated that the group should concentrate primarily on what the previous committee had described as the A-model and the C-model.[7]

This committee worked comparatively quickly and completed its report in 1972. Its proposal was that the relations between the Church of Sweden and the state should be changed in a manner which largely corresponded to the previous C-model: church and state should be separated, the church should take its own decisions on all matters, it should retain its property and, for a period of transition only, the state should aid the church in the collection of membership fees. Two social functions that the church had hitherto handled should be transferred to the responsibility of secular society, namely the maintenance of civil registration and, at least in principle, the provision of burials and the maintenance of cemeteries. The committee argued on the basis of the principle of religious liberty, but it was not so much the religious liberty of the individual as that of the denominations that guided their conclusions. The fact that the state had the right to make decisions on a number of ecclesiastical issues implied in some sense that the religious liberty of the Church of Sweden was limited. The obvious differences with regard to the public status of the various denominations – the Church of Sweden, the Free Churches and the so-called Churches of Immigrants – also implied an offence against the principle of religious liberty and religious equality. A time schedule for the proposed alterations was drawn up. It envisaged that the process would be completed in ten years, that is, from the beginning of 1983 the work of the Church of Sweden would no longer be regulated though public legislation.[8]

The members of the commission jointly supported the proposal described above. Some of them however reported divergent views on some details. The most significant of these was the view proffered by the representative for the Centre Party and thus also for rural interests. He did not share the majority views that the right for the church or the parish to levy taxation on its members should cease, and that the responsibility for the provision of burials should be transferred to secular authorities.

When the committee had submitted its proposal and various agencies and organisations were given an opportunity to express their views it soon became clear that the negative voices were many and strong. The various state authorities and the secular boroughs were largely positive. The same applied to an even greater extent to the Free Churches and the Churches of Immigrants. The dioceses and the parishes of the Church of Sweden itself, however, took a negative view. And this negative view prevailed not only in rural areas. Only in a minority – less than 20 per cent – of the parishes asked did the representatives consider the proposal acceptable. The majority of the other parishes made it clear that they did not want any changes at all, or that they would only accept changes on condition that the right for the church to levy taxes would remain.[9] It thus became clear that a cleavage existed, not so much between representatives for the various political parties as between the politically elected representatives for the state and the local boroughs on the one hand and the mainly politically elected representatives for the parishes on the other. The unity behind a relatively generous proposal that the Social Democrat government had hoped for did not exist, and even within its own party there were many people at the parish level who were very critical. Church–state matters ran the risk of becoming an issue in the parliamentary elections due to be held in 1973. In this situation, Palme, now Prime Minister, declared that the government had no intention of putting forward any legislative proposal for a separation of the church from the state. The matter was thereby not written off but was left to rest.

While the 1968 Preparatory Commission on State and Church had been at work, the Church Assembly had taken an initiative of its own, so indicating that the church had no desire to remain passively outside the political process. The bishops were unanimously behind a proposal which also had the support of many other members of the 1968 Church Assembly. The favoured view was that the Church of Sweden should continue as a state-church, but that its legal status should be constitutionally regulated. The church ought to have more influence on its own internal affairs, and both its democratic features and its leadership structures ought to be strengthened. The Church Assembly and those who signed this proposal added a theological dimension by underlining that baptism, rather than the parents' membership, should determine whether or not a child be considered a member of the Church of Sweden. The Church Assembly also appointed a special working group, called 'the Archbishop's Working Group on Church and State', in order to clarify some of the issues.

The question of the future status of the Church of Sweden was seen as determining the opportunities that would be open to the parishes to work at the local level. The National Association of Parishes was very active in lobbying in favour of a system that would preserve a legally regulated status for the Church of Sweden. In 1968 this association approached every parish, asking the elected lay representatives to respond to a questionnaire. The result showed that, of the 2,356 units that replied, only five per cent were in favour of church–state separation.[10] The Association of the Parishes also sponsored a survey that sought to clarify the views of the Swedish people on the issue of church and state. The main result was that less than half of the respondents (47 per cent) said 'Yes' to the question 'Do you consider it to be in the interest of the people of Sweden that the church has a structural connection with the state?' whereas a quarter (24 per cent) said 'No'.[11] Surprisingly few people were decidedly in favour of the status quo, and the minority was by no means insignificant.

THE RESISTANCE PHASE: 1973–79

The writing off of the church–state issue from the immediate political agenda did not mean that it had been completely left aside. The considerations of the government and the church leaders in this new situation, and the identity of those actively engaged in finding ways ahead, belong to the least known aspects of this long process. The situation can be described as follows: several actors in leading positions, within the political as well as within the religious system, wanted to change the relations between the church and the state, but they had to proceed with great care, since there was strong opposition, not least among those linked to the point of intersection between religion and politics represented by the parish councils and their national organisation.

In this new situation, the group appointed by the Church Assembly in 1968 continued its work. In 1975, the Social Democrat government appointed another working group, consisting of civil servants and other officials, for the purpose of clarifying, together with the group appointed by the Church Assembly, what possibilities there might be of breaking the existing deadlock. The minister acting on this issue was not an ideologically driven Social Democrat, but rather a person with a pragmatic attitude, deeply rooted in the everyday reality in which both the local authorities and the parishes had to work. Both the minister and the archbishop personally participated in the introductory soundings, and the archbishop also took part in the discussions at a later stage. The process became more complicated later when in 1976 the Social Democrats lost power, since the three Centre, Liberal and Moderate (Conservative) parties that then made up the government took very different views on the church–state issue. The group appointed by the Social Democrat government nevertheless continued its work with only minor changes of personnel, and in 1978 this group and the group appointed by the Church Assembly jointly submitted a proposal for the ordering of the future status of the Church of Sweden.[12]

The joint proposal implied that, by and large, the suggestion made by the 1968 Preparatory Commission on State and Church still stood, but it was amended to provide a more generous deal for the church at the time of the separation. Thus, the help from the state to collect membership fees should be permanently rather than temporarily offered, and the state should also make an annual financial contribution to the church. A new idea introduced in this proposal was the suggestion that the Riksdag should adopt a special Law for the Church of Sweden, and thus guarantee its religious as well as its structural identity. Besides this joint proposal, the report submitted in 1978 also included a proposal from the Archbishop's Working Group on how the organisation of the Church of Sweden should be structured at diocesan and national levels.[13] There should be a representative body for each diocese as well as for the church as a whole. The Church Assembly should no longer consist of a certain number of priests and a certain number of lay people. The bishops should not be eligible for election but should participate in the Church Assembly *ex officio*. A central governing body of the church should be set up under the leadership of the archbishop. On the question of membership of the church, the church-based working group suggested that, in the future, baptism should be required as a condition for membership, but also that all current members at the time of separation should be able to retain their membership of the Church of Sweden.

This new proposal implied a generous deal for the Church of Sweden as part of the separation which major parts of the political establishment wanted to achieve. It was financially generous and it was possible to foresee what the organisation of a church, structurally separated from the state, would look like. The Law for the Church of Sweden would guarantee that the church did not change its identity but would continue to display the same (or a similar) public appearance as it had done for a long time. Nevertheless, much anxiety still existed in many parishes in the face of the proposed changes. This anxiety focused largely on financial issues, but there were also fears that the character of the Church of Sweden as a 'folk-church' (or national church) open to everyone would be replaced by that of an elitist church, demanding active commitment from its members and ascribing a more dominant role to the clergy.

Such views became evident when the new proposals were sent to the parishes for comments. The efforts at reform were not received with any enthusiasm at the local level. The number of parishes that took a positive view on the proposed change of relations (27 per cent) was considerably smaller than those which expressed a negative attitude (45 per cent).[14] Negative attitudes to the various partial issues relating to the main proposal were even more obvious: 70 per cent of the parishes wanted the church to retain responsibility for civil registration – both for church members and for others. This is an illustration both of the strength of the perception of the identity between the church and society that still existed and the perception of the responsibility of the national 'folk-church' for all Swedish citizens and not only for its own members.

The Minister for Church Affairs, who was a member of the Liberal Party and who personally was strongly in favour of a change, chose, in spite of public opinion, to submit this proposal to the 1979 Church Assembly. It was clear even before the meeting of the Church Assembly that it would be rejected. More than half of the members rallied to a counter-proposal favouring instead partial reforms within the framework of continued links between the church and the state. The debate was long and intense, and the voting resulted in 54 against – thus indicating that the Church Assembly should use its right of veto – and 42 in favour,[15] including ten (of which the archbishop was one) of the 13 bishops. Among the priests there were 20 in favour and six against. There was thus a massive majority among the lay members (45–12) against the proposed change of relations.

THE EXPLORATORY PHASE: 1980–91

The Liberal Minister for Church Affairs took advantage of an opportunity that the Church Assembly had opened up. A new committee was appointed. Although both the government and the parliamentary majority was non-Socialist, a Social Democrat – a well-known expert on constitutional matters – was appointed chairman and, besides him, the committee consisted of two Social Democrats and one representative each from the three non-Socialist parties. All the members were deeply rooted within their own parties and, except the chairman, they were also known to be active lay members of the Church of Sweden. Their work quickly issued in a proposal (1981) that brought a new dimension to the entire question of the future status of the Church of Sweden: its character as a state-church should be marked even more clearly while the church should at the same time be given greater liberty as well as a more democratic structure for decision-making.[16]

The established, state-related status of the Church of Sweden – which meant that it was ultimately dependent on decisions by public agencies of the state – was underlined by the provision that in future the government and the Riksdag would pass legislation relating to church matters without any opportunity for the Church Assembly to influence the decisions. Only consultation would be required. At the same time, while all the principal issues were left entirely to the politically based agencies of state, the Riksdag would be required to delegate to the Church Assembly the right to take decisions on a number of internal church matters. The constitution of the Church Assembly should also be changed. Rather than consisting of all the bishops *ex officio*, priests elected by all the priests and lay members elected by the parishes – altogether 96 people – the Church Assembly should henceforth consist of 251 members, all elected indirectly by electors appointed by the parishes. No places were reserved for bishops or priests, but they could be elected. The bishops should attend the meetings of the

Church Assembly and their views on doctrinal issues would be accorded particular significance.

The government immediately submitted this proposal to the Church Assembly, which was thus given the opportunity to decide whether or not it should dispossess itself of its right to veto legislation on church matters in the future and whether or not its own character should be entirely changed. There was no unanimity, but, following long debate, the proposal was accepted by a majority of 71 votes to 22.[17] The opposition was particularly strong among the priests: 16 out of the 25 priests who voted were against. Priests sympathetic to the idea of a 'folk-church' were, however, largely in favour. The majority of the bishops were in favour (9–2 of those who voted) and the positive majority among the laity was overwhelming: 53–4. Although the issues were not immediately linked to the issue of church–state relations, many people were well aware that this decision could mark a major step on the way towards the dissolution of the previous link. Following the decision by the Church Assembly, the government and the Riksdag were entirely at liberty to alter basic matters relating to the status of the Church of Sweden without taking further notice of the Church Assembly. Of course, nobody expected such a one-sided decision within the foreseeable future.

In accordance with the legally required period between elections to the parish councils, elections to these bodies were held in the autumn of 1982. The first task of the newly elected members was to choose the electors who would in turn elect the members of the new Church Assembly. The elections followed, to a greater extent than in the past, party-political lines. Many active church members, not least many priests, were opposed to this further politicising of the church elections and therefore nominated 'non-aligned' candidates. Table 1 shows the party distribution of members of the Church Assembly and the Swedish Riksdag in the autumn of 1982.

The Non-Aligned Group, according to whose view the parish councils and the Church Assembly should be independent of the political system, constituted a minority, although a large and, as it turned out, active minority. Within this group, priests made up almost two-thirds of the members. There were, however, many priests also within the other groups, and altogether priests made up 36 per cent of the total membership of the new Church Assembly, while they had accounted for 40 per cent of the previous one, which had been elected according to status categories. The largest group in the new Church Assembly was the Social Democrats, but their position in this body was nowhere near as strong as that which they held in the simultaneously elected Riksdag. The Centre Party, focused as it was in rural

TABLE 1

THE COMPOSITION OF THE SWEDISH CHURCH ASSEMBLY AND
THE SWEDISH RIKSDAG 1983 (%)

	Church Assembly (N=251)	Swedish Riksdag (N=349)
Non-Aligned Group	21	–
Moderate (Conservative)Party	19	25
Centre Party	24	16
Liberal Party	5	6
Social Democrat Party	31	47
Left Party	–	6
Sum	100	100

Source: G. Gustafsson: *Kyrkomötet 1983–1985* (Stockholm: Religionssociologiska institutet, Religion och Samhälle 1987), pp.7 ff.

areas, was represented in relatively larger numbers in the Church Assembly than in the Riksdag.

Not much happened with regard to the church–state issue during the rest of the 1980s. With hindsight it could be said that the internal organisation of the church was being consolidated, particularly at diocesan level, in preparation for a new situation in which the status of the church would be different compared to the past. That the same political will prevailed within the government, which was again Social Democrat, was made obvious through the decision at the end of this decade to transfer the responsibility for civil registration from the duties of the priests to that of the taxation authority. Thus the church lost one of its remaining general social functions. This change took place in 1991. As a result of an initiative in the Church Assembly, an investigation was set up within the church to consider its rules about membership. The requirement that baptism should be necessary for membership of the Church of Sweden encountered fierce opposition at local level.[18] However, church leaders and contacts with international ecumenical organisations managed to make people aware of the peculiar stance taken by the Church of Sweden by accepting as members such a large number who had not been baptised. When a proposal was put forward by the Church of Sweden Central Board in 1994 suggesting that baptism should be a basic requirement for membership of the church – except for those who were already members – only very few, or less than ten per cent, of the members of the Church Assembly were opposed.[19]

In 1988 the Church Assembly requested that the government set up an investigatory commission for the purpose of clarifying the legal and financial framework for the work of the Church of Sweden after the reforms of the early 1980s. The Social Democratic government appointed a prominent lawyer as sole investigator, but both the civil servant who had primarily handled ecclesiastical matters for the government office and the General Secretary of the Church of Sweden, were made available to him as experts. The task requested from the investigator was considerably wider than the Church Assembly had intended. A key sentence in the remit makes it clear that the investigation should consider 'what, from the state's and from the church's point of view respectively, it seems appropriate to alter in this relationship'. The result was a report in 1992, which listed various problems and unclear issues, but also defined 'three different models as a basis for discussion about alternatives to the present order'.[20]

The first model envisaged that the Church of Sweden should be granted a status 'as independent as possible within the framework of a continued constitutional link to the state'. The second model envisaged that the Church of Sweden should be granted very extensive liberty, but should be the object of framework legislation. The right for the parishes to levy taxation on its members should cease, but the state should assist the church in the collection of tax-like membership fees. The third model envisaged that the Church of Sweden should be granted the same status as all other denominations, that is, that there should be no particular legislation and that all the denominations should have financial equality. They could all be given grants from the state for particular purposes, for example for the maintenance of historic buildings of cultural significance. According to all three models, the Church of Sweden would retain its property.

Within the framework of this investigation, an extensive survey of the views of members of the Church of Sweden on the church–state issue was also undertaken. The central question was 'Do you in principle view a separation between the state and the church as something positive or negative?' A few more respondents (46 per cent) took a positive view than those who replied negatively (34 per cent). A significant result was that both among those who replied 'positive' and those who replied 'negative' there were several who chose the weak alternative 'fairly' rather than the strong 'very'.[21] In other words, this was not a very important issue for the majority of the church members.

THE DECISION PHASE: 1992–

The shift from a Social Democratic to a non-Socialist government in 1991 hardly affected the course of events. Following the presentation of the results of the experts' investigation, the new Minister for Church Affairs,

herself a member of the Christian Democrats and with personal links to the
Pentecostal Movement, appointed a new investigatory commission almost
immediately. The efficient lawyer was re-appointed and took the chair, but
otherwise the committee had a parliamentary membership, including
representatives from all the seven parties that in the early 1990s were
represented in the Swedish Riksdag. The majority of the members were well
known for their Christian commitment. This investigation, known as the
Preparatory Committee on Church Matters, presented its results in 1994.
The proposal corresponded in many aspects to the second model presented
by the 1958 investigation, and thus to a fairly large extent, also to the
B-alternative presented by the 1968 Preparatory Committee on State
and Church.[22]

Now finally there was a specific proposal for how relations between
church and state in Sweden should be changed. The proposal was that the
Church of Sweden should in future be free from the state, but a new Law
for the Church of Sweden should be promulgated, stating that the Church of
Sweden should remain an Evangelical-Lutheran denomination, that it
should work across the entire country – that is, that every part of Sweden
should belong within a territorial parish – that each individual should belong
to the parish of his or her residence, and that it should have a democratic
organisation linked to an episcopal structure. Besides the Law for the
Church of Sweden, the investigation also proposed a Law for Religious
Denominations, which would regulate the public and legal status of other
religious associations, but which would in part also apply to the Church of
Sweden. The parishes' right to levy taxation would cease, but the state
would help with the collection of the membership fee, calculated in
proportion to income. Public grants for the maintenance of historic
buildings of high cultural value (old churches) would be made. The parishes
of the Church of Sweden would continue to take full responsibility for the
provision of funerals and for the maintenance of cemeteries for its own
members and for everyone else. This would ensure that Christians as well
as people of other faiths or none would be guaranteed the opportunity of a
dignified burial in accordance with their own beliefs.

The representatives of the political parties in the commission were not
entirely in agreement. The representative for a populist party, New
Democracy, which temporarily held a not insignificant number of seats in
the Riksdag, did not support the proposal but favoured the status quo. The
representative for the Liberals did not want any special deal for the Church
of Sweden, but considered one law dealing with all denominations
sufficient. By and large, the representative for the Left Party shared this

view. The representative for the Centre Party also held a leading position in the Association of Parishes and therefore claimed that the Law for the Church of Sweden ought to be more detailed than was proposed by the majority of the committee. He also thought the parishes should retain the right to levy taxation on its members.

Neither the Social Democratic nor the Moderate members of the commission made any alternative proposals, and thus the majority proposal had a firm political foundation. As part of a general reorientation away from cultural conservatism towards neo-liberal values in the 1980s, the Moderate Party had changed its views on the church–state issue and took a favourable view on the proposed changes. It could therefore be expected that almost two-thirds of the members of the Riksdag would support the proposal, and when it was sent for comments to a number of legal and administrative public agencies as well as to various church agencies and organisations, no major objections were raised. In the spring of 1995, in preparation for the final decision on the church–state issue, the government, which was once again Social Democrat, gathered the leaders of the other political parties for negotiations concerning the proposition to be submitted to the Church Assembly and then to the Swedish Riksdag. Political unanimity was achieved, and even the leader of the Centre Party supported the government proposition, which in all essential details followed the proposals made by the Preparatory Committee on Church Matters.

The Church Assembly considered the proposal in August 1995. Criticism was noted referring to various details and some issues that needed further clarification prior to any change were pointed out, but apart from that, the reception was positive. The Social Democrats, the Liberals, the Christian Democrats, the Moderates and the Non-Aligned Group all supported a positive reply from the Church Assembly to the government legislative proposal, though the Centre Party group was not all in agreement. A minority of this group, constituting a tenth of all members of the Church Assembly, registered their dissent.[23] The Riksdag discussed the matter in December 1995, and there was widespread agreement on the main issue. Representatives for the Left Party, however, took the view that the proposal did not go far enough, and the voting figures on the proposal were 282–19.[24]

Following the historic decision, the investigatory work was continued both by the state and the church. One result was that a tax-like fee, which non-church members and church members alike would be required to pay for funerals and cemetery maintenance, should be given directly to the parish in which they were resident and not to the state as the Preparatory

Committee on Church Matters had proposed. The Riksdag accepted that proposal. That decision is interesting in principle, as it means that the Church of Sweden continues, even after the completion of its separation from the state, to be responsible for the provision of a service which, although frequently linked to a religious – Christian or other – ceremony, is nevertheless ultimately a public, social duty: to ensure that there are opportunities for the care and disposal of the dead.

The church's preparatory work took on great proportions, since an entirely new Church Order, including regulations of a number of very different issues, had to be worked out. It is interesting to note how it was envisaged that the democratic process in a church with greater liberty relative to the state would work. The church should have decision-making bodies representing its members at three levels: the national level (the Church Assembly) the regional level (the diocesan church council) and the local level (the parochial church council). Formerly, it was only the representatives at the local level that had been elected through general, direct elections. The turnout at these elections had decreased since the 1930s, when elections to the parochial church councils began, and when about 20 per cent of those entitled to vote would do so. In the 1997 elections only about ten per cent of the church members voted. Representatives to the diocesan church council and to the Church Assembly were elected through indirect elections by electors appointed by the parochial church councils. The proposed new Church Order envisaged direct elections to the parochial and diocesan church councils, and the Church Assembly should, as previously, be elected indirectly. However, during the debate in the Church Assembly it became apparent that the Social Democrats, the Moderates and the Liberals wanted direct elections to the Church Assembly as well, whereas the Centre Party and the Non-Aligned Group wanted to stick to the proposal. The former view won the day by 144 votes against 95.[25] The independent church-to-be was thus given an electoral system that was by and large parallel to that which is used in the political system, and which is clearly different from the electoral system that applied to the church prior to the change of church–state relations.

The change in the relationship between church and state took place without any drama on 1 January 2000. In the immediate aftermath, membership figures of the Church of Sweden have hardly been affected. Many people had expected a major exit when the church no longer had the same official character. During the last 'normal' year, 1998, the number of exits was 13,000, in 1999 it was 34,000 and in the year 2000 it was 19,000.[26] So far no major decrease in the number of members has been noted, since

the highest exit figure, for the year 1999, represents less than half a per cent
of the total number of members of the Church of Sweden. Elections to the
different levels of representation took place in September 2001. The turnout
was 14 per cent, which is somewhat higher than in previous elections. Table
2 shows the distribution of seats in the Church Assembly following this
election. For the purpose of comparison, figures showing the distribution of
seats in the Church Assembly prior to the change of church–state relations
and in the Riksdag following the 1998 elections are also given.

The relative strengths between the various groups in the Church
Assembly did not change very much following the introduction of the new
electoral system. The political parties still dominate and the Non-Aligned
Group enjoys the same strength as before. The Social Democrats remain the
largest group. The Centre Party and the Moderates have lost a little, but this
is compensated by the gains of the Christian Democrats. The distribution of
seats in the Church Assembly corresponds fairly well to that in the Riksdag,
especially if the Non-Aligned Group is left aside, although the Centre Party
continues to have a much stronger position in the Church Assembly. The
results of this first Church Assembly election indicated that the power
structure in the Church of Sweden is likely to remain more or less the same
as in the past. It also shows that, although the Church of Sweden has gained
greater liberty from the state, it has not gained any greater independence
from the political system that prevails in Swedish society.

TABLE 2
THE COMPOSITION OF THE SWEDISH CHURCH ASSEMBLY 2001
AND 2002 AND THE SWEDISH RIKSDAG 1998–2002 (%)

	Church Assembly 2002–5 (N−251)	Church Assembly 1997–2001 (N−251)	Swedish Riksdag 1998–2002 (N=349)
Non-Aligned Group	14	15	–
Moderate (Conservative) Party	19	24	23
Centre Party	17	24	5
Christian Democrat Party	10	4	12
Liberal Party	6	6	5
Social Democratic Party	29	27	38
Left Party	2	–	12
Green Party	–	–	5
Other Groups	3	–	–
Sum	100	100	100

Source: For the Church Assembly 2002: Data from the Secretariat of the Church of Sweden.
Other data: G. Gustafsson, *Tro, samfund och samhälle* (Örebro 2000), p.211.

A CONSENSUAL OUTCOME

The Church of Sweden often describes itself as a church with a 'double line of responsibility'. This is evident also in the Law for the Church of Sweden, which says that the work should be carried out 'in co-operation between a democratic organisation and the ordained ministry of the church'. That statement emphasises the two structures of authority within the church, each of which is legitimate in its own way. Bishops and priests have authority based on theological tradition and because of acts of ordination. The local parish council, the Church Assembly and other elected bodies also have responsibility for the church, but their authority is built on the same democratic values which prevail in the rest of society. It may be worth noting this 'double line of responsibility' when summarising the evolution of the church–state issue in Sweden.

When the state brought the church–state issue onto the agenda in the 1950s, public opinion took a negative attitude to any change. When a relatively far-reaching proposal for a separation was available in 1972, it emerged that, had a government proposition been put forward, it would not only have led to a conflict between the political parties, but would also have encountered fierce opposition from the Social Democrats holding elective offices within the parishes. Thus there was no legislative proposal, and after a demonstration of strength, particularly from those democratically elected within the church, the Social Democratic leaders became inclined to seek solutions based on broad political agreement. Events at the end of the 1970s showed that the government, regardless of its political colour, stood a better chance of finding allies within the church among those whose authority was based on theological formation than among the elected representatives of the laity. Many priests and bishops were in favour of seeking greater liberty for the church and they were willing to pay the price, whereas the elected lay representatives often took a negative view of every proposal made. The final result was a compromise acceptable to all parties: those who were theologically aware gained a church with much greater liberty. The representatives for parish interests gained a structure that guarantees the continuity of more or less the same financial framework for the work of the church as in the past. The politicians were able to wind up a state-church that had become increasingly obsolete as Swedish society had become more multi-cultural. The political parties can still, through the Church Assembly and its other elected bodies, retain a certain amount of influence in the church. The Swedish people seem hardly to have noticed the change of church–state relations since the work of the church has not changed at all. The drawn-out process has probably meant that the change has not come across as dramatic, but as something foreseen and expected. What would have been experienced as a very dramatic change in the 1960s appeared at the turn of the millennium to be a step in a natural process of development.

Translation: The Revd Sr Gerd Swensson, Te Deum

NOTES

1. Besides the author's general knowledge of these developments, the first two parts are built on a number of works that describe various circumstances or provide a survey of earlier or more recent Swedish church history. With reference to the first part I would draw attention particularly to A. Jarlert, *Romantikens och liberalismens tid* (Sveriges kyrkohistoria 6, Stockholm 2001); S. Thidevall, *Kampen om folkkyrkan; Ett folkkyrkligt reformprograms öden 1928–1932* (Stockholm 2000); J. Alwall, *Muslim Rights and Plights: The Religious Liberty Situation of a Minority in Sweden* (Studia Theologica Lundensia 53, Lund 1998); H. Tingsten, *Den svenska socialdemokratins idéutveckling*, 2 (Stockholm 1967 (1941)); and C. Dahlgren, 'Sverige', in G. Gustafsson (ed.), *Religiös förändring i Norden 1939–1980* (Malmö 1985), pp.196–237. When describing developments since the 1950s I have made great use of L. Ejerfeldt, 'Das Verlhältnis von Staat und Kirche in Skandinavien, dargestellt am Beispiel Schweden', *Essener Gespräche zum Thema Staat und Kirche* 17 (Aschendorf 1983), pp.128–43; S. Ekström, *Svenska kyrkan i utveckling. Historia, identitet, verksamhet och organisation* (Stockholm 1999); T. Ekstrand, *Folkkyrkans gränser. En teologisk analys av övergången från statskyrka till fri folkkyrka* (Stockholm 2002); *Svenska kyrkan i förnyad gestalt – 1995 års beslut om kyrka och stat* (Stockholm 1996).
2. SOU, *Betänkande med förslag angående vidgad rätt till utträde ur svenska kyrkan och därmed sammanhängande frågor 13* (Stockholm 1927), pp.65 ff.
3. T. Pettersson, *Utträdesbenägenhet och utträde ur Svenska kyrkan* (Religionssociologiska institutet, Forskningsrapport no. 149–50, Stockholm 1979), pp.4 ff.
4. Riksdagens protokoll 1956, motion FK 163 and AK 214.
5. SOU, *Religionens betydelse som samhällsfaktor. Möjligheter och metoder för en sociologisk undersökning 26* (Stockholm 1963), pp.7 ff.
6. SOU, *Svenska kyrkan och staten 11* (Stockholm 1968), pp.21 ff.
7. SOU, *Samhälle och trossamfund 36* (Stockholm 1972), pp.29 ff.
8. Ibid., pp.12 ff.
9. SOU, *Samhälle och trossamfund. Sammanställning över remissyttranden över betänkanden av 1968 års beredning om sat och kyrka 9* (Stockholm 1974), p.385.
10. I. Ström, I. Stoltz and P.-O. Nilsson, *'En kraftig uppryckning av kyrkan?'* (Stockholm 1970), p.50.
11. Ibid., p.81.
12. SOU, *Stat- Kyrka Ändrade relationer mellan staten och Svenska kyrkan 1* (Stockholm 1978).
13. SOU, *Stat – Kyrka. Kyrkans framtida organisation 2* (Stockholm 1978).
14. Kyrkomötets protokoll 1979, Regeringens skrivelse no. 2, p.202.
15. Kyrkomötets protokoll 1979: 20, pp.583 ff.
16. SOU, *Reformerat kyrkomöte, kyrklig lagstiftning mm 14* (Stockholm 1981).
17. Kyrkomötets protokoll 1982: 19, p.622.
18. SKU, *Vägen till kyrkan. Om dop och kyrkotillhörighet 1* (Stockholm 1988), p.223.
19. Kyrkomötets protokoll 1994: 8, p.140.
20. SOU, *Ekonomi och rätt i kyrkan 9* (Stockholm 1992), pp.401 ff.
21. J. Alwall, G. Gustafsson and T. Pettersson, Svenska kyrkans medlemmar och kyrka-statfrågan (SOU:102, Stockholm 1991), p.45.

22. SOU, *Staten och trossamfunden* 42 (Stockholm 1994).
23. Kyrkomötets protokoll 1995:10, pp.263 ff.
24. Riksdagens protokoll 1995/96:34, p.49.
25. Kyrkomötets protokoll 1999:7, pp.166 ff.
26. Data from the Secretariat of Reseach, Church of Sweden, Uppsala.

The Illusion of State Neutrality in a Secularising Ireland

BILL KISSANE

On 6 March 2002 the Irish public went to the polls for the third time in 20 years to vote on a constitutional amendment which would limit the circumstances under which Irish women could avail themselves of an abortion. Not only would the threat of suicide be removed as a legal ground for abortion, but tough new penalties would be introduced for those performing abortions. Remarkably, the section of the electorate that voted, by a margin of less than 11,000 votes, rejected the government's proposals, leaving open the possibility that a future Irish government might legislate for abortion under certain circumstances. It was the first time that an alliance between the Fianna Fail party, the Catholic Church, and the official pro-life movement was defeated in a referendum on abortion, suggesting that the liberal minority among the Irish electorate may one day become a majority. The results showed a clear urban–rural divide, with all 11 Dublin constituencies and the other large population centres having 'no' majorities. A similar pattern had been evident in the divorce referendum of 1995, suggesting that large sections of Irish society are becoming secularised. Indeed, in the six referenda on moral issues which have taken place since the 1960s, the liberal argument has prevailed in four, albeit by small margins in two of them.

In this context, the question of whether Irish state policy reflects these changes or defends the values of a declining 'moral majority' becomes an important issue. In matters of religion, the liberal ideal of state neutrality demands of the state that it (a) does not justify its policies on the basis of the intrinsic superiority or inferiority of particular conceptions of the good life and (b) does not attempt to influence people's judgements of the value of these different conceptions.[1] If this is so, then it is clear that the Irish state has never been a neutral state: as is evidenced by the existence of a long section in its constitution entitled 'Directive Principles of Social Policy'. On the other hand, the idea of state neutrality is not absent in contemporary

Irish politics either. A recent Supreme Court decision ruled that the state broadcasting service RTE had acted unlawfully in its disproportionate allocation of broadcasting time to the liberal side in the 1995 divorce referendum. According to the Chief Justice, in a fair referendum the broadcasting service had an obligation to see 'that the scales should be held equally between those for and against' the proposed constitutional amendment.[2] This suggests that the state should indeed be neutral between rival conceptions of the good and should not use public resources to influence peoples' autonomous evaluation of those conceptions.

The question becomes one of assessing how far the undoubted social changes that have affected Irish society during an era of rapid 'Celtic Tiger' economic change have resulted in a process of 'neutralisation'. The rise in prosperity, a huge expansion in third-level education, and the beginnings of mass immigration have all definitely set the scene for changes in the nature of the church–state relationship in Ireland.[3] Despite this, the Irish Republic was recently derided by the Unionist leader, David Trimble, 'as a sectarian, mono-ethnic, mono-cultural state'. In contrast, Conor Cruise O'Brien sees the March 2002 referendum result 'as the last high watermark of the Church's influence' in the Irish Republic.[4] Arguably, however, the Irish state has not yet reached a position of neutrality on religious issues and recent trends suggest that if any kind of state neutrality is to be achieved, it will take the form of the state intervening to equalise the conditions under which various religions operate, rather than a regime of church–state separation. If this is so, the Irish state will become more committed to social pluralism than to classical liberalism, terms typically confused in Irish public discourse.[5] Irish liberals often see recent changes to be heralding the advent of a more 'liberal and pluralist' society in the Republic, but the nature of the present church–state relationship suggests that the particular form of pluralism that is evolving is anything but liberal. If this is so, neutrality may be a less coherent organising principle of public life than many think.[6]

THE 1937 CONSTITUTION

The starting-point for any consideration of state neutrality in Ireland today is the 1937 constitution. Not only did it attempt to reconcile secular traditions of thinking about politics with Catholic social teaching, it also attempted to specify the precise relationship between church and state. On the one hand, the constitution re-established a greater degree of majority-restraining features in the political system than had hitherto obtained in practice.[7] On the other, it reflected the values of the majority of the population, and while a recent review of the constitution has concluded that the constitution has stood the test of time well, it also recommended changes in the constitution in precisely those areas where the influence of Catholic social teaching is most obvious.[8] Because the constitution can only be amended by referenda, differences over its component parts have become a central part of Irish public life in a way that was not envisaged when it was introduced.

The nature of the relationship codified in 1937 had been forged under the Union with Britain, when a close identification between Irish nationalism and the Catholic religion developed, and nationalists defended the prominent role accorded the church in areas of public policy. For example, an attempt by the British government to introduce a non-denominational primary education system in the early 1900s was frustrated by an alliance between the new Sinn Fein party and the Catholic hierarchy.[9] After independence, the Catholic Church retained its control over primary and secondary education, and in 1929 passed a decree stating that no Catholic could attend a non-Catholic primary or secondary school without special permission, a policy that also applied to attendance at Trinity College Dublin. Not only were most schools owned and staffed by the Catholic Church, the training of primary teachers was also largely under the control of the Catholic Church: the only non-denominational teacher-training college closed in 1922.[10] The state made little effort to interfere in the running of the educational system, which was largely a private enterprise: one Education Minister compared his role to that of a plumber who was called in only when something went wrong.[11]

For educated Catholics, the idea that the state should be neutral when it came to religion was anathema. In 1927 John Marcus O'Sullivan, the Minister of Education, summarised the official view:

As an instance I might cite the claim so often put forward that the state should have a monopoly of the control and direction of Education. Indeed on the whole question of the relations of Church and state and the latter's functions, there has steadily become dominant in modern times a view, which when adopted as a dogma of universal application is certainly unCatholic but which receives support from many Catholics. This development is all in the direction of the secularisation of the state – the normal being regarded as a condition of affairs in which the state stands neutral and indifferent between belief and unbelief. In fact this neutrality frequently develops a distinct bias against belief. In many quarters the tendency is to regard religion as a weakness to be tolerated; a concession to facts and to the slowness of the masses to accept progress.[12]

Independence spelt a greater degree of co-operation between church and state than before; sessions of the Irish parliament began with prayers in Irish; it was customary for elected representatives to attend a special mass before any new parliament was convened; and on the feast day of St. Patrick, government ministers attended Mass at the Catholic Cathedral in Dublin. When the first President of Ireland, Douglas Hyde, died, no government minister attended his funeral service since attendance at Protestant services was considered a sin by the Catholic Church. It became standard practice for public works to be blessed on completion, and the attendance of both state and clerical figures became the norm.[13] During the civil war of 1922–23 security measures passed by the state were followed by statements by the hierarchy emphasising the duty of the population to support the government in every way possible. After the civil war it became customary for the Irish army to parade up the aisle of Catholic churches during morning mass on Easter Sunday, an event that was followed by a ceremony at the local graveyard to commemorate IRA men who had lost their lives during Ireland's struggle for independence. Thus the forces of militant Republicanism and conservative Catholicism, which had been bitterly opposed to each other during the civil war, were reconciled in a church ceremony.

By 1937 legislation on divorce, contraception, and freedom of expression had already been brought into line with Catholic teaching. The collusion between a puritanical political elite keen to be seen to be doing its best to defend Catholic values, and a church anxious to ensure that the new state would not limit its power, is best reflected by the fact that the state's Censorship of Publications Board was usually chaired by a priest. Under the new constitution, it became obligatory for the President, now the head of state, to make a religious declaration when taking up office. The preamble to the constitution adopted in 1937 reads:

> *In the name of the Most Holy Trinity, from Whom is all authority and to Whom, as our final end, all actions both of men and states must be referred,*
> > *We, the people of Eire,*
> > *Humbly acknowledging all our obligations to our Divine Lord, Jesus Christ, Who sustained our fathers through centuries of trial,*
> > *Gratefully remembering their heroic and unremitting struggle to regain the rightful independence of our Nation,*

> *And seeking to promote the common good, with due observance of*
> *Prudence, Justice and Charity, so that the dignity and freedom of the*
> *individual may be assured, true social order attained, the unity of our*
> *country restored, and concord established with other nations,*
> *Do hereby adopt, enact, and give ourselves this Constitution.*

This clearly suggests that the 'common good' should be evaluated by religious criteria and implicitly identifies the Irish nation with the Catholic religion. The preamble can be considered part of the constitution since the title *Bunreacht na hEireann* precedes the preamble, and the preamble itself uses the phrase 'this constitution'.[14] Moreover, in 1984 the preamble was cited in the Supreme Court to justify the prevention of a decision rendering unconstitutional certain nineteenth-century statutes criminalising homosexual conduct between consenting adult males. The court considered that the preamble indicated an acceptance of Christian values, and that the state was entitled to discourage conduct 'morally wrong and harmful to a way of life and to values which the state wishes to protect'.[15]

Article 44.1.2 read that 'the state recognises the special position of the Holy Catholic Apostolic and Roman Church as the guardian of the Faith professed by the great majority of the citizens', although other religions were also recognised. Since de Valera resisted pressure to recognise the Catholic Church as the 'true' church, or 'the Church established by Christ', this latter acknowledgement has been seen as a generous gesture.[16] However, this article, alongside the preamble, was cited in a Supreme Court decision in 1951, upholding a decision of a judge in the High Court which ruled that as a result of the special position accorded the Catholic religion in the constitution, the child of a failed mixed marriage should be awarded to the mother, contrary to practice at the time, because she was a Catholic, rather than to the father, who was a Protestant.[17] The recognition of the Catholic religion only as the faith of the majority, while falling short of establishing that church, and bearing in mind its Napoleonic precedents, cannot be construed as an example of state neutrality.

In other respects, the constitution was more liberal. In line with its predecessor, the 1922 constitution, the state was also prohibited from endowing any religion, from discriminating against people on the basis of religious belief, and from acquiring church property by compulsion, except for certain specific public works, and then only on payment of compensation.[18] Article 44.1 reads that 'the state acknowledges that the homage of public worship is due to Almighty God. It shall hold His Name in reverence and shall respect and honour religion'. Taken with the preamble, this has been taken by the courts to mean that the citizens of the Irish state are a religious people, but 'in terms which do not confine the benefit of that acknowledgement to members of the Christian faith'.[19] However, article 44.1 also provides a broad justification for the state's participation in religious ceremonies, the playing of the Angelus on state television and radio each day being an obvious example.

What proved more controversial was article 41.3.2, which declared that 'no law shall be enacted providing for the grant of a dissolution of marriage'. Up to 1996 divorce was impossible in Ireland and the primacy of church law over state law with regard to marriages was demonstrated by the fact that throughout the whole period the church continued to annul marriages which the state regarded as still valid, leading to the situation where remarriages of Catholics who had been granted an annulment 'were potentially bigamous in the eyes of the state'.[20] The constitution's emphasis on protecting the family was also reinforced by two clauses, article 41.1.1, recognising the family as 'the natural and fundamental unity of Society', and article 41.1.2, stating that the state 'guarantees to respect the Family in its constitution and authority'. The rights of the family were also extended to education, article 41.2 stating that the state must 'respect the inalienable right and duty of parents to provide, according to their means, for the religious and moral, intellectual, physical and social education of their children'. The state had no right to insist that children must attend schools established by the state or any particular type of school 'designated by the state'.

By the time the constitution was drafted, clerical control over education was so entrenched that the only outstanding question was how to secure the status quo by constitutional legislation.[21] At the heart of the system were two principles enunciated by canon law; (1) that Catholic parents should send their children to schools which provide a Catholic education; (2) that the state should provide the parents with the freedom to make such a choice.[22] Both were achieved under the 1937 constitution, which provided constitutional protection for 'a system of public funding of private schools'.[23] As late as 1992/93 2,988 (93.1 per cent) out of 3,209 primary schools were Roman Catholic and just under three-quarters of second-level students attended denominational schools.[24] The saving grace of the provisions for education was article 44.2.4, which read: 'Legislation providing state aid for schools shall not discriminate between schools under the management of different religious denominations, nor be such as to affect prejudicially the right of any child to attend a school receiving public money without attending religious instruction at the school.'

Such a provision, preventing religious discrimination in the admission of pupils to publicly funded schools, had several precedents, having been present, in different forms, in the 1922 constitution, the 1921 Anglo-Irish Treaty, and two of the Home Rule Bills.[25] Similarly, state instructions to national schools required that they were to identify clearly which periods were for religious instruction in order to facilitate any child whose parents wanted to exclude it from religious instruction.[26] However, there was no provision in the constitution requiring schools to attenuate the religious ethos of the school, so that obvious manifestations of that ethos, such as the presence of crucifixes in classrooms, the saying of prayers in advance of each class, or the holding of school masses, were perfectly constitutional. As a result, Protestant parents who could not send their children to a nearby Protestant school had no option but to send their children to a school where the ethos would be emphatically Catholic, even if they were exempted from religion classes. In other respects, too, the denominational character of state schools was accentuated over time. In 1956 the denominational character of all national schools was explicitly recognised by the state, despite the fact that not all such schools were attended only by people of the same religion. In 1965 a rule requiring that teachers be 'careful in the presence of children of different beliefs not to touch on matters of controversy' was deleted from the rules for primary teachers. Then in 1971 a new curriculum for primary school teachers encouraged the integration of secular and religious components of the curriculum, hitherto kept separate, on the grounds that 'the separation of religious and secular instruction into differentiated subject compartments serves only to throw the whole educational function out of focus'.[27] As a result, the possibility of parents choosing to remove their children from religious influence was no longer present.

If state neutrality is achieved when a state refrains from encouraging or discouraging religious belief or disbelief, then it is clear that the Irish state has never been neutral with regard to religious belief.[28] Rather, it has left non-believers in particular with extremely curtailed rights within the system. Indeed, the 1971 primary teachers' handbook stated that 'religious instruction is, therefore, a fundamental part of the school course, and a religious spirit should inform and vivify the whole work of the school', thus undermining efforts to keep secular and religious instruction separate in primary schools that date back to the 1830s.[29] Neither was the state neutral between religions, since the ban on divorce infringed the rights of the small Protestant minority whose religion did not insist upon the indissolubility of marriage.[30] Thirdly, if a requirement of state neutrality is that there be no disabilities associated with adherence to a particular religious or secular belief system, then the Irish state has also failed to meet this criterion.[31] A case in 1985 saw the High Court uphold the validity of a legal decision to justify the dismissal of a secondary teacher on the grounds that her lifestyle implied a rejection of the values and the behaviour that her employers, a Catholic school, sought to promote. The judge commented that the plaintiff 'knew from her upbringing and previous experience the sort of school in which she sought employment, and should have been aware of the obligations she would undertake by joining its staff'.[32] The reality that a teacher educated in a state university, with a teaching qualification recognised by the state, and in receipt of what was in effect a state salary, had little option but to work in a denominational school, was not alluded to by the judge in this statement.

AMENDING THE CONSTITUTION

De Valera's constitution failed to reconcile universal rights with Catholic teaching and when the liberalisation of Irish society began in the 1960s, the constitution became a fundamental issue in political debate. With regard to religious matters, the constitution was first amended in 1972, when the deletion of article 44 was approved by an overwhelming majority of voters. This decision makes sense only in the context of the Northern Ireland conflict, then in its most serious phase. The Taoiseach Jack Lynch argued that the proposed changes would contribute towards Irish unity and would be indicative of the 'outward-looking' approach of the government and the people towards Irish unity.[33] One Fianna Fail TD told an audience that:

> The opportunity is to display their generosity of heart and mind in openly declaring before the world, and before the people of Northern Ireland and Britain in particular, that they have no interest in a position in which the Catholic Church could have any status or privileges which are not equally extended to all religious denominations, or even to persons of no religious convictions whatever.[34]

The 1972 amendment was opposed by a new movement called 'defend 44', which saw the proposed changes as the prelude to the introduction of the permissive society to Ireland.[35] However, the opposition parties agreed to support the amendment, which was passed with the approval of over 70 per cent of the voters. Nevertheless, the Fine Gael leader Liam Cosgrave believed that an entirely new constitution was needed to attract the North, while the Labour leader Brendan Corish argued that de Valera's constitution should be replaced by 'a genuinely Republican document without any taint of sectarianism'.[36]

Evidence that the relationship between modernisation and liberalisation was not a linear one is provided by the fact that it took over ten years before the next amendment was introduced, and then its effect was to make abortion, which had been illegal before 1983, unconstitutional. The fear that abortion could be introduced into Ireland by the Dail or the courts was at the heart of a campaign launched by the Pro-Life Amendment Campaign formed after the Pope's visit to Ireland in 1979. PLAC argued that article 40 of the constitution, which guaranteed life to the citizen but not to the unborn, should be amended to cover the period between conception and birth.[37] The three main political parties initially proved responsive to this campaign, the Fianna Fail leader promising the electorate not only a referendum, but also an airport at a major religious shrine.[38] Ultimately pressure from PLAC, the Catholic Church, and the Fianna Fail party led the government to propose the following amendment: 'The state acknowledges the right to life of the unborn and with due regard to the equal right of life of the mother, guarantees in its laws to protect, and as far as practicable, by its laws, to defend and vindicate that right.'

This was subsequently opposed in the campaign by the Labour Party, Fine Gael, and the Church of Ireland. The Catholic Church became involved in the campaign, stressing that Catholics had an obligation to vote and highlighting the danger of abortion being introduced in Ireland. A statement by the Irish Bishops Conference also stating that Catholics could, in conscience, vote no, was followed by a number of intransigent statements on behalf of more conservative Bishops. The amendment was passed by a two to one majority: 66.45 per cent voting yes, and 32.87 per cent voting no. Despite the low turnout of 54.6 per cent, the result was clearly a vindication of the Catholic Church's authority and demonstrated the vulnerability of the political process to a campaign orchestrated by well-organised interest groups.

Having been defeated in 1983, it may have been unwise for the Taoiseach, Dr Garrett FitzGerald, to proceed only three years later with a referendum to amend the clause prohibiting divorce. However, FitzGerald had already publicly committed himself to such a move, he was under pressure to do so from his coalition partner, the Labour Party, and opinion polls showed large majorities in favour of divorce under carefully defined circumstances.[39] Moreover, although the voters had accepted the anti-abortion clause in 1983, in 1985 an important bill permitting the open sale of contraceptives was passed by the Dail, a morale-boosting victory for the liberal camp. What the 1986 campaign again showed, however, was that any constitutional amendment which lacked cross-party support was vulnerable to the pressures of well-organised interest groups. In particular, the activists of the Anti-Divorce Campaign were able to rely on the support of the Catholic clergy and members of the Fianna Fail party in their efforts to frustrate the passing of the amendment.[40] As later campaigns would also show, the tactic of playing on the public's fears of what would happen to property rights if divorce were permitted proved a decisive one. By 63 to 37 per cent the amendment was rejected by the electorate, leading many people to doubt the viability of the whole liberal project.

Politically, it was of the utmost importance in 1986 that the supposedly 'neutral' Fianna Fail party and the Catholic Church came out, in the end, against divorce. By 1992, not only were left–right differences becoming more pronounced but,

> there is a second explicit cleavage between fundamentalist Catholics
> on the one hand, and liberal Catholics, Protestants and secular citizens
> on the other. On this cleavage Labour and the Progressive Democrats
> are almost entirely in the liberal and secular camp; Fianna Fail
> (especially its supporters) is far more fundamentalist than liberal
> while Fine Gael is somewhat more liberal than fundamentalist.[41]

However, the simplification and intensification of this cleavage did not alter the fact that liberalising amendments would only succeed if they had all-party support. Indeed, such support was not forthcoming when the next amendments were proposed, the effect of which would be more to qualify the right to life of the unborn, introduced into the constitution in 1983, than to broaden the basis on which abortion would be permitted. The major catalyst for the 1992 referendums was that of 'the X case', that of a 14-year-old girl, pregnant as a result of a rape, who in February 1992 was denied the legal right to travel to Britain to obtain an abortion. This decision was then reversed by the Supreme Court in a judgment which ruled that under the terms of the 1983 amendment abortion would be permissible in Ireland 'if it is established as a matter of probability that there is a real and substantial risk to the life as opposed to the health of the mother, which can only be avoided by the termination of her pregnancy'.[42] The judgment cast doubt on efficacy of the 1983 amendment, and raised the possibility that the constitutional right to travel could be overridden if it conflicted with the right to life of the foetus. Not surprisingly, the church and the anti-abortion movement demanded a new referendum to reinforce the objective of the 1983 amendment.

While conceding the need for a referendum to clarify issues left over by the Supreme Court decision, all the political parties shared a permissive attitude to freedom of travel and its concomitant, freedom of information, and were determined to exclude the interest groups from the policy-making process.[43] Since 1983 the outlook of the electorate itself had shifted on the issue of abortion. Opinion polls showed that in 1990 a majority of adults, and a huge majority of young adults, were prepared to accept abortion if the mother's health was at risk.[44] The election in the same year as President of Ireland of a liberal lawyer, Mary Robinson, who had opposed the 1983 amendment, also suggested that there was a growing constituency of opinion who identified with the liberal agenda. Finally, the authority of the Catholic Church was considerably dented in 1992 by the revelation that the Bishop of Galway, Eamon Casey, had fathered a child and used church funds to help raise it in America. Nevertheless, Fianna Fail was the dominant partner in government and the Taoiseach, Albert Reynolds, while accepting the Supreme Court judgment, was determined to legislate for it in the most conservative way possible.[45]

As a result, the proposed amendments distinguished between permitting abortion when the life as opposed to the health of the mother was at stake, the probability of suicide not being considered a basis for a threat to the life of the mother. All the other parties opposed this distinction, but Fine Gael, the Green Party, and Sinn Fein equivocated on it during the campaign. The Catholic Church again stated that the individual could in conscience vote either way, but criticised the government for not allowing a clear choice between abortion and no abortion. However, as before, individual members of the hierarchy argued for a no vote on all three issues, and the pro-life campaign followed suit. By large margins, freedom to travel and freedom of information were accepted by the electorate, but the wording on abortion was rejected. The political parties and interest groups had not accepted the Taoiseach's claim that the wording represented a nuanced attempt to reconcile existing positions on a complex issue: the conservatives wanted a wording returning to the *status quo ante*, while the liberals recognised that the new wording did not represent an advance on the Supreme Court decision. The consequence of the referendums was stalemate: although abortion was now legally permissible under certain conditions, in practice no abortions are likely to have taken place. Indeed, the Irish Medical Council changed its ethical guidelines after the vote, so that any doctor who performed an abortion under the guidelines outlined by the Supreme Court could be struck off the medical register.[46]

An aspect of the 1992 referenda was the political parties' determination to wrestle control of the policy-making process from the interest groups by trying to achieve some consensus on how to move forward. When the next issue, that of divorce, came up, in December 1995, there was all-party consensus on an amendment to the article prohibiting divorce put to the electorate by the 'rainbow coalition' of Fine-Gael, Labour, and the Democratic Left. Fianna Fail's acceptance of the change can be explained partly as a consequence of the fact that the government had decided to write into the constitution the conditions under which divorce would be tolerated, specifying the number of years a couple had to be separated in order to qualify for divorce.[47] Nevertheless, once the campaign had begun, public support for divorce declined considerably, and 'those opposed to divorce proved to be very successful in persuading traditional sectors of the electorate to change their mind'.[48] The Catholic Church adopted a strong position against change, leaving little room for the individual conscience. The anti-divorce campaign skilfully played on the public's anxieties over the implications of the amendment for property rights. The slight margin of the victory for divorce (less than one per cent), was all the more remarkable considering how strongly supportive of divorce public opinion had been six months before the vote. If it had not rained heavily in those areas in the West of Ireland where the turnout was low, the no vote may well have exceeded the yes vote.

The period between 1995 and 2002 was one of rapid economic growth in the Irish Republic, but the circumstances in which the next referendum on abortion took place, on 6 March 2002, indicated that the confusion inherent in the 1992 result was still very much present in Irish public life. Five years previously, the coalition government under Fianna Fail's Bertie Ahern had promised the four independent TDs who supported his administration a referendum which would reverse the situation created by the Supreme Court's decision in 1992 whereby a pregnant woman, on grounds of possible suicide, could lawfully have an abortion in Ireland. After an extensive consultation process, the amendment offered pro-life campaigners their wish for a ban on abortion in cases of threatened suicide, the criminalisation of abortion, and protection of current medical practice. However, the amendment was opposed by Fine Gael and Labour, the medical establishment became divided during the campaign, and the ranks of the pro-lifers themselves became split because hardliners felt that the amendment failed to protect the unborn from the moment of conception. The voters narrowly rejected the amendment, leaving the effect of the Supreme Court judgment on the X case intact. With a new election only months away, Fine Gael and Labour then signalled their intention to legislate for abortion in limited circumstances. However, it is clear that any government will have to resolve a bundle of outstanding constitutional, legal, and medical issues if it is to legislate for abortion. Such legislation would have to quantify the risk to the life of the suicidal mother, state what procedures should take place before she be referred to an abortion clinic or hospital, and decide what type of medical certification would be necessary. Attention will obviously focus on the Irish Medical Council, which changed its guidelines on the area of reproductive medicine last autumn to accept that 'termination of pregnancy can occur when there is real and substantial risk to the life of the mother'.[49] However, it is clear that the medical profession as a whole is divided on the issue and the prospect exists that some doctors would accept a limited abortion regime while others would remain uncooperative.

The narrow margin of the liberal victory in March is indicative yet again of how weak the impulse towards the secularisation of the law has been since the 1960s.[50] For example, the Censorship of Publication Board, now under lay control, still derives its authority from legislation passed in 1929 and 1946. Clearly, the Irish Republic has remained much more insulated from secularising influences than its Western counterparts.[51] On the other hand,

> Ireland has moved from banning all artificial contraception to allowing all forms of contraception, including the sale of condoms without any lower age limit; from laws criminalising homosexuality to laws on homosexuality which rank among the most liberal in the world; from a total ban on divorce to the possibility of the introduction of no-fault divorce into Irish law, all in just sixteen years.[52]

The Church itself has retreated from the position it adopted in 1953 when it opposed a Health Bill on the grounds that universal health provision without a means test was contrary to Catholic social doctrine.[53] The religious commemoration of the 1916 rising was discontinued in 1974, a sign that the close identification of the nation with the Catholic faith was unravelling.[54]

Moreover, there have been a number of legal judgments which have rejected the natural law interpretation of the Irish constitution and defended instead a pluralist interpretation of Irish law, a position that is explicitly rejected by the Catholic Church. In 1995, for example, the Supreme Court ruled that a family had the right to withdraw a woman from a life-support system which has been keeping her alive since 1972. However, the hospital, under church control, refused to discontinue the system, and the woman's family had to have her removed to another hospital in order to carry out the court's ruling.[55] Like schools, the Catholic Church controls most Irish hospitals and imposes strict ethical guidelines on the staff. That the balance of power between church and state remains in question is also borne out by a case in 1997 in which the Children's Court upheld the right of a 13-year-old rape victim to leave the country for an abortion on the grounds that the risk to her life would increase substantially if the pregnancy continued.[56] However, the right of the girl, who had been under the care of the Eastern Health Board, to leave for an abortion, had been challenged by the parents, whose lawyers' fees were paid by the anti-abortion organisation called Youth Defence![57] A clearer example of the tragic dimension to Ireland's church–state relationship could not be found.

TOWARDS RELIGIOUS NEUTRALITY

With at least a third of Irish voters now committed to a liberal stance on moral issues, with another third pragmatic in the way in which they evaluate those issues, and with another third committed to a traditional Catholic viewpoint, it may be argued that the Irish state is not only now in a position to meet the requirements of theorists of state neutrality, but has also gone a considerable way to meet those requirements already. The fact that the current Taoiseach, a separated man, is seen regularly at official functions with his partner, is itself unprecedented, and, according to a Catholic newspaper, is 'constitutionally untenable' on the grounds that article 41 of the constitution pledges the state 'to guard with special care the institution of marriage, on which the family is founded, and to protect it against attack'. However, no Catholic organisation has challenged this situation in the courts, although some argue that there is a legal basis for doing so.[58] The ambiguities in the Taoiseach's position were clarified in May 2001 on the occasion of a state ceremony to celebrate the elevation of Cardinal Desmond Connell, the first time since independence an Irish Catholic priest was made Cardinal. The invitation was issued in the format 'The Taoiseach, Mr. Bertie Ahern, TD and Ms. Celia Larkin request the pleasure of the company of', and was criticised by the Protestant Dean of St Patrick's Cathedral for putting 'lesser relationships' on a par with marriage. The ensuing public row was embarrassing for both church and state, but the unambiguous nature of article 41 may return to haunt Irish political elites.

Equally controversially, the decision of the President, a committed Catholic, to take communion in a Protestant Church in December 1997, in defiance of canon law, is another example of the shift in attitudes among the political elite. This shift is best illustrated by the inauguration of a National Day of Commemoration in 1986 to commemorate the lives of all Irish people who have lost their lives in wars, including those who died fighting in the British army. The day centres around a multi-denominational prayer service which the President, the Taoiseach, TDs, and representatives of the various churches attend. Since 1996 representatives of the Islamic faith have also been attending. In legal terms, in July 1999 the Supreme Court upheld a High Court judgment that a newspaper could not be prosecuted for blasphemy for portraying, in the wake of the divorce referendum, a portly priest in vestments pursuing three senior government figures under the caption of 'Hello progress – bye bye Father?' Since the 1937 constitution did not define what the offence of blasphemy actually consisted of, the Supreme Court ruled that 'the state is not placed in the position of an arbiter of religious truth'.[59]

The growth of a more neutral interpretation of the role of the state is best illustrated by educational policy. Up to 1998 the state did not fully fund the establishment of primary schools, but expected the sites and 15 per cent of the new school's capital cost to be funded privately. In areas where a new school was needed, it became customary for the Catholic Church to organise the financing of such schools, and to provide a site, often from its own lands. This system placed those small groups of parents in urban areas which wanted multi-denominational education for their children at a disadvantage, since they lacked church support. Furthermore, it usually took five years for new multi-denominational schools to be recognised by the Department of Education: only then would they be entitled to an 85 per cent building or renovation grant. The system was also discriminatory since the state provided full funding for new *gaelscoileanna*, schools where the medium of instruction would be Irish. In the 11 years up to 1997, while only two new Catholic schools were recognised by the Department of Education, 56 *gaelscoileanna* and 13 multi-denominational schools were recognised.[60] In the period between 1994 and now the number of multi-denominational schools has risen from 14 to 23. There are now around 3,578 pupils attending multi-denominational schools compared to 2,765 in 1994.[61]

In response to this growth, the state has undertaken to provide full funding for multi-denominational schools. In January 1998 the Minister of Education agreed to pay the costs of a site and 100 per cent building cost for a multi-denominational school in Galway, thus placing these schools on the same footing as the *Gaelscoileanna*. The following year the Minister announced that the state would pay for all new school sites, which meant that the state would become the owner of all new school sites and buildings.

Furthermore, the passing of a new Educational Bill in 1997 allowed for the first time the recognition of non-denominational schools and is expected to lead to a quick growth in secular primary schools. According to the general secretary of the Irish National Teachers' Organisation, Senator Joe O' Toole,

> This is bound to erode the influence and control of the main churches over primary education. In future parents will have the choice of a variety of schools for their children. Teachers will have a wider range of options in deciding the ambience in which they will work and new groups will join the ownership and management of primary schools.[62]

A recent case where state funding was denied to a Steiner school in Co. Clare ruled that the state was entitled to refuse funding in February 1995 on the grounds that the school failed to employ teachers with proper qualifications, and provided inadequately for the teaching of Irish. However, the judge ruled that the state's argument that it had discharged its obligation to provide free primary education in the area by funding 15 denominational schools within a 12-mile area of Coleenbridge was untenable. This suggests that the parents had a constitutional right to non-denominational education regardless of the existence of publicly funded denominational schools in the same area. Secondly, the court did not base its judgment on religious or philosophical criteria, which again suggests that parents have the right to receive state funding for any type of primary education they choose.[63]

For the moment, what these changes imply is less a process of secularisation, and more a variation on the main theme of denominational schooling, since in 1997 the government also negotiated a new agreement on the ethos and governance of primary schools which the Catholic hierarchy welcomed as 'a historic development in ensuring the continuation of the ethos of schools of different religious denominations'.[64] What was agreed was a new board of management for primary schools with two elected parents, two teachers, two owner representatives, and two representatives of the wider community agreed unanimously by these six. This certainly spells greater parental input, but a key demand of the Church of Ireland was its insistence on having 'absolute discretion' as to what pupils they allowed in. Section 29 of the Education Bill of 1997 states that where a school board of management refuses to enrol a student for reasons other than lack of accommodation, a parent or student over 18 can appeal the decision to the Secretary General of the Department of Education, which has the authority to direct the school board in a certain way.[65] However, it is debatable whether the Department has the constitutional right to overrule the school. What is clear is that denominational schools have the right under the 1998 Employment Equality Act to discriminate in favour of a teacher of its own religion in order to protect its denominational ethos. As a result, many minority religions may set up their own schools employing only teachers with their own worldview. However, with a chronic shortage of primary teachers it is clear that the vast majority of the new teachers planned by the Department of Education are going to be educated in one of the country's four denominational teacher training colleges.[66] In addition, under the new curriculum announced in 1999, the content of religious instruction will be left to the individual primary school, although secular and religious instruction are separated in a way that did not apply in the 1971 curriculum.

Given the growth in multi-denominational schools and the influx of around 1,000 asylum seekers a month, the long-term effect of these changes may well be to allow for the emergence of a more pluralist society in the Irish Republic. It was pointed out in 1998 that for the first time in the history of the state God has not been mentioned in the philosophical introduction to the new primary school curriculum. Indeed, a very different educational ethos from that of 1971 was spelt out:

> Children come from a diversity of cultural, religious, social, environmental and ethnic backgrounds, and these engender their own beliefs, values and aspirations. The curriculum acknowledges this pluralism in society and caters for a variety of differences while at the same time promoting tolerance and respect for diversity in both the school and the community.[67]

In secondary education, the Catholic Church is preparing for an unprecedented degree of lay participation in the management of the country's 360 voluntary Catholic schools. Figures for 1997/98 show that while there were 2,300 members of religious orders in secondary education in 1969/70 (34 per cent of the total), by 1997/98 this figure had dropped to just over 660 members (5.2 per cent of the total). It is widely believed that within five to ten years all Catholic voluntary secondary schools will be owned by trusts on which lay people are heavily represented, increasingly in the majority.[68] In 1998 the Conference of Religious of Ireland predicted that within 25 years the religious orders would cease to be directly involved in schools.[69] The extent to which they are retreating from education is also borne out by the decision of the Holy Ghost Fathers to hand over the management of five elite schools to a private firm. An historical irony is also provided by the fact that one of these schools, Blackrock College, was the *alma mater* of none other than Eamon de Valera.

In recent years the Irish state has moved in the direction of greater neutrality between religions, but with regard to non-believers neutrality is a chimera. The ruling by the Supreme Court in March 1998 that a religious denomination was 'not obliged to change the general atmosphere of its school merely to accommodate a child of a different religious persuasion who wishes to attend that school' places clear limitations on the educational choices of secularists.[70] Moreover, the new scheme for the management of primary schools allows the patron of the school, usually the Catholic Church, to dismiss the board of management if the denominational ethos of the school has been put at risk by the admission of too many pupils of a different outlook than that of the school.[71] In October 2000, Bertie Ahern was lobbied by representatives of the four main churches who were worried about the possible impact of an EU equality directive on denominational schooling. Subsequently, the Minister of Justice, Mr O' Donoghue, got an amendment to the directive which would preserve the right of denominational schools and hospitals to uphold a religious ethos when recruiting. Responding to claims by teacher unions that the directive would infringe the right to privacy of Irish teachers, the Minister responded that under the Employment Equality Act of 1998 there was an obligation on employees not to actively undermine the ethos of the institution in which they were employed.[72] This interpretation of the Act contrasts with that of the US State Department, which concluded the following year that it outlawed discrimination on religious grounds in relation to employment.[73]

In short, the Irish state has begun to practise a form of 'religious neutrality' which falls far short of any genuine 'liberal neutrality'.[74] Little effort has been made to alter the basic tenets of the educational system, which is based on the parental right to have their children educated in a manner they see fit, and which allows private schools to maintain their denominational ethos despite receiving public funding. In 1998 the Supreme Court also ruled against a claim by the Campaign to Separate Church and State that the payment by the state of chaplain's salaries in voluntary schools breached article 44 2.2 prohibiting the endowment of a religion.[75] The court ruled that the system was 'merely a manifestation, under modern conditions, of principles which are recognised and approved by Articles 44 and 42 of the Constitution'.[76] With regard to the preamble, the Archbishop of Dublin, Dr Desmond Connell, has rejected the argument that the proposed removal of any positive affirmation of religious belief from the constitution would be an act of neutrality. Instead, he argued that 'it substitutes for the views of the vast majority of Irish citizens a view which implicitly rejects the deep and personally held belief of so many Irish people in the existence of God and the religious dimension of life'.[77] With vocations having fallen dramatically, the church may be retreating from its position of dominance in education, but remains a powerful voice when it comes to formulating state policy.

CONCLUSION

Despite not having a tradition of endowing or establishing any religion, the Irish state has never been neutral with regard to religion. As with other perfectionist regimes, the elevation of one conception of the good life, Catholicism, over all others, served to 'distort the free evaluation of different ways of life, to rigidify the dominant ways of life, whatever their intrinsic merits, and to unfairly exclude the values and aspirations of marginalised and disadvantaged groups within the community'.[78] This situation was tenable when over 95 per cent of the population were devout Catholics, but with weekly mass attendance falling to 66 per cent by 1996, the values and aspirations of 1937 can no longer command obedience.[79] More recently, there have been moves towards neutrality in the vital area of education, but this could be characterised as the state being neutral in favour of religion. Monsma and Soper might regard such changes as an example of 'positive neutrality' – whereby the state enables the various churches to enjoy equal opportunities to act in public – but it is difficult to square such an approach with their belief in pluralism.[80] In 1992/93 there were 2,988 Catholic primary schools out of a total of 3,209 in the state, and there is no doubt that the Catholic Church will ensure that the denominational ethos of such schools will be maintained as far as practicable.[81] This is also the intention of the state, as was revealed by a statement of the Minister of Education and Science in 1998:

> I want to emphasise that the pooling of power which is at the centre of any meaningful partnership is in no sense a threat to denominational education, rather in my view it represents a new opportunity. An opportunity for denominational schools to grow and develop in partnership with the key stakeholders in the school without any diminution of their mission. Key to that mission is the fostering in denominational schools of an ethos or characteristic spirit based primarily upon religious beliefs. The legal right of schools to do that is secure.[82]

The idea of neutrality may be compelling in a society where the state has already established its predominance over civil society, but otherwise the argument for neutrality may well be an argument for the status quo, with modifications. Neutrality requires 'a certain faith in the operation of nonstate forums and processes for individual judgement and cultural development', but in independent Ireland the non-state sector has never been a level playing field.[83] De Valera's solution to the dilemma of separating church and state in a religiously dominated society was for the state to allow civil society huge autonomy. This did not result in a separation of church and state, but in an elaborate if discreet system of state support for a private institution, the Catholic Church. The extent to which this still is the case is evident from the state's decision in January 2002 to pay a large portion of the compensation to be paid by the Catholic Church to victims of sexual abuse in institutions that were run by religious orders but financed by the state.[84]

This raises the question of whether the Irish Republic should be regarded as a secularising state. To employ a Marxist analogy, the past 40 years have seen fundamental change in the religious 'base' of society, but changes in the 'superstructure' have been slow to follow. The Irish state now seeks a *modus vivendi* between the various faiths existing in Ireland but remains a 'neutral ally' of religion in general. The current government has also been party to an agreement maintaining denominational education in Northern Ireland, and it is difficult to see how it could defend one system in the north while undermining its counterpart in the south.[85] Paradoxically, the main constitutional guarantee of pluralism today is provided by constitutional articles that were intended to enshrine denominational education in 1937, but it is doubtful whether the Fianna Fail party is aware of this irony. In the contemporary Irish context, state neutrality can only be construed as even-handed intervention in the religious sphere, and there is little prospect of a separation of church and state on the American model. To those who have campaigned for a more plural society in Ireland, the changes that have been made are welcome. What is remarkable, however, is the tenacity with which traditional values have thus far maintained their grip on the political system.

NOTES

1. W. Kymlicka, *Contemporary Political Philosophy: An Introduction* (Oxford: Clarendon Press 1990), p.205.
2. *Irish Times*, 27 Jan. 2000.
3. On the history of church–state relations since independence, see J. Whyte, *Church and State in Modern Ireland 1923–70* (Dublin: Gill & MacMillan 1981).
4. *Irish Times*, 11 March 2002.

5. On the relationships between pluralism and liberalism, see J. Gray, *Two Faces of Liberalism* (Cambridge: Polity 2000).
6. For a trenchant critique, see B. Barry, 'How Not to Defend Liberal Institutions', *British Journal of Political Science* 20 (1990), pp.1–15.
7. See B. Kissane, *Explaining Irish Democracy* (Dublin: UCD Press 2002), pp.214–16.
8. Constitution Review Group, *Report of the Constitution Review Group* (Dublin: Stationery Office 1996).
9. N. Browne, 'Church and State in Modern Ireland', in T. Murphy and P. Twomey (eds.), *Ireland's Evolving Constitution 1937–1997: Collected Essays* (Oxford: Hart Publishing 1998), p.44.
10. Ibid.
11. Ibid., p.45.
12. J.M. O'Sullivan, *Defending the Truth* (Dublin: Catholic Truth Society 1927).
13. B. Chubb, *The Politics of the Irish Constitution* (Dublin: Institute of Public Administration 1991), p.37.
14. Constitution Review Group, *Report of the Constitution Review Group*, p.3.
15. J. Casey, *Constitutional Law in Ireland* (London: Sweet & Maxwell, 2nd edn. 1992), p.317.
16. Chubb, *The Politics of the Irish Constitution*, p.28.
17. Browne, 'Church and State', p.46.
18. Chubb, *The Politics of the Irish Constitution*, p.26.
19. Casey, *Constitutional Law*, p.556.
20. J. Coakley, 'Moral Consensus in a Secularising Society: the Irish Divorce Referendum of 1986', *West European Politics* 10/2 (1987), p.291.
21. D.M. Clarke, 'Education, the State, and Sectarian Schools', in Murphy and Twomey (eds.), *Ireland's Evolving Constitution 1937–1997*, p.66.
22. Ibid., p.69.
23. Ibid., p.66.
24. Ibid.
25. A. Hyland, 'The Multi-Denominational Experience', in Constitution Review Group (ed.), *Report of the Constitution Review Group* (Dublin: Stationer's Office 1996), pp.631–2.
26. Clarke, 'Education, the State, and Secondary Schools', p.74.
27. Hyland, 'The Multi-Denominational Experience', p.634.
28. S. Monsma and C. Soper, *The Challenge of Pluralism: Church and State in Five Democracies* (Lanham, MD: Rowman & Littlefield 1997), p.6.
29. *Irish Times*, 22 Aug. 1998.
30. Coakley, 'Moral Consensus', p.291.
31. Momsa and Soper, *The Challenge of Pluralism*, p.202.
32. Casey, *Constitutional Law*, p.529.
33. *Irish Times*, 3 Nov. 1972.
34. *Irish Times*, 11 Nov. 1972.
35. *Irish Times*, 13 Nov. 1972.
36. *Irish Times*, 3 Nov. 1972.
37. B. Girvin, 'Social Change and Moral Politics: The Irish Constitutional Referendum 1983', *Political Studies* 34/1 (1986), p.69.
38. Ibid., p.71.
39. Coakley, 'Moral Consensus', p.292.
40. Ibid., p.293.
41. B. O'Leary, 'Affairs, Partner-Swapping, and Spring Tides: The Irish General Election of November 1992, *West European Politics* 16/3 (1993), p.410.
42. B. Girvin, 'Moral Politics and the Irish Abortion Referendum 1992', *Parliamentary Affairs* 47/2 (1994), p.206.
43. Ibid., p.210.
44. Ibid., p.205.
45. Ibid., p.213.
46. B. Girvin, 'Church, State and the Irish Constitution: The Secularisation of Irish Politics', *Parliamentary Affairs* 49/4 (1996), p.603
47. Ibid.

48. Ibid.
49. *Irish Times*, 8 March 2002.
50. For an application of the secularisation thesis, see T. Inglis, *Moral Monopoly: The Rise and Fall of the Catholic Church in Modern Ireland* (Dublin: UCD Press 1998), pp.201–41.
51. M. Corish, 'Aspects of the Secularisation of Irish Society 1958–1996', in E. Cassidy (ed.), *Faith and Culture in the Irish Context* (Dublin: Veritas 1996), p.169.
52. Corish, 'Aspects of the Secularisation', p.141.
53. Chubb, *The Politics of the Irish Constitution*, p.41.
54. T. Garvin, 'Patriots and Republicans: An Irish Evolution', in W. Crotty and D.E. Schmitt (eds.), *Ireland and the Politics of Change* (London and New York: Longman 1998), pp.144–56.
55. Girvin, 'Church State and the Irish Constitution', p.608.
56. *Irish Times*, 29 Nov. 1997.
57. Ibid., 22 Nov. 1997.
58. Ibid., 15 Jan. 1999.
59. Ibid., 31 July 1999.
60. Ibid., 2 Feb. 1998.
61. Ibid., 10 Feb. 2000.
62. Ibid., 24 Dec. 1997.
63. Ibid., 17 April 1999.
64. Ibid., 2 Oct. 1997.
65. Ibid., 23 Jan. 1998.
66. Ibid., 13 April 1998.
67. Ibid., 22 Aug. 1998.
68. Ibid., 7 June 1999.
69. Ibid., 26 Jan. 1998.
70. Ibid., 26 March 1998.
71. Ibid., 10 June 2000.
72. Ibid., 19 Oct. 2000.
73. US Department of State, *Annual Report on International Religious Freedom for 1999: Ireland* (Washington DC: State Department 1999).
74. To an extent it has always aspired to such a stance. For example before a new Dail was convened in the 1930s special services were also held for Protestant and Jewish members, a custom not always acknowledged by liberal scholars.
75. *Irish Times*, 14 Jan. 1998.
76. Ibid., 26 March 1998.
77. Ibid., 2 April 1998.
78. W. Kymlicka, 'Liberal Individualism and Liberal Neutrality', *Ethics* 99 (July 1989), p.900.
79. G. Whyte, 'Some Reflections on the Role of Religion in the Constitutional Order', in Murphy and Twomey (eds.), *Ireland's Evolving Constitution*, p.52.
80. Monsma and Soper, *The Challenge of Pluralism*.
81. Constitution Review Group, *Report of the Constitution Review Group*, p.339
82. Speech by Michael Martin, Minister for Education and Science, at the Conference on the Role of Denominational Schools in a Pluralist Society, Trinity College Dublin, 18 Sept. 1998.
83. Kymlicka, 'Liberal Individualism and Liberal Neutrality', p.899.
84. *Irish Times*, 4 April 2002. Crucially, the notorious 'industrial schools' where sexual abuse was rife were inspected by state inspectors.
85. B. O'Leary, 'Comparative Political Science and the British–Irish Agreement', in J. McGarry (ed.), *Northern Ireland and the Divided World* (Oxford: Oxford University Press 2001), p.55.

The Italian State:
No Longer Catholic, no Longer Christian

MARK DONOVAN

The church–state relationship has been a central theme of Italian historiography. Two themes in particular can be highlighted: the role played by the Catholic Church in the failure of successive political regimes to consolidate themselves, and the relationship between the church, the state and political parties. Thus, a prominent interpretation of the political crisis of the 1990s sees it as a third case of state failure, following those of liberalism, which collapsed in the early 1920s, and of Fascism, which disintegrated in 1942/43.[1] Second, the most significant aspect of the 1990s crisis was probably the collapse of the Christian Democratic Party (DC) which dominated Italian governments from 1947 to 1994. This collapse was accompanied by a major shift in church–party relations and confirmed a shift already taking place in church–state relations.

What follows builds on Kalyvas' conclusion that Christian Democratic parties were formed against the opposition of the Catholic Church to argue that the transformation of the Italian party system in the 1990s obliged and enabled the Vatican finally to break its nearly 50-year-long support for Catholic party politics in Italy.[2] The specific perspective adopted thus comes from an understanding of the prominent role of party politics in Italy in shaping church–state relations rather than from an analysis of the nevertheless important changes taking place within Italy's Catholic world. From this party perspective, Italy's 1990s state crisis centred on the transformation of the party system and in particular on the disintegration of the government parties – meaning primarily the dominant Christian Democratic Party. In the early stages of the crisis, and beyond the collapse of the DC, the Vatican and many grass-roots Catholic activists continued to support party political mobilisation on the basis of Christian inspiration. Only in 1995 did official church separation from party politics and the assertion of 'neutrality', in the sense of partisan non-alignment, become definitive. The Vatican's new stance followed the failure of the attempt by the DC's successor party, the Italian Popular Party (PPI), to build a Catholic centre party able to hold the balance of power in processes of government coalition formation and hence reunify the post-DC Catholic party fragments. In the emerging bipolar party system, it was not in the church's interest to apparently be aligned with either half of the spectrum.

Whilst the Vatican's position *supra partes* has helped consolidate the formation of a substantially secularised party system in Italy, it is not the case that the church is neutral regarding public policy. Indeed, the absence of a dominant, Christian-inspired party arguably both enables and requires the church directly to address, variously, 'the state', the parties and public opinion. Moreover, the Vatican's determination to reassert its leadership of a politically divided and restive Catholic world in and after 1995 led it to champion positions regarding abortion and other bio-ethical issues which were described by observers as 'neo-intransigent'.[3] The end of the confessionally ambiguous 'DC-state' (1948–94) thus sees a 'normalisation' of church–state relations in Italy in which the Catholic Church now acts as a cross between an independent state, a territorially ramified and organisationally complex array of powerful pressure groups, and a highly articulated social movement.

Several factors continue to make church–state relations controversial. First, Catholic-inspired political parties continue to play a significant and visible role in the policy process. Second, the state is widely perceived to be weak, and prominent political issues are believed to contribute significantly to defining in religious terms the nature of the state and Italian society. This perception reflects the high profile of church–state relations in Italy and the continuing, if far from unchallenged, mobilisational capacity of the church, exemplified by the spectacular millennium events in Rome. Examples of issues which see a variety of church organisations either directly active in public policy and/or lobbying for change include bio-ethical and life style matters such as human fertility treatment; public funding for private (essentially Catholic) schools, and immigration. The last of these, furthermore, is itself introducing a religious pluralism into Italy, which is fundamentally new and is thus changing the very meaning of church–state relations in Italy.

CHURCH, STATE, NATION AND POLITICAL PARTIES: FROM THE RISORGIMENTO TO THE REPUBLIC

The church–state relationship in liberal Italy was profoundly antagonistic for most of the period 1860–1924. The kingdom of Piedmont, which provided the core of the state-building process in the formation of Italy, had pioneered the reduction of church privileges by liberal states whilst the construction of Italy brought the destruction of the papal states and, in 1870, the military occupation of Rome.[4] Pius IX (1846–78) became a self-proclaimed 'prisoner' in the Vatican, thus initiating the 'Roman question', which remained a thorn in Italian church–state relations until 1929. Pius demanded the non-participation (the '*non-expedit*') of devout Catholics in the new state's elected institutions and the consequent denial of legitimacy which exacerbated the regime's difficulties in winning elite and public support led many liberals to regard the church as a hugely powerful, subversive organisation. Similar considerations reflecting the enduring weakness of the Italian state continue to underlie residual anti-clerical sentiment in the twenty-first century.

In the late nineteenth century, the rise of mass politics created the possibility of a *rapprochement* between conservative liberals and the church on the basis of anti-socialism. This did not happen. As per Kalyvas, the era of mass mobilisation challenged Vatican authority as well as that of the liberal state. In 1904, Pius X dissolved the Opera dei congressi, the 'first Christian Democracy', because of its tendency to political autonomy. In 1913, the church again sought to pre-empt autonomous Catholic political organisation following the introduction of universal suffrage in 1912 by offering support to conservative liberals in the Gentiloni Pact. Christian Democrats denounced this arrangement as 'prostituting' the Catholic vote. When the Libyan and then First World Wars accentuated the politicisation of Catholic mobilisation, the formation of a Catholic-inspired party, the Italian Popular Party (PPI), followed, in 1919. The PPI won 20.5 per cent of the vote and rapidly acquired a quarter of a million members. The emergence of an autonomous political party had been forced on the Vatican.

The emergence of a competitive, democratic, state-building architecture, a multi-party system, did not lead to the consolidation of democratic politics. Rather, the post-WWI collapse of the nascent liberal democracy saw the PPI undermined by the Vatican, which conspired in Mussolini's destruction of Italy's liberal regime.[5] The Vatican went on to effect a *rapprochement* between church and state via the so-called Lateran Pacts of 1929. By then, the new regime had recognised Catholic participation in school examinations and the degrees of the new Catholic university (Sacred Heart, Milan); restored the crucifix to school and courtrooms; repaired churches, raised clerical salaries; closed down anti-clerical journals and banned freemasonry. Further to this, the Pacts: (1) established the sovereign Vatican city state; (2) gave financial compensation for the loss of papal territories; and (3) agreed a Concordat granting various privileges: (a) religious instruction was extended to secondary schools; (b) church marriages were deemed legally sufficient; (c) seminarists were exempted from military service; (d) Catholic action associations were guaranteed operation; (e) modest state stipends were instituted for priests and bishops.[6]

Fascism repressed the Catholic political and social organisations that were developing autonomously of the church, but the church's ecclesiastical organisation was reinforced and even developed as a rival to Fascism. A competitive, rarely antagonistic, relationship between Catholicism and the state was created. When Fascism broke down in 1942/43, two popularly rooted forces were poised to govern Italy: the Catholic and the Marxist. Historically, both had tended to form anti-state, autonomous sub-cultures. Now both developed 'ethical parties' which demanded loyalty to the party as the incarnation of a set of values.[7] These parties were flanked by an array of social, cultural and economic institutions, each creating semi-autonomous national dimensions, the so-called 'institutionalised traditions',[8] whilst being inserted in competing international, universalist camps. By the time of the first parliamentary election campaign in 1948, the Vatican had reversed its anti-party stance to provide invaluable support to the Christian Democratic Party (DC), which was seen as the essential political instrument to defeat the Socio-Communist challenge in Italy.

Initially, in 1944–47, the two traditions worked together alongside Italy's other, minor anti-Fascist forces in the CLN (the Committee for National Liberation), laying the basis for the unification of an Italian people with an Italian state. However, severe domestic tension plus the Cold War led to the formation of a state governed by the Catholic-inspired DC, whilst the Socio-Communist sub-culture was confined to the role of opposition. The ethical party nature of these forces, plus the presence of minority liberal and Fascist nostalgia traditions, undermined the construction of an Italian people owing allegiance to an impartial state. Rather, the so-called 'First Republic' (c.1948–94), was largely synonymous with Christian Democratic domination of both the formal processes of government and of the party penetration and dominance of civil society. Most Italians never identified with the new state and almost immediately the new republic became identified by nationalist and then liberal critics as a 'partyocracy', that is self-serving and partial, rather than impartial. This term did not win a wide audience until the 1970s, however. Rather, well into the 1970s, the state was usually identified by critics as the 'DC-state', and this state was seen, particularly through the 1950s, as a clerical one.

The 'Christian Democratic state', nevertheless, was strongly contested and secularisation made steady progress, although this was not widely perceived until the 1970s. Then, referendums on divorce (1974) and abortion (1981), both of which produced majorities in favour of maintaining new and permissive legislation, clarified the situation. At the same time, the DC was shown to be unable to block such legislation whilst, simultaneously, it was becoming synonymous with corruption and policy immobilism. The newly active Italian Episcopal Council (CEI) sought more clearly to demarcate itself from the party, emphasising the primacy and distinctiveness of its religious mission. Nevertheless, concern that government alternation would give the Italian Communist Party (PCI) a dominant role in coalition formation and the making of public policy led the Vatican to maintain strong links with the DC, seeking to encourage its reform. In the event, the party eventually collapsed.

THE 'FIRST REPUBLIC': CHRISTIAN DEMOCRATIC?

Many Catholic historians argue that the DC was, despite and even because of, its many faults, a profoundly national party.[9] Thus, although the DC's dominant elites, from De Gasperi onward, eschewed nationalist terminology in order, variously, to bolster what remained of anti-Fascist unity after the exclusion of the left from the cabinet in 1947, to weaken the linkages between intransigent Catholicism and the right, and to contest the ethical Catholic nationalism of the Dossettiani on the DC-left, the party nevertheless became, in many respects, a statist, social Catholic party from the 1950s.[10]

According to Guido Formigoni, the ideological roots of Catholic understandings of the nation state in Italy are to be found in the 1840s debate between Vincenzo Gioberti and Luigi Taparelli d'Azeglio.[11] This debate provided a cultural template comprising two ideological poles that dominated debate over the next century. The liberal-nationalist, or 'guelphist' pole, symbolised by Gioberti, fused religious ideals with national sentiment. Italy's identity was located within Catholicism, as guided by Rome and the papacy, thus providing the Italian state with the mission of spreading Christian civilisation. Taparelli, by contrast, lamented modernity's dissolution of the ties between states and its undermining of the juridical and moral status of the papacy, and, whilst national identity formation in socio-cultural terms was not unreasonable, the conjunction of nationalism and liberalism in state-building projects violated natural and universal law. Notwithstanding this more hostile view of the state, the strength of nationalism was such that not even the most intransigent conservative analysis could frontally oppose the national idea.[12] Consequently, the liberal and intransigent Catholic positions tended to interpenetrate each other over time. Formigoni concludes that the national idea was integral to Catholic thinking about modern politics. Thus, the argument that Catholic universalism is one of the major causes of the weakness of national identity in Christian Democratic Italy, as propounded by conservative liberals in the 1990s, is unfounded.[13] Certainly, the Vatican provided strong support for the principle of Italian national unity in the 1990s against the secessionism of the Northern League.

In an analysis of the 'collective myth' of Catholic political unity established by the Vatican in order to support the DC, Enzo Pace helps explain the liberal-reactionary symbiosis identified by Formigoni.[14] Analysing the stances adopted by Catholics towards modern politics, he distinguished two forms of socio-political activism. The 'fundamentalist' refuses any compromise with the mundane structures of the world and sees state institutions as permanently lacking legitimacy. All forms of the state need a superior ethical principle to underpin them, and this must be a religious guarantee. By contrast, the 'pragmatic' strand accepts the legitimacy of the state, identifies church and state as two separate spheres, and sees the structures of the modern state as a means for promoting the common good. As such, the state is subordinate to society. Since nineteenth-century Catholic liberals sought to use the instruments of the modern state to reconquer society, bringing it back to the lost faith, Catholic liberalism could appear reactionary. On the other hand, even Taparelli's fundamentalist distinction between the state and the religious sphere provided the state with relative autonomy. It was not directly subordinate to the church, and the church would not seek to make it so.[15] Given these complexities, it is not surprising that the DC was an ambiguous conglomerate of an institution whose contribution to the consolidation of a liberal and democratic state in Italy has been construed in widely diverging ways.

The Lateran Pacts had made Italy a confessional state under an unconstitutional regime. The Republic apparently brought a constitutionally confessional state.[16] This reflected the Lateran Pact's incorporation into the 1948 constitution (article 7); the church's highly effective mobilisation on behalf of the DC (voting now became a moral duty) and, more generally, Pius XII's dynamic drive to rechristianise Italy, Europe and, indeed, the world; plus the apparent domination of Catholic and DC political and cultural preferences. The persistence of DC government through the turbulent 1960s and 1970s caused frustrated radicals to see the church as keeping a steady grip on Italy.

In fact, the DC and the Catholic Church were distinct; the limits to the authority of both were significant; and the ambiguity of Italy's confessional identity continued.[17] The DC, indeed, was one party of many, and held only a plurality, not a majority, of the vote (c. 40 per cent, 1953–79), and the role of the other parties, including the PCI, in governing Italy, albeit not via the cabinet in the latter's case, was great.

Whilst Catholic political unity cemented by anti-Communism was the core of the DC's electoral triumph in 1948 – the party gained 48.5 per cent of the vote and over a half of the Chamber of Deputies (but not Senate) seats – the party's leadership wanted to avoid the vulnerability to papal authority of the PPI. So, whilst the DC relied on the Pope's authority to establish the principle of the political unity of Catholics and on the organisational power of the church's parish-based, nationwide electoral mobilisation, the party nevertheless sought to establish both its organisational independence and the autonomy of the political sphere. The DC was not the 'long-arm of the Church'.[18] Whereas the PPI's dominant figure, Luigi Sturzo, had been a priest, the leadership of the DC was lay, and in the 1940s it set about establishing mass organisations loyal in the first place to it, even if religiously inspired. The Catholic Italian Workers' Association (ACLI) was built with this intention, and when the 'Catholic' trade union (CISL) was established, it linked with the American AFL-CIO in ICFTU, the International Confederation of Free Trade Unions, rather than the Catholic International (IFCTU), whilst the farmers' movement, Coldiretti, gave the party an explicitly non-confessional, mass rural base. In the 1950s, Amintore Fanfani reinforced the party's independence from the church (and business interests) by promoting the interpenetration of state and party. For example, the state monopoly of the new medium of television was put to party work, with DC party sections providing prompt popular access to the new communications medium.

The DC's autonomy of clerical and indeed papal influence was confirmed by its coalition strategies. The alliance with the Marxist parties, 1944–47, was maintained despite the opposition of the Catholic right and the displeasure of Pius XII. Subsequently, from 1947/48, the party governed with the so-called 'lay parties' (Liberals, Republicans and Social Democrats) rather than with the monarchists and the MSI, again despite the Catholic right's preference for such a coalition. From December 1963, the party formed a series of governments with the Socialists (PSI), whereas in 1959 the Vatican reiterated the 1949 decision that Socialist, as well as Communist, party (or trade union) membership warranted excommunication. And yet the DC's political independence was ambiguous. The DC's symbiotic relationship with the church was clearly visible. Moreover, the centrist coalition strategy and the consequent exclusionary nature of the democracy it established was highly paradoxical. Until 1963, when the Socialists (PSI) entered the so-called 'Centre-Left' governments, nearly half of the electorate supported parties excluded from government as a matter of principle, and political discrimination against individuals was rife after the so-called 'cold civil war' of c.1947–50, with its dozens killed and thousands injured by armed police intervention in civil disorders.[19] Furthermore, many saw Fanfani's understanding of the alliance with the PSI as effecting a strategic leftward shift by the DC in order to win the PSI's more moderate electorate and so consolidate its hold over the median voting position and hence its domination of coalition formation and government. In this way, a Catholic-dominated exclusionary democracy would have persisted indefinitely. Despite these fears and the significant weakening of the PSI during the 1960s, including by unconstitutional means, the DC's coalition strategy helped modernise the Catholic world and break down barriers between Catholics and non-Catholics, thus promoting democratic consolidation in Italy. These processes were confirmed and accelerated by the Second Vatican Council, organised by John XXIII partly to free him of the influence of the still highly conservative cardinals of the Vatican Curia.[20]

With the benefit of hindsight, the 1950s can be portrayed as seeing only the semblance of Catholic authority.[21] Indeed, Scoppola sees the presence and power of the church in Italian society as declining from 1948 – not least thanks to the nature of the DC and the church's relation to it.[22] Thus, as early as 1952, the Inter-Regional Bishops' Conference (the fore-runner of the CEI) identified support for the DC as causing problems for clerical recruitment and morale, and sought to assert the distinction between the party and the church. However, the conference simultaneously sought to promote the popularity and effectiveness of the DC by 'renewing' it internally.[23] The latter strategy was repeated intermittently over the subsequent decades, with medium-term success.[24] Membership crises in the late 1970s and early 1990s were confronted in this fashion, but only on the first occasion with success.[25] To sum up, what was built from the 1940s was not a confessional state but a DC state, and this state was in many respects independent of the church and even damaging to it. Nor did the DC state govern a homogenous Catholic nation, for this ignores the prominence of anti-clericalism, not least in the 'Red Belt' and, indeed, the growing pluralism of Catholicism itself.[26]

The ambiguity of Italy's religious identity was ended by the divorce referendum of 1974.[27] The pro-divorce victory was a massive shock to most

Italians as well as to international observers, and the unexpected revelation of Italy's rejection of Catholic teaching further fuelled the process of change. In 1978, abortion was legislated for and it too confirmed by referendum, in 1981. The church's recognition of these changes and of the fact that it was vain to rely on the DC to promote church policy led the Vatican to re-emphasise the formal church–state relationship. However, given changed expectations in the Catholic world, following the Second Vatican Council, and the social changes underpinning the divorce and abortion legislation and referendums, it was also clear that the Concordat governing the relationship itself needed revision. This soon followed, in 1984. For the first time, the principle of church–state separation was formally accepted. Italy ceased to be even formally a Catholic state. And in fact, since 1984, Italy's growing religious pluralism has found formal recognition: in 1987 an agreement was signed with Italy's Jewish community; in 1991 an Orthodox Christian metropolitan was established in Venice;[28] in 1994, the Berlusconi government signed an agreement with the Baptists; and in March 2000 the D'Alema II government signed an agreement with both the Italian Buddhist Union and the Jehovah's Witnesses, both of which remained subject to parliamentary ratification when the thirteenth legislature (1996–2001) ended. In the spring of 2002, parliamentary pressure was strong for some formal relationship to be established between the state and its Muslim population.

Like other concordats, the 1984 revision had an exchange logic.[29] It ended compulsory religious teaching in schools, making it voluntary, and over 90 per cent of parents opt for their children to receive it. It placed the scandal-ridden Vatican bank (IOR) under legal regulation, made church properties fully taxable and ended state stipends but introduced tax breaks on donations and enabled the payment of voluntary contributions via income tax. At a rate of 0.8 per cent (that is, 'eight per thousand'), some 40–45 per cent of taxpayers choose to make such contributions. Notwithstanding this evolution in church–state relations, from 1984 until 1996 the church continued to play a direct role in the process of party system change. In particular, the CEI, and more specifically its papally appointed president, came to play a prominent role in Italian politics. The reasons for this include the symbolic importance of Italy as, in some sense, the 'home' of the Catholic Church and the opportunity to do so thanks to the profundity of the state and political crisis of the 1990s. Nevertheless, the beginnings of the church's shift away from the DC can be traced in the CEI's relationship with the DC from the 1970s.

CHURCH, STATE AND PARTY: BEYOND CHRISTIAN DEMOCRACY

The 1952 Inter-Regional Bishops' conference cited above was the first step towards creating an autonomous national organisation of the Italian episcopacy. Hitherto, Italy's national religious identity had been pre-empted by the domination of the Vatican and the enduring localism of Italy's churches.[30] Preparations for the second Vatican Council reinforced the trend towards recognising a specifically Italian episcopal identity, and the CEI was formally instituted in 1972. It enabled a process of papal disengagement from Italian politics, the core of which was the disengagement of the church itself from the DC. However, because of, variously, the centrality of Rome to Italy and to Catholicism, the Pope also being Bishop of Rome and Primate of Italy and, finally, Paul VI's (1964–79) intimate relationship with the DC, it was possible for John Paul II (1979–) to assert his authority over the CEI and to re-engage the church in Italian party politics. Indeed, strategic disagreement between the Pope on the one hand and the bulk of the CEI and Catholic world on the other led to a reassertion of Papal influence in Italian politics, executed by the CEI President. This process can be seen in the CEI's decennial assemblies.

Since its inception, the CEI has organised three decennial assemblies of the Italian 'Catholic world', in 1976, 1985 and 1995. In 1976, episcopal division and Papal caution led the Assembly to postpone the expected definitive break with the DC. These were the years of the divorce referendum and the electoral advance of the PCI, which, it was feared, would outvote the DC in 1976. This did not happen, even though the Assembly established the legitimacy of not voting DC. By 1985, the ecclesiastic elite, led by Cardinal Carlo Maria Martini, was expected entirely to overthrow the surviving model of partnership with the DC. However, one consequence of this was expected to be to encourage left Catholicism, and therefore the recently elected John Paul II blocked this development.[31] By 1995, the DC was no more and its successor, the PPI, was in crisis. Now, the pope asserted the end of Catholic political unity and hence political alignment, replacing it with cultural unity and political non-alignment. Whilst this development reflected the church's historic antipathy to Catholic parties and more recent changes within Italian Catholicism, they were precipitated by party political developments.

In 1993/94, the DC disintegrated. The collapse of the Soviet Union with its ruling party the CPSU and the traumas suffered by the Italian Communist party had briefly appeared to confirm the triumph of political Catholicism. However, the failings of the DC both as a Catholic party and as an effective party of government had left anti-Communism as its principal glue. When the Northern League emerged as a new mass party in 1992, it did so in precisely the areas of the DC's greatest success during its heydays in the 1950s and 1960s – the areas of the so-called 'white subculture' created in opposition to the liberal state in the late nineteenth century.[32] In 1993, the DC disintegrated under the impact of massively publicised judicial investigations, notably the 'Tangentopoli' investigations into systemic political corruption, and allegations of association with the mafia and collusion in murder against the party's greatest living statesman, Giulio Andreotti. The party's formal successor party was the PPI, but the right split to form the Christian Democratic Centre (CCD), which allied with Silvio Berlusconi's newly founded Forza Italia. Other minor splits to the left had already taken place: Leoluca Orlando's Network in 1990, and the Christian Socials in 1993, whilst Mario Segni had formed the Popolari for Reform in 1992/93.

The Vatican continued to support the DC through its travails. It attacked Orlando, a DC reformist whose small party achieved national and international prominence in the 1992 election, and suspended his advisor, Father Ennio Pintacuda, from teaching in the Jesuit school for political education in Palermo. Subsequently, the Vatican isolated Mario Segni despite his popular prominence as the champion of political reform via referendums to change the country's electoral systems. By contrast, it took an intense interest in the DC, now led by a northerner noted for his honesty, Martino Martinzzoli, and its attempt to renew itself by annulling its membership and recruiting in the Catholic world.

In the 1994 election, the PPI and Segni were, ironically, forced into an alliance in an attempt to survive the consequences of bipolarisation and the new electoral rules. These latter now awarded three-quarters of parliamentary seats on a plurality ('first-past-the-post') basis and alliances formed on both the left and the right threatened to crush third forces. On the left were the Progressives, dominated by the post-Communist Democratic Party of the Left (PDS). On the right were two electoral alliances dominated by Silvio Berlusconi and his new party, Forza Italia (FI). Forza Italia and the CCD allied with the Northern League to form the Freedom Pole in the north, and with the MSI-AN to form the Pole of Good Government in the south. Media coverage of the election campaign ignored the 'Catholic' centre pole and the election result destroyed Segni. The PPI fared little better. The defeat was a major blow to the Catholic world, for a combination of grass-roots' wishful thinking plus the authoritative backing given to the PPI had led many to believe that at long last Catholics would have the party they had wanted but never had.[33] The aim of creating a Catholic centrist party holding the balance of power between left and right, thus able to become a quasi-permanent party of government, had failed. Worse was to come.

Following Berlusconi's election victory, Camillo Ruini, the President of the CEI, appeared to identify the victorious centre-right as the natural home for Catholics, large numbers of whom had switched their vote to Forza Italia.[34] The PPI was invited to shift rightward, overcoming the gap that separated the party from 'its' electorate. Poll evidence, however, indicated that the party was likely to lose whichever way it went, left or right. By mid-1994, most conservative voters had already shifted to supporting Forza Italia and/or its CCD allies.[35] In any event, the exit of the CCD had left the old DC-left the major component of the PPI, and no deal with Berlusconi was possible for it. Berlusconi's entry into politics was unwelcome in itself, and both his major allies, the Lega Nord and the 'neo-Fascist' MSI-AN, were seen as unacceptably extremist. Even the CEI had signalled repeatedly and clearly its opposition to the Northern League's proposals to dismember Italy, and whilst the CEI called for the country to give Berlusconi's government and the new electoral system a chance to work, it also made clear its preoccupation regarding the threat Berlusconi's government presented to the constitution and social cohesion.[36]

Far from moving rightward, from late 1994 the PPI sought to develop links with the PDS and even the Northern League (which abandoned Berlusconi's government) in order to challenge Forza Italia's ever closer relationship with what formally became, in January 1995, the 'post-Fascist' National Alliance. The CEI warned against PPI-PDS-LN co-operation leading to the replacement of the elected government (a so-called *ribaltone*). In fact, whilst the government was brought down, the formation of an alternative coalition proved impossible. Instead, in January 1995, a non-parliamentary government led by Berlusconi's Treasury Minister, the Bank of Italy technocrat Lamberto Dini, was formed. The PPI's split was then precipitated by the need to define a coherent nationwide alliance strategy in that spring's regional elections, and in particular by the PPI-left's promotion of Romano Prodi as Prime Minister candidate for a future national alliance with the left. Rocco Buttiglione, who had replaced Martinazzoli as party secretary after the 1994 election disaster, vetoed PPI support for Prodi. Grass-roots support, however, mushroomed throughout the country and polls indicated two-thirds of the PPI's electorate supported Prodi's candidacy.[37] The party split.

The PPI allied with the left from the 1995 regional elections, whilst Buttiglione's CDU (as it became) joined the right, now known as the

Freedom Pole. The internal logic of the split was only partly a left–right one. It was also between the traditional DC, both left and right, which emphasised the autonomy of the political, and the recent influx from the Catholic world, epitomised by Buttiglione, whose political culture was widely seen as clerico-conservative.[38] The mid-1990s saw a resurgence of Catholic conservatism, which many feared could take on fundamentalist tones, asserting the absolute nature of Catholic values.[39] Another dimension of the CDU's strategic position, however, was the intention to moderate, perhaps even supplant, the radical forces (the MSI-AN and FI) dominating it.

The situation confronting the Vatican was unprecedented. The DC had never been the party of all Catholics, but it had been the only party for Catholics. Now, several parties claimed Christian inspiration and they spanned the left–right spectrum. The bulk of the organised Catholic world, or at least its elites, moreover, tended to identify with the nascent centre-left Olive Tree coalition, whereas the country's minority, now, of practising Catholics was divided much more evenly across the political spectrum and, if anything, tended to the right (see Tables 1 and 2). In these difficult circumstances, the Vatican adopted a position of non-alignment, seeking to disarm the move towards supporting the left.[40] A decisive moment in imposing this stance on the Catholic world was the third decennial assembly of the CEI which took place in Palermo in November 1995.

The location of the assembly symbolised the Italian church's newfound, anti-mafia pro-state position and was linked to the church's mission to 'save Italy'. The CEI and the pope himself had already strongly opposed Bossi's separatism. Now this national stance was used to provide a framework within which the church could be *super partes* in the new party environment. The Catholic associations which had been prominent in the first two assemblies were silent. Proceedings were dominated by figures nominated by Ruini, the Pope's personal appointment as President of the CEI. The figure called upon to lead the section of the assembly devoted to political affairs was the historian Giorgio Rumi, himself politically unaligned and a supporter of the move towards cultural unity as a social force rather than political unity. In the meantime, *Famiglia cristiana*, Italy's largest circulating paper (not counting tv guides) had been 'purged' for its criticism of the new line which appeared to discriminate against the Olive Tree in favour of Berlusconi's Freedom Pole.

In the run-up to the 1996 election, Rumi confirmed the church's position of non-alignment whilst arguing that this did not mean neutrality.[41] Rather, the church sought the robust defence of its autonomously defined supreme values, and this meant support for candidates who would guarantee: (1) the

TABLE 1

PROPORTION OF 'PRACTISING CATHOLICS' COMPRISING PARTIES'
ELECTORATES, 1996 ELECTION

	Weekly[1]	Regularly[2]
PPI	66	68.8
CCD-CDU	63	76.7
Dini list	42	51.4
Forza Italia	22	45.5
PDS	19	28.7
National Alliance	19	42.2
Communist Refoundation	13	15.3
Northern League	11	40.4

Notes: 1. Franco Garelli, 'Cattolici senza partito', *Il Mulino*, 45/367 (1996), p.890. The category comprised 27.5 per cent of the population.
2. Ilvo Diamanti, 'L'identità cattolica e comportamento di voto 1997', p.348, based on a pre-electoral survey. The category (defined as attending at least 2–3 times per month) comprised 46 per cent of the population.

TABLE 2

DISTRIBUTION OF 'PRACTISING CATHOLICS', 1996 and 2001

	1996			2001	
	Weekly[1]	Regularly[2]		Weekly[3]	Regularly[3]
Non or spoilt vote	29	N/A	Non/spoilt	N/A	N/A
PPI + CCD-CDU	23	13 + 6	Margherita	16.6	11.9
Forza Italia	12	20	Forza Italia	37.9	36.4
PDS	11	20	DS	12.8	19.9
AN	8	17	AN	10.4	13.1
Dini list	5	5	in Margherita	–	
Communist Refoundation	5	3	CR	3.3	5.8
Northern League	3	8	other C-R	6.2	5.5
	–	–	other C-L	1.5	3.4
Pannella list	2	–		–	–
Other	3	8		11.2	4.0
	100	100		100	

Notes: 1. Franco Garelli, 'Cattolici senza partito', *Il Mulino*, 45/367 (1996), p.891. Definition as Table 1
2. Ilvo Diamanti, 'L'identità cattolica e comportamento di voto 1997', p.348. Definition as Table 1
3. ITANES (Italian National Election Survey), *Perché ha vinto il centro-destra* (Bologna, Il Mulino 2001), p.85. 'Other C-R' includes the CCD-CDU and LN.

primacy and centrality of the person; (2) the defence of human life at all stages of its existence; (3) the promotion of the family founded on marriage; (4) the dignity of women and woman's role in social life; (5) the effective liberty of education and of schooling; (6) a correct equilibrium of powers within the state; (7) support for local government and intermediate social structures in a context of national unity; (8) the centrality of work, social justice, liberty and efficiency in the economic system and in the development of employment; (9) prioritisation of attention to depressed geographical areas and the weaker social strata; (10) international peace and solidarity and Italy's consequent responsibilities in Europe and the world; (11) respect for the environment and the safe-guarding of future generations.

The disappearance of Catholic political unity was not accepted without a fight by Catholic political entrepreneurs. In the thirteenth parliament (1996–2001), all the Catholic party fragments were divided by projects to reunite them. The most notable of these was the formation of the UDR (Democratic Union for the Republic) by former Christian Democrat and ex-President of the Republic (1985–92), Francesco Cossiga, in February 1998. This party was formed mostly from MPs elected on the right in 1996, in particular by the majority of the CDU, and at the end of 1998 it supported the formation of a new centre-left government. This coalition was formed by the leader of the Left Democrats (DS), and former Communist, Massimo D'Alema following the defeat of Romano Prodi's minority government in a vote of confidence. That defeat resulted from Communist Refoundation withdrawing its external support for Prodi's government. Now, whilst the bulk of the new parliamentary majority came from the parties of Prodi's Olive Tree alliance, the UDR provided the vital missing votes. Cossiga's aim was to unify the UDR and PPI, creating a centre-left independent of the Communists. The enhanced visibility of Catholic forces and the project of 'normalising' Italian politics by removing Communist influence was intended to persuade the other Catholic political forces, notably the CCD, to join Cossiga, recreating a Catholic centre pole. In the longer run it is likely that Cossiga hoped to create the potential for centre-right governments comprising this new Catholic party and Forza Italia, that is excluding the Northern League and National Alliance, both regarded by many Catholics as extremist parties. As part of this strategy, Cossiga promoted the passage of Berlusconi's party towards becoming a member of the European People's Party (EPP).

Cossiga's initiative was contested in particular by Romano Prodi, who responded to his government's defeat and the formation of the UDR by building his own party, the Democrats for the Olive Tree. Its principal aim was the maintenance of the bipolar structure of Italian politics, whereas Cossiga's 'neo-centrism' risked recreating a tripolar party system such as had underpinned the so-called 'First Republic'. Prodi's party proved popular with voters in the 1999 European parliament election, outperforming the PPI (7.7 per cent compared to 4.2 per cent). The merger of the UDR and PPI was blocked. In any case, it was not clear that the DS leadership could risk alienating much of its membership and electorate by turning their back on the Communists. And on the right, Berlusconi showed no willingness to jettison National Alliance, whilst the CCD remained loyal to Berlusconi.

In the end, Cossiga's party broke up. His initiative caused further fragmentation and turmoil in the world of party Catholicism, rather than reaggregation. The CDU returned to the centre-right and re-allied with the CCD, whilst a remnant, led by Clemente Mastella, formed the Udeur (European Democratic Union) and joined the left. In the meantime, at the end of 1999, Forza Italia's claim to the DC's inheritance, challenging the Catholic parties, was reinforced by the party's admission to the European People's Party. This development was strenuously opposed by the PPI and former Prime Minister Dini's strongly religiously identified Italian Renewal party (RI). But with no fewer than four Italian parties in the EPP providing only eight MEPs between them, and these divided between left (PPI and RI) and right (CCD and CDU), the pressure to admit FI's 22 MEPs was overwhelming.

In the run-up to the 2001 election, a further attempt was made to create a Catholic centre party. Sergio D'Antoni, the former General Secretary of the Catholic trade union CISL (1991–2000), founded European Democracy, attracting the support of Giulio Andreotti (now acquitted of the charges against him) and limited support in the PPI. The party had minimal success in the election, obtaining just two Senators. In the new parliament, it formed an alliance with the CCD-CDU, founding the UDC – the Christian Democratic and Centre Union. This party has 69 MPs (40 Deputies and 29 Senators), a little over seven per cent of the total, and risks 'cannibalisation' by Forza Italia, which considerably increased its appeal to Catholic voters between 1996 and 2001 (see Table 2). Electoral considerations also forced a process of Catholic reaggregation on the left. In the autumn of 2000 the PPI, the Democrats, RI and the Udeur formed an electoral list, the Margherita, and obtained an unexpected success, receiving 14.5 per cent of the proportional vote. In parliament they formed a single group and in the spring of 2002 the first three of these parties moved towards forming a single party of the same name. The fragmentation of the post-DC Catholic parties, their marginalisation and, above all, their location on both sides of the left–right spectrum means that Catholic politics can no longer take place in and via a dominant party. Rather, they have to take place via pressure group activity, the influence of key individuals, and/or formal church–state relations.

CATHOLIC POLITICS AND PUBLIC POLICY

From the early 1990s, the church in Italy has consistently highlighted its national and pro-state identity, for example challenging the Northern League's proposals to fragment the country, and adopting a clear position against the mafia. It has supported constitutional reform both specifically, as in the proposal to introduce a French-style semi-presidential system of government in early 1996,[42] and in general, as in the formation of the Bicameral Committee for Constitutional Reform in 1997. Some have argued that the church is seeking to substitute itself for the crisis-ridden state.[43] Perhaps more realistically, the church has vigorously promoted its own policy agenda whilst keeping its hands free of direct responsibility for managing the difficult reality of modern government.

Education has been perhaps the major issue of dispute between the church and the modern state. The topic is back on the agenda in Italy, and is no less controversial for that very fact. The issue bites deep into the question of the Republic's identity with Norberto Bobbio, sometimes described as Italy's 'lay pope', rejecting any form of state support for Catholic education as subverting the constitution. Article 33 states that private schools and institutes should have 'no costs for the state'. Approximately seven per cent of the school population attends Catholic schools. Nevertheless, the need for educational reform at all levels is generally acknowledged and the centre-left governments launched a major school reform in March 2000 whilst the centre-right government suspended its implementation in favour of its own project. Within the more general debate, a liberal strand has emerged which argues that public–private competition in a framework regulated by the state can only be of benefit, so that Bobbio's position is an unhelpful interpretation of the constitution and even illiberal. Moves towards a mixed system were contained in the 2000 legislation, which was welcomed by the Association of Catholic Teachers (AIMC) and the association of Catholic Infant Schools (FISM), although the CEI found it inadequate. The legislation envisaged a 'national education system' which left syllabi and teaching with no further regulation beyond not infringing constitutional norms whilst stipulating requirements about access, infrastructure, management, national pay rates and bargaining, as well as acceptance of the state teaching audit system. In return, private infant and elementary schools opting for parity would obtain state funding, the disadvantaged parents of parity private schools would be able to access study awards or obtain tax benefits, and all such schools would be treated as charities for tax purposes. The centre-right has declared its intention to 'equalise' conditions fully for public and private schools.

Bioethics was only established as a separate discipline in Italy in the 1970s and was initially perceived essentially as the reapplication of the unity of morality and religion according to official Catholic doctrine. A minority of lay forces turned to the internationally dominant Anglo-American paradigm. From the mid-1980s an autonomous approach developed which recognised the immense differences either side of the religious cleavage. Nevertheless, until the late 1990s, a Catholic veto resulted in a legislative vacuum, since regulation itself was seen as state recognition of, and participation in, immoral practice.[44] Since this absence permitted some controversial developments to take place, including embryo implantation in post-menopause women, an attempt at legislation was made by the centre-left. However, the bill approved in the Chamber of Deputies resulted from Catholic co-operation across the government–opposition divide at a time when the PPI was under intense pressure to break with the left. It was, thus, 'particularly ideological and restrictive',[45] for example banning donor insemination for infertile couples, and the government did not proceed with it. In the spring of 2002, substantially similar legislation was presented by the new government. Again, cross-bloc parliamentary co-operation was a feature of the legislation's progress, resulting in non-married couples obtaining the right to state fertility treatment.

Finally, the Italian church's health and welfare role has been reinforced by recent legislation. A universal national health service was introduced in Italy only in the late 1970s. Unfortunately, the new system caused costs to soar and although generous pensions rather than health care costs were the major cause of public debt and high taxes, the new NHS did dramatically reinforce systemic political corruption.[46] Especially against the background of the Tangentopoli revelations from 1992, local government reforms since 1990 have challenged the local party oligarchies and major cost-cutting reforms have been introduced. The general impact of the double blow of appallingly corrupt health care and then painful reform was to reinforce anti-universal and anti-state sentiment to the benefit of the voluntary, essentially Catholic, sector.[47]

A citizenship-based, universal, mixed (public–private) and plural (lay and Catholic) welfare system has now won broad elite acceptance, and the church's role in it is extensive, not least in the care of drug-abusers, the young and the elderly, the handicapped and immigrants. This welfare role is highly regarded by the public. However, the public repeatedly affirms its dislike of the church giving advice on political or even public welfare matters and this distinction, and the more general public disinclination to follow Catholic moral teaching, has led prominent ecclesiastics to fear the reduction of the church to little more than a welfare agency. Nevertheless, as in education, the state's inability to fund health care to the extent desired and the acceptance of the need to introduce markets and competition is likely to benefit the voluntary sector and religious institutions. These developments have probably reinforced the 'intermediate' nature of Italy's church–state relationship as defined by Robbers (see Minkenberg below).

CONCLUSION

Since Italy's foundation, church–state relations have undergone a series of transformations, and both the state and the church have themselves changed. When Italy was founded, the church lost its territorial power and reacted by reinforcing its internal authority structure and seeking to organise society without the state and against it. Later, challenged ideologically and organisationally by the rise of Socialism, it co-operated with state elites whilst still hoping to subvert, or convert, the state to its own ends. Via Mussolini, the church reached a legal accommodation with the state, yet maintained a certain competitive autonomy, managing to emerge from the Fascist period strengthened, whilst Fascism collapsed. The church largely filled the subsequent vacuum, but the state survived, although the political parties became so dominant as apparently to supplant it. Nevertheless, with the triumph of the Christian Democrats in 1948, it was the church that appeared dominant. Only in the 1970s did it become clear that 'the DC-state' was not the church's state. Indeed, it became clear, not least following the Second Vatican Council, that both 'the church' and 'the state' are too complex phenomena, and in a pluralist democracy their interpenetration with society too significant, to ignore the role of opposition parties and broader social forces in fully defining the nature of the relationship.

For the bulk of the period in which Italy has had a democratic state, the church (generalising to its elite structures, and not least the papacy specifically) has supported Italy's dominant 'state' party, the Christian Democrats. Indeed, despite a substantial change in this 'church–state party' relationship from the 1970s, Vatican and ecclesiastical support for the DC continued until 1995. Thus, at the same time that the church–state concordat was revised (1984), John Paul II reaffirmed the church's close relationship with the DC at the second decennial ecclesiastical assembly in Loreto (1985). Since 1995, however, the church has been coming to terms with Catholic party pluralism, describing its position as one of 'non-alignment'. This is a major change. Yet the church eschews the term 'neutrality', since this would deny that it has an agenda of its own. In roughly the same period, religious pluralism has grown in importance, and both the state and the church have shown a clear awareness of this, with the Italian state actively supporting the pluralisation of religion in Italy.

To sum up, the church–state relationship in Italy has evolved from one of subversive non-participation in the liberal period through competitive collaboration under Fascism to critical alignment with the hegemonic state party in the Christian Democratic period and, finally, to non-alignment. The latest development aroused intense opposition within part of the Catholic world since the emergent right, led by Berlusconi, was viewed by many Catholics as idolatrous and capable of undermining the 'shared civil ethos which lies at the foundation of every democratic society'.[48] However, the centripetal evolution of Berlusconi's Home of Freedom alliance (as it has been known since the return to it of the Northern League in 2000) since 1995/96 has been marked. Thus, notwithstanding the concerns raised by the alliance's electoral victory in 2001, many hope that Catholic activism across the political spectrum will help finally to construct the ethico-political myth of there being a unified, democratic nation-state in Italy.[49]

NOTES

1. M.L. Salvadori, *Storia d'italia e crisi di regime* (Milan: Il Mulino, 3rd edn. 2001).
2. S.N. Kalyvas, *The Rise of Christian Democracy in Europe* (Ithaca and London: Cornell University Press 1996).
3. S. Magister, *Chiesa extraparlamentare* (Napoli: L'ancora del mediterraneo 2001), pp.71–83.
4. Kalyvas, *The Rise of Christian Democracy*, pp.215–16.
5. J.N. Molony, *The Emergenceof Political Catholicism in Italy* (London: Croom Helm 1977).
6. M. Clark, *Modern Italy, 1870–1996* (London: Longman 1996).
7. A. Lepre, *Storia della prima Repubblica. L'Italia dal 1942 al 1992* (Bologna: Il Mulino 1993), pp.53–4.
8. S.H. Barnes, *Representation in Italy: Institutionalized Tradition and Electoral Choice* (Chicago: University of Chicago Press 1977).
9. A. Giovagnoli, *Il partito italiano. La democrazia cristiana dal 1942 al 1994* (Rome: Laterza 1996); A. Lombardo, *DC e questione nazionale* (Milan: SugarCo. 1981).
10. The Dossettiani were the followers of Giuseppe Dossetti. See G.B. Bozzo, *Cattolici e Democristiani* (Milan: Rizzoli 1994); A. Becchi, 'Democrazia cristiana e idea nazionale: la memoria e il progetto', *Storia Contemporanea* 25 (1994), pp.887–928.
11. G. Formigoni, *L'Italia dei cattolici: Fede e nazione dal Risorgimento alla repubblica*

(Bologna: Il Mulino 1998).
12. Ibid., p.31.
13. Ibid., p.155.
14. E. Pace, *L'Unità dei cattolici in Italia. Origini e decadenze di un mito colletivo* (Milan: Guerrini e Associati 1995).
15. Ibid., pp.27–8.
16. A.C. Jemolo, *Church and State in Italy, 1850–1950* (Oxford: Blackwell 1960).
17. Formigoni, *L'Italia dei cattolici*, p.166; Andrea Riccardi, 'Il cattolicesimo della Repubblica', in G. Sabbatucci and V.Vidotto (eds.), *L'Italia Contemporanea* (Rome: Laterza 1999), pp.233–319.
18. D. Sassoon, *Contemporary Italy. Politics, Economy and Society since 1945* (Harlow: Longman 1986), pp.143–5.
19. Lepre, *Storia della prima repubblica*, pp.127–9.
20. G. Martina, *La chiesa in Italia negli ultimi trent'anni* (Rome: Studium 1977); A. Riccardi, *Il 'partito romano' nel secondo dopoguerra, 1945–54* (Brescia: Morcelliana 1983); A. Riccardi, 'La nazione cattolica', in A. Giovagnoli (ed.), *Interpretazioni della Repubblica* (Bologna: Il Mulino 1998), pp.47–61.
21. Riccardi, 'La nazione cattolica'.
22. P. Scoppola, *La 'Nuova cristianità' perduta* (Rome: Studium 1985), p.20 and *passim*.
23. Riccardi, *Il 'partito romano'*, pp.177–84.
24. A. Arian and S.H. Barnes, 'The Dominant Party System – A Neglected Model of Democratic Stability', *Journal of Politics* 36/2 (1974), pp.592–614.
25. F. Anderlini , 'La DC: iscritti e modello di partito', *Polis* 2 (1989), pp.277–304.
26. P. Allum, 'Uniformity Undone: Aspects of Catholic Culture in Postwar Italy', in Z.G. Baranski and R. Lumley (eds.), *Culture and Conflict in Postwar Italy. Essays on Mass and Popular Culture* (Basingstoke: Macmillan 1990), pp.79–96.
27. Riccardi, 'La nazione cattolica', p.54.
28. A. Riccardi, 'Culti nuovi e tradizionali, movimenti emergenti', in P. Ginsborg (ed.), *Stato dell'Italia* (Milan: Il Saggiatore 1994), pp.347–49
29. Pace, *L'Unità dei cattolici in Italia*, p.16.
30. A. Riccardi, *Le Chiese di Pio XII* (Laterza: Rome-Bari 1986).
31. Magister, *Chiesa extraparlamentare*, p.56.
32. G. Gangemi and G. Riccamboni, 'Introduzione', in G. Gangemi and G. Riccamboni (eds.), *Le Elezioni della Transizione. Il sistema politico italiano alla prova del voto 1994-1996* (Turin: UTET 1997), pp.vii–xxvi; P. Messina, 'Persistenza e mutamento nelle subculture politiche territoriali', in Gangemi and Riccamboni (eds.), *Le Elezioni della Transizione*, pp.19–55.
33. L. Accattolli, 'Ruini: Cattolici al Centro, se potete', *Corriere della Sera*, 15 March 1994, p.6; G. Brunelli, 'La scommessa perduta sul partito cattolico', *Il Mulino* 44/358 (1995), pp.237–43; S. Magister, 'The Church and the End of the Catholic Party', in M. Caciagli and D.I. Kertzer (eds.), *Italian Politics: The Stalled Transition* (Oxford: Westview Press 1996), pp.223–40.
34. F. Garelli, 'Una nuova stagione per la Chiesa e i cattolici in Italia?', *Il Mulino* 43/354 (1994), pp.581–94.
35. R. Mannheimer, *Corriere della Sera*, 12 Dec. 1994; 23 Jan. 1995; 6 Feb. 1995.
36. *Corriere della Sera*, 23 April, 1994.
37. *Corriere della Sera* 13 March 1995.
38. O.M. Petracca, *Corriere della Sera*, 3 Aug. 1994.
39. E. Marzo, 'Ma la Vandea non é un'eredità politica', *Corriere della Sera*, 24 Sept. 1994, p.33.
40. Magister, *Chiesa extraparlamentare*, p.67
41. *La Repubblica*, 3 April 1996.
42. *Corriere della Sera*, 13 Feb. 1996
43. R. Cartocci, *Fra Lega e Chiesa. L'Italia in cerca d'integrazione* (Bologna: Il Mulino 1994).
44. G. Berlinguer, 'Bioetica all'avanguardia ma la legislazione é bloccata', in P.Ginsborg (ed.), *Stato dell'Italia* (Milan: Il Saggiatore 1994), pp.321–4.
45. C. Flamigni, *La procreazione assistita* (Bologna: Il Mulino 2002).

116   CHURCH AND STATE IN CONTEMPORARY EUROPE

46. U. Ascoli, 'Le prospettive dello stato sociale', in P. Ginsborg (ed.), *Stato dell'Italia* (Milan: Il Saggiatore 1994), pp.538–41.
47. M. Ferrera, 'The Partitocracy of Health. Towards a New Welfare Politics in Italy?' *Res Publica* 38/2 (1996), pp.447–59.
48. Magister, 'The Church and the End of the Catholic Party', p.238.
49. Pace, *L'Unità dei cattolici in Italia*, p.172.

Orthodoxy and Nationalism in the Greek Case

GEORGE TH. MAVROGORDATOS

RELIGION AND NATIONALISM

How does a particular religion become literally identified with a particular nationality? How does the odd notion arise that one cannot be, for example, truly Irish or Polish without being *also* (even nominally) a Roman Catholic?

Despite the prolific literature on nationalism, and the growing literature on religion, there seems to be no general theoretical framework or systematic discussion focusing specifically on the linkage between the two. The issue here is 'filiation' rather than mere affinity or covariance, according to the three terms used by Anthony D. Smith in his more narrow analysis of 'election myths'.[1] Most, apparently, regard this linkage as given, or as incidental. Their secular outlook may lead them to neglect the impact of religion as such. Such neglect, however, masks the complexities involved.

Both logically and historically, the most obvious starting point stems from the logic of differentiation and separation inherent in nation-building. Religion provides a primordial line of demarcation, which may be far superior to any other. It is certainly more readily identifiable, clear-cut, exclusive, and impermeable than language, ancestry, or any other relevant criterion. Occasional syncretism notwithstanding, it does not even make sense to say that one is of 'mixed' religion, whereas many are bilingual or of mixed blood. Religion is, moreover, by definition value-laden and breeds a sense of superiority and mission, unlike language as such. To use the kind of argument dear to Benedict Anderson in his classic book, people may be prepared to fight and die for the 'true' religion long before (if ever) they are prepared to do so for the 'correct' language, especially as long as they remain illiterate. In this respect, the emphasis he placed on the 'primordialness' of language may be exaggerated or else anachronistic, insofar as it applies to a *later* stage of nation-building.[2]

The superiority of religion over language in nation-building is best demonstrated by the Low Countries, which broke up twice, in 1579 and again in 1830, according to religion and not language. The Calvinist component of Dutch national identity repelled irremediably the staunchly Catholic population of what was to become Belgium, irrespective of actual linguistic boundaries. Subsequently, the increasing importance accorded to the language question by Catholic Flanders has been threatening to break up Belgium without ever inducing the notion of a common nationality (even less of 'national reunion') with the Dutch, despite the common language. Religion and not language also threatened to break up the Swiss nation in 1847 in the *Sonderbund* war, which may be regarded as the final stage of its formation. Religion and not language also served to construct an Austrian national identity during the inter-war years.

This intrinsic and enduring superiority of religion as a primordial line of *national* demarcation deserves a far more central place in theories of nationalism. Nationalism has often been compared to a 'secular' or 'civil' religion.[3] The implication has been that it supersedes religion as such. The reverse side of the same coin, however, is that religion has often provided a ready-made initial core of national identity, which has proved remarkably resilient over the centuries.

The weight of religion as an essential core of national identity has often been reinforced by a history of defence against external foes, or else by a history of discrimination and deprivation within multinational states and empires. A prime example is Catholic Poland, perennially squeezed (and eventually partitioned) between Orthodox Russia and Protestant Prussia (although Catholic Austria also took its part). Examples of the latter kind are offered by the situation of the Orthodox in the Ottoman Empire, and of the Catholics in eighteenth-century Ireland. In both instances, one had simply to change one's religion in order to have immediate access to property, wealth, and power. For those who refused this 'diabolical' bargain, the religious and thereby doubly 'sacred' core of national identity was certainly reinforced. The latest example of religion serving as a surrogate and an eventual nucleus of national identity according to the scheme imposed by a multinational state is, of course, that of the Muslims in Bosnia, who were treated as the equivalent of a separate nationality in what used to be Yugoslavia.

Less obvious than the logic of demarcation is the logic of integrity, independence, and sovereignty linking religion and nationalism. Few denominations actually coincide with a single 'chosen people' or nation. In such cases, the particular denomination may be easily and directly construed as a constituent of a unique national identity. Anglicanism provides the most obvious example, as the name itself proclaims. Exactly the same is true of the Armenian Apostolic Church. Outside Christendom, Judaism corresponds by definition to the Jewish nation, Hinduism to the Indian nation (irrespective of secular versions of nationalism in both cases). Finally, Iran remains for centuries the only country identified with Shiite Islam, which, therefore, may fit and fuel Iranian nationalism without the incongruities created by Sunni Islam elsewhere.

In most cases, however, a religion or denomination is common to several nations. How can it become identified with any one among them in particular? It is here that differences between religions in terms of authority structure and organisation become crucial. Among Christian denominations, Catholicism and Protestantism represent the two extremes in this respect.

Ever since the Middle Ages, the Catholic Church has been a single worldwide organisation transcending both state and national boundaries, and obeying a single worldwide centre, which is normally independent of any other authority. Once this independence was won and secured, the supranational authority of the Pope has been incompatible, first with dynastic, later also with national loyalties. This conflict of loyalties was to plague Catholic countries well into the twentieth century, and Italy was bound to be the foremost case, since its national unification also required the elimination of the Papal States. Consequently, it was primarily in Catholic countries that the separation of church and state became a paramount and urgent issue. It was also primarily in Catholic countries that strictly secular nationalism developed, which came to be regarded as a universal model of the new 'civil religion'. Insofar as Catholic countries like Poland or Ireland remain exceptional or 'retarded' in this respect, this is no doubt because of the protracted struggle for national liberation from non-Catholic oppressors.

Protestantism, of course, is the exact opposite. Arising in rejection of the supranational authority of the Pope, Protestantism and especially Lutheranism was not merely compatible with, but actually inseparable from incipient nationalism from the very beginning. Luther's first pamphlet was addressed to the nobility of the 'German Nation' alone. In the case of England, it has even been argued that Protestantism served as the 'midwife' of nationalism.[4] Calvinism played a comparable role in the case of the Netherlands.[5] Moreover, Protestantism and especially Lutheranism promoted the conception of a state church, imposed by secular authority. The principle that was originally defined as '*Cuius regio, eius religio*' could be easily transferred later from the dynastic to the national state, as in Scandinavia. Consequently, the state church also became a national institution – the embodiment and guardian of national identity and sovereignty in the religious sphere. Furthermore, as a powerful agent of socialisation, it came to play an essential role in national education.

If Catholicism and Protestantism constitute two opposite poles in this respect, the Greek case serves to illustrate the intermediate position of the Eastern Orthodox faith, which has moved over the centuries from one extreme to the other. It also serves to illustrate the enduring limitations on religious freedom stemming from the identification of a particular nation with a particular religious denomination.

AN ODD CASE IN THE EU?

For a country that has been a member of the EU since 1981, contemporary Greece appears quite anachronistic with respect to religious freedom. A most telling recognition of this contradiction was the recent appointment by Foreign Minister G. Papandreou of an advisory group on religious freedom. This task force was supposed to make recommendations on such issues as church–state relations, religious instruction in schools, preconditions for the establishment of places of worship, the mention of religion on identity cards, conscientious objectors, proselytism, the content of oaths, and so on.

Under attack by the Archbishop of Athens (head of the Orthodox Church of Greece), the Foreign Minister lamely invoked the international obligations of Greece, especially under the European Convention on Human Rights and before the European Court of Human Rights, where it is his department's responsibility to represent Greece – and usually lose.[6] Critics objected, nonetheless, that these are domestic issues and the preserve of other ministries.[7] Eventually, both the advisory group and its recommendations were quietly forgotten.

This controversy bears ample witness to the fact that pressure to change is external rather than domestic. By an overwhelming parliamentary majority, including both major parties (PASOK and ND), the separation of church and state was excluded (in 1998) from the constitutional revision that was eventually completed in April 2001. No new revision of the Constitution is allowed before five years have elapsed since the previous one. Hence, the present constitutional status is expected to remain unchanged until at least 2010.

What this status implies is provided by the list of tasks assigned to the controversial advisory group, supplemented by the most relevant recent developments:

1. The 'productivity bonus' instituted for civil servants was extended to the Orthodox clergy, after much pressure from the church. The fact that this raised no objections except ironic comments reflects the unquestioned acceptance of the church's status as a 'special branch' of the state and of its civil service. According to the Constitution, church administration in general is regulated by state law.

2. State honours due to a Head of State were staged not only for the funeral of the previous Archbishop of Athens, and for the repeated visits of the Patriarch of Constantinople, but also for the visit of a holy icon from Mount Athos to Athens.

3. The construction of *any* religious building still requires the permission of the local Orthodox bishop. Consequently, despite pressures from Arab countries and despite the presence of many Muslims (both immigrants and internal migrants), there is no mosque operating in the Greater Athens area, nor anywhere else in Greece, for that matter, except Thrace, where the native Muslim population enjoys minority status by international treaty. Internal migrants from Thrace living in Attica, however, are not only deprived of religious services, but also of valid baptisms and marriages, since the (state-appointed) muftis of Thrace do not have jurisdiction outside their area. Moreover, Muslim cemeteries operate only in Thrace.[8] The construction of a single mosque in Attica became unavoidable only because of the requirements of the Olympic Games, to be held in Athens in 2004. Its peripheral location, outside the city, was calculated to minimise reactions (which have been limited to protests by neighbouring towns).

4. For its part, the Orthodox Church reserves the right to issue building permits for its own churches and chapels without interference by civil authorities. Abuses have involved even the construction of villas beside chapels, in gross violation of general regulations.[9] In a country (and countryside) perennially plagued by unauthorised building, this is perhaps the most tangible manifestation of the effective role of the church as a state agency, or, worse, as 'a state within the state'.

5. In 1998, the Council of State (supreme administrative court on the French model) ruled unconstitutional a reduction in the hours of religious instruction in the schools, which is exclusively in the Orthodox faith. According to an earlier decision of the same court, in 1995, pupils may be exempted only if they or their parents make a formal request invoking specifically different religious beliefs.

6. Civil marriage was introduced in Greece only in 1982, and only as an alternative to religious marriage. The overwhelming majority still

marries in church. Orthodox clergymen sometimes refuse burial rites and other rights to those who were not married in church.

7. Cremation of the dead is not allowed in Greece, because of church opposition. Cremation has to be performed abroad, and even then the return of the ashes may face obstruction from official channels.[10] It now seems that cremation will be allowed at last, but only for those who make a formal request beforehand, or who can prove that they do not belong to the Orthodox Church.

8. Leaving the Orthodox Church of Greece, however, may not be as simple as it sounds. For almost 80 years, the church has refused to acknowledge the exit of Old Calendar supporters (self-designated as 'Genuine Orthodox Christians'), and still considers them rebellious members. It protested vehemently when the leadership of the Old Calendar Church was received by the President of the Republic in 1998.

9. Although conscientious objectors (mainly Jehovah's Witnesses) have acquired since 1998 the right to alternative service, harassment has continued under many guises. Some of them are even placed in welfare institutions run by the Orthodox clergy, which often refuses to accept them.[11]

10. Although ostensibly both proselytism and blasphemy are criminal offences with respect to any recognised religion, in practice such repressive legislation is invoked only by Orthodox zealots, on behalf of the church.[12] Most recently, in 2000, the church openly condemned a novel by M. Androulakis, and condoned both the legal and illegal actions of those seeking to ban it (unsuccessfully, as it turned out).

It is telling that the latest issue over which the church chose to mobilise its supporters was that of identity cards. Until recently, birth certificates, compulsory identity cards, and other official records in Greece routinely included religious affiliation: 'Christian Orthodox' for almost 97 per cent of Greek citizens. This was the material underpinning of every argument justifying the special position of the Orthodox Church as the 'prevailing' religion in the land, according to the wording of the Constitution.

In May 2000, however, the competent Authority for the Protection of Personal Data outlawed the mention of religion on identity cards, and the Simitis government immediately endorsed this ruling as final. The church apparently perceived this move as a first step in the gradual erosion of its institutional monopoly, and refused to accept it. Insisting that Orthodoxy is inseparable from the Greek identity, the church assumed suddenly the appearance of a political movement, headed by the aggressive and demagogic new Archbishop Christodoulos. Mass rallies were organised in Thessaloniki and Athens, to which he spoke. In every detail, these imitated (or reproduced) party rallies in the days of triumphant populism under Andreas Papandreou.

The church also took the unprecedented step of organising the collection of signatures demanding that a referendum be held on the issue of the new identity cards and their mention of religion. This initiative was conceived as a show of force and a means of pressure, since the Constitution does not allow referenda except by decision of parliament (a dead letter so far).

The collection of signatures dragged on for several months, well into 2001. In the end, the church claimed to have collected over three million signatures (although this claim could not be corroborated independently). Even so, this number fell short of what would have been required to claim a majority, since seven million had voted in the parliamentary election of April 2000, out of an electorate of nine million. The issue was then set aside, but not forgotten. Archbishop Christodoulos appears determined to revive it on the eve of the next parliamentary election.

In terms of the various models of church–state relations,[13] Greece is a clear-cut case of 'formal establishment', involving not only the Orthodox Church of Greece, but also two religious minorities: the Muslims of Thrace (whose muftis are appointed by the state as civil servants) and the Jews (whose communities and central council are established and regulated by state law). To speak of 'plural establishment', however, would be misleading, since no equal treatment is implied. All other faiths are usually treated as private associations. Even so, the status of the Catholic Church as a legal person has been disputed until recently.[14]

It is fair to conclude that, from the point of view of the individual and especially of the non-believer, religious freedom remains quite limited in Greece by the standards developed and applied in other Western democracies. Unless one is willing to bear very substantial costs, one can neither live nor die outside the church(es): the Orthodox Church and the few others recognised or tolerated. The question is whether this situation stems from factors specific to the Eastern Orthodox tradition. After all, Greece is the only Orthodox country in the EU.

A STATE CHURCH

The contradiction between the promise of religious freedom and the establishment of a state church was built into the very first constitution of independent Greece, adopted in Epidaurus on 1 January 1822. It has remained at the heart of the matter under successive constitutions until the present day.

The establishment of a state church was certainly in keeping with the Eastern Orthodox tradition. 'In Orthodoxy, God is Caesar's junior partner' according to Huntington's lapidary formulation.[15] As a prominent Greek theologian was to argue in 1852, 'the Eastern Church is everywhere joined to the state, never being separated from it, never divided from the sovereigns since Byzantine times, and always subordinate to them'.[16]

The status of the Eastern Church as a state church subordinate to Caesar had been firmly established from the very beginning, under Constantine the Great. This relationship was never questioned nor challenged throughout the Byzantine millennium, in sharp contrast to the course taken by the Western Church, especially after the Great Schism of 1054.

The Byzantine Emperor, at least, was considered 'equal to the Apostles' (*isapostolos*). The same relationship persisted, nonetheless, when his place was taken by an *infidel*, the Ottoman Sultan, after the fall of Constantinople in 1453. Previously a Byzantine dignitary, the Patriarch of Constantinople now became an Ottoman official, responsible for the *'Rum millet'*, that is, all the Christian Orthodox subjects of the Ottoman Empire.[17]

When Greece declared (in 1821) and eventually won (by 1830) its independence from the Ottoman Empire, precisely the logic of a state church required that the Orthodox Church in Greece should also be independent of the Patriarch in Istanbul (that is, 'autocephalous' in ecclesiastical terms). Formally proclaimed in 1833, this independence was eventually accepted by the Patriarchate in 1850. With each subsequent expansion of the Greek state, the corresponding dioceses were effectively removed from the Patriarchate and added to the Church of Greece. Only the Dodecanese, annexed by Greece in 1947, remains under the jurisdiction of the Patriarchate, together with the autonomous Church of Crete.[18] A lingering dispute involves the other 'New Lands' (annexed by Greece between 1912 and 1923), over which the Patriarchate claims to retain purely 'spiritual' authority. On the other hand, Archbishop Christodoulos and his associates reportedly aspire to elevate the autocephalous Church of Greece (and themselves) to the rank of a patriarchate, and thereby make complete independence from Constantinople even more manifest.

Although exploited at the time for political purposes, the subordination of the new autocephalous church to the first king of Greece, a Bavarian Catholic, did not, in fact, represent an anomaly with respect to the Ottoman past, since it perpetuated church subordination to the secular ruler. If anything, it was an improvement if viewed from a Christian angle. By 1844, in any case, the constitution that was forced upon the king required his successors to be Christian Orthodox, although a new royal dynasty had to be imported (from Denmark in 1863) before this requirement could be met. The same is now required of the President of the Republic (although some argue that the oath of office prescribed by the Constitution might be compatible with other Christian denominations or even adaptable to other religious beliefs).

Ever since 1833, the Orthodox Church of Greece continues to perform the primary function of a state church: it is essential for the formal legitimation of state authority. No regime and no government ever did without religious ceremonies performed by the Orthodox clergy: oaths of office (typically administered by the Archbishop of Athens), masses celebrated in the Athens Cathedral, and so on.

Consequently, the Greek state has always sought to protect its official church as a matter of self-preservation. A case in point involves the Old Calendar movement.[19] The change from the old (Julian) to the new (Gregorian) calendar in Greece coincided with the proclamation of the inter-war Republic, in 1924. Until its overthrow in 1935, the repression of Old Calendar supporters (*palaiohemerologites*) not only aimed at preserving the integrity of the established Church of Greece. It also aimed at safeguarding the authority of church leaders loyal to the regime, and at suppressing agitation openly hostile to the supposedly sacrilegious Republic.[20]

Early subordination to the state may have bred certain traits which, in turn, have always helped the Orthodox Church maintain its collaboration with Caesar, and thereby safeguard its position as a state church. Foremost among these are (a) the lack of doctrinal rigidity and consistency, and (b) the concomitant lack of corporate solidarity and discipline. The Orthodox Church has never been as monolithic as the Catholic Church has always aspired to be, under a single 'infallible' leader. Consequently, the Orthodox Church has never experienced anything like the Reformation or the Counter-Reformation.

The impression of immutable traditionalism usually associated with Orthodoxy may mask its malleability. Over the centuries, there is not a single issue on which the church has absolutely refused to compromise with the state, except one: their separation. Only in such an eventuality, when the church would have nothing more to lose, would it risk a total break with the state. Otherwise, the church has been apparently willing to compromise on practically everything.

Marriage is a case in point. If the Orthodox Church allows three valid marriages in a lifetime, this is obviously arbitrary, and not the logical outcome of theological argument, as in the case of the Catholics (one marriage) or the Protestants (as many as you need). At one time, the church allowed up to four valid marriages, simply because the Byzantine emperor Leo VI wished it.[21] Then the number went back to three, and has stayed there ever since. Perhaps no other issue illustrates better the historic contrast with Catholicism. In a similar situation, the Pope was willing to risk a break with Henry VIII of England, with momentous consequences.

In more recent times, abortion is another case in point. Although the Orthodox Church of Greece did protest against the legalisation of abortion in 1986, its reaction was distinctly subdued in comparison to its major confrontation with the PASOK government in 1987, over the issue of church property and church administration. By now, abortion as a religious issue is rarely mentioned.

In practice, the Orthodox Church demands nothing of its nominal members in terms of their daily lives. Fasting may look like an exception, but it has long become merely a custom associated with certain holidays – a tradition devoid of actual religious meaning. Short of other arguments, the current archbishop recently chose to promote fasting as a superior diet formula.

On the other hand, the absence of corporate solidarity has meant that, in any situation of conflict with the state, part of the clergy has *always* been available for collaboration. On the very day that Patriarch Gregory V was ignominiously executed in 1821, as responsible for the Greek revolt that he had vainly excommunicated, a willing successor was found. 'On the way to the sultan's palace to seek confirmation of his election, he had to pass through the gate from which the body of his predecessor still hung.'[22] In occupied Athens, in 1941, Archbishop Chrysanthos may have refused to swear in the first Quisling government appointed by the Germans, but his rival Damaskinos was ready to take his place (which Damaskinos had considered rightfully his ever since 1938). Finally, no less than two archbishops were willing to accede to their throne thanks to the last dictatorship (1967–74), the latter serving until his death in 1998. Out of 12 archbishops of Athens during the twentieth century, hardly one can be identified whose accession and tenure was not affected by state intervention.[23] Only the election of the current incumbent, Archbishop Christodoulos, in 1998 may be considered free of such interference.

Under these conditions, no regime and no political party in Modern Greece ever had cause to break with the church as such, and opt for its separation from the state. For its part, the church as such was never identified with any single regime or party. At all times, there were clergymen friendly to each and every side, including the Communist-controlled National Liberation Front (EAM) during the Occupation, in World War II. Only briefly, in the ensuing Civil War (1946–49) and its immediate aftermath, was the church more narrowly identified with anti-communism. This was precisely the time when the project of a political party on the Christian Democratic model found some support, although it was quickly abandoned.[24] Again, after the last dictatorship (1967–74), what saved the church from a potential re-examination of its constitutional status was the fact that only some of the contending personalities and factions in its midst had been unambiguously identified with the military regime.

When all is said, however, the obvious contrast with the Catholic Church in all these respects does not amount to a specificity of the Eastern Orthodox tradition. As a state church, the Orthodox Church of Greece has a lot in common with Protestant state churches. Indeed, the settlement of 1833 has often been regarded, then and later, as a distinctly Protestant scheme. The Orthodox Church of Greece also has in common with these churches the character of a *national* church. Therein lies today the most insuperable obstacle to religious freedom.

A NATIONAL CHURCH

As a state church, Eastern Orthodoxy or, more concretely, the Patriarchate of Constantinople could entertain ecumenical pretensions with some plausibility only as long as it was identified with an *empire*: first the Byzantine, then the Ottoman. Both thwarted repeatedly the aspirations of Bulgarians and Serbs to break away from the Patriarchate. Only the Russians were in a position to do so irrevocably, after 1453 – setting a precedent.

In the nineteenth century, however, the rise of nationalism in the Balkans and the progressive dismemberment of the Ottoman Empire dealt a fatal blow to ecumenical pretensions, as each breakaway nation-state required its own independent ('autocephalous') Orthodox Church. For the liberated Greeks, it was essential that their state church should not be under the jurisdiction of an Ottoman official (the Patriarch). For the other nations, it was essential also that their respective churches should not remain under the jurisdiction of a Patriarchate perpetually controlled by the Greeks.

From the start, the Patriarchate of Constantinople was bound to oppose and condemn 'the ethnic parochialism of secular nationalism, which threatened, and eventually did destroy, the ecumenicity of transcendental values which held Balkan society together within the fold of Orthodoxy during the centuries of captivity'.[25] The key word here is 'captivity'. Over and above its concern for 'ecumenicity' as such, the Patriarchate was bound to safeguard its own position within the Ottoman Empire, and to protect the Orthodox populations for which it was responsible. Being in the hands of Greeks, it was also bound to oppose competing nationalisms (like that of the Bulgarians in particular).[26] 'Captivity' preserved 'ecumenicity'. Otherwise, the preservation of ecumenicity required the liberation of the entire Orthodox flock, or, at the very least, the liberation and independence of the Ecumenical Patriarchate itself. Had this happened, a conflict between Orthodox and national loyalties might have developed, as in the Catholic case, and Balkan nationalisms, consequently, might have acquired a secular and even anticlerical character.

As it happened, however, the Ecumenical Patriarchate remained forever captive, while its ecclesiastical jurisdiction was dismembered piecemeal along with the Ottoman Empire, to the benefit of national states jealous of their hard-won sovereignty. These did not have to make a total break with tradition, as in the Protestant case. The Eastern Orthodox tradition was that of a state church, and could be readily adapted to the requirements of a national state. There was, moreover, the unquestionable Russian precedent, more than three centuries old. Consequently, thanks to the available option of 'autocephalous' national churches, Orthodoxy not only remained compatible with nationalism, but even became its champion, *despite* the lasting but helpless opposition of the Patriarchate of Constantinople.

In Greece, the identification of the Nation with Orthodoxy proved irresistible from the very beginning. During the War of Independence itself, religion was the *only* fixed line of demarcation between the warring sides, in full conformity with the pre-existing Ottoman system of religiously defined 'millets'. To change sides irrevocably, one was typically required to convert. The religious split within the large population of Albanian ethnic stock proved particularly decisive: whereas Muslims identified with the Ottoman Turks, Orthodox Christians readily identified with the Greek cause, even if they did not speak Greek. The same was also true of other ethnic groups, like the Vlachs (or Koutsovlachs). Accordingly, the first constitution in Epidaurus simply stated that all the native inhabitants who 'believed in Christ' were *ipso facto* Greek.

Although the wording could be understood to embrace all Christians, it was not persuasive enough for the Greek Catholics, concentrated in the Cyclades. Despite their Greek language and culture, they refused to recognise themselves as part of the newborn nation and join the struggle.

Under the protection of the King of France in Ottoman times, they did not expect to be accepted on an equal footing in a Greek state dominated by the Orthodox.[27] Its evolution down to the present was to prove them right.

With the exception of these Catholics (and a few Jews), the religious homogeneity of the initial Greek state was complete from the start, after the forcible departure of all the Muslims. In sharp contrast, linguistic homogeneity remained entirely to be created by the new state and its educational system. An early comedy (in 1836), aptly entitled *Babylonia*, tells of a motley group assembled (in 1827) to celebrate Greek independence, whose members are incapable of understanding each other's tongue, with fatal consequences. Despite the linguistic emphasis of early Greek nationalism, therefore, Orthodoxy and not language was bound to provide the ready-made initial core of Greek national identity.

A century later, an unprecedented and momentous event, which was to complete the process of national integration for Greece (save the Dodecanese), again equated religion with nationality. This was the compulsory exchange of populations between Greece and Turkey, agreed in 1923 following the Greek defeat in Asia Minor. In the absence of any other indisputable criterion for a compulsory process of expatriation, the Christian Orthodox population of Turkey was considered Greek and resettled in Greece (although many spoke only Turkish). Conversely, the Muslim inhabitants of Greece were considered Turks and resettled in Turkey (although some also spoke Greek). Only the Chams in Greek Epirus were eventually exempted, thanks to the argument that, although Muslims, they were in fact Albanians and not Turks.[28] This is enough to prove that religion was treated merely as a substitute for nationality. Otherwise, the very idea of an exchange of purely religious minorities between Greece and Turkey would have been patently absurd.

Even today, Orthodoxy serves as a convenient test of Greek national identity. It serves, for example, to sort out those immigrants from Albania who can be classified as members of the Greek minority there, and are entitled to special treatment in Greece.

For their part, Orthodox clergymen have continued to serve as national leaders, especially for the Greeks outside the Greek state. The most recent and notorious example was Archbishop Makarios in Cyprus.

Can one be fully Greek and not be, even nominally, an Orthodox, that is, a 'Greek Orthodox'? Although many would accept it in principle, and some have even proved it in practice, with their own lives, the overwhelming majority of the nation would still respond in the negative, if they did not reject the question as meaningless.[29]

In all these respects, however, the Orthodox Church in Greece and elsewhere (Serbia or Russia, for example) is far from unique as a national church. Protestantism has also been identified with the nation in several cases, such as England, the Netherlands, and the Scandinavian countries. Even Catholicism, despite its unique supranational organisation (and its ultramontanism), remains the equivalent of a national church for the Irish or the Poles.[30] What may still distinguish the Orthodox Church today is that it is *not* likely to follow the path of other national churches towards pluralism – at least not in the foreseeable future.

A SIEGE MENTALITY

Inevitably, the identification of a particular church with the state, the nation, or both has always been at the expense of religious freedom. Although intolerance may be more readily associated with Catholicism, in Protestant countries as well Catholics and various nonconformists were first persecuted and later discriminated against, until as late as the end of the nineteenth century. The ever closer approximation of religious freedom and state neutrality, under various models of church–state relations, was adopted in most cases only in the twentieth century.[31]

Several factors have been responsible for this evolution, including the irresistible advance of secularisation. One should not overlook, however, that all this became possible only long *after* religion-related historic challenges to the national state and its security were over. The one case in Western Europe where this has not yet happened is Ireland, and it is highly instructive. Ireland is indeed the single non-Orthodox but Christian case that most resembles Greece.

An 'Orthodox revival' has been under way for several years in Greece, spearheaded by various 'neo-Orthodox' thinkers, and eventually crowned by the accession of Archbishop Christodoulos in 1998. Despite some renewed interest in spirituality and monasticism, centred on Mount Athos, this revival is quite unlike that in the United States, for example. In content, it is not a revival of religion as such, but rather of *nationalism* identified with Orthodoxy. Exactly the same has been true in other Orthodox countries, like Serbia or Russia.

This is why secularisation, on which Greece compares with Western countries, appears quite irrelevant in this context. Christodoulos won the highest popularity ratings (after the President of the Republic) not as a defender of the faith or morality, but rather as an outspoken guardian of national identity under imminent threat. The issue of 'identity' cards was ideally suited to this purpose, since the name itself of the official document in question coincided with that of the cherished concept. Facile but persuasive rhetoric could equate the omission of religion on the former with the eradication of Orthodoxy from the latter. Beneath a trendy style beloved by the media, Christodoulos assumed the traditional role of an Orthodox clergyman as national leader (*ethnarch*).

Recourse to tradition might prove ineffectual by itself without the continuing linkage between religion and critical issues of foreign policy, and even national security. The status of Muslims in Greece is a prime example. It cannot be addressed simply and abstractly as a matter of religious freedom, since most of the country's Muslim citizens are Turks, living near the border with Turkey. On the other side of the same border, the Patriarchate of Constantinople remains a captive of the secular Turkish Republic, just as it was a captive of the Ottoman Empire.[32]

Why should the Patriarchate be a concern of Greek foreign policy, and why should it remain in Istanbul in the first place? These are assumptions that are best left unspoken and unquestioned in Greek public life. For more than 1,000 years, the Patriarchate has embodied a glaring contradiction: an Ecumenical Church in Greek hands. As the dictionary attests, 'Greek Orthodox Church' is still a popular name for the Eastern Orthodox Church as a whole. The contradiction could stand as long as it was backed by imperial power, both Byzantine and Ottoman, but not thereafter.

Unlike the Papacy, moreover, the Patriarchate of Constantinople never acquired a secure territorial base from which to exercise its nominally 'ecumenical' leadership, even after the demise of empire. Perhaps its only real chance to do so was in 1922, when the victorious Turkish Republic demanded that it be removed from Turkish soil, to Mount Athos. An autonomous monastic commonwealth within the Greek state, Mount Athos surely had the potential to become the Orthodox equivalent of the Vatican, especially if its status was guaranteed by international treaty. Nevertheless, this eminently practical scheme was rejected by Greece with the backing of all the Western powers, in a rare show of Christian unity. Clinging to the fiction of an Ecumenical Church in Greek hands, Greece chose, instead, to keep a Turkish population in Western Thrace as a Muslim minority, so that the Patriarchate could remain in Istanbul, surrounded by an equivalent Greek Orthodox minority.[33] This was a momentous breach in the logic of the compulsory exchange of populations, which was supposed to remove completely past causes of friction between the two countries.

Under Turkish pressure, in successive stages, the Greek Orthodox minority has practically vanished from Turkey, but the Patriarchate remains.

It is no longer permitted to operate its printing house (since 1964), nor its theological seminary (since 1971). On the other hand, it is allowed to recruit its clergy, including the Patriarch himself, only from a rapidly dwindling pool of Greek Orthodox Turkish citizens. Under these conditions, its extinction is only a matter of time.

Trying to make the best out of a desperate situation, the incumbent Patriarch Bartholomeos has argued that the location of the Patriarchate prevents it from becoming a national church, like all the other Orthodox churches, and preserves its ecumenical character. If it is not a national church, it is, nonetheless, an *ethnic* church. Although nominally 'Ecumenical', it has become in fact the church of diaspora Greeks, in America, Australia, and Western Europe. For them, the Orthodox Church indeed provides the principal and, increasingly, the *only* vehicle for the preservation of their ethnic identity. A Greek cannot be a Protestant or a Muslim in Australia either. Insofar as the Greek state expects diaspora Greeks to maintain manifold ties with the mother country, and to serve as pressure groups for Greek national interests, it retains a perpetual and vital interest in the Patriarchate, which has ecclesiastical jurisdiction over them. That the Patriarchate should remain in an alien and hostile environment, hostage to the secular state of a Muslim nation (and subject to slow strangulation by that state), is, of course, a political absurdity. It reflects, nonetheless, the enduring and inextricable embrace between the Greek nation-state and Orthodoxy on a worldwide scale.

Ever since 1923, the Ecumenical Patriarchate of Constantinople remains a pawn in Greek–Turkish relations, including the bitter conflict over Cyprus. Any move against it evidently runs counter to Greek national interests. It is mostly in this connection that the credibility and wisdom of Archbishop Christodoulos posing as a national leader have been undermined. Over and above his petty quarrels with the Ecumenical Patriarchate over matters of spiritual jurisdiction, the very idea of turning the autocephalous Church of Greece into a Greek Patriarchate like the Russian, Serbian, Romanian, Bulgarian, and Georgian, although ostensibly nationalist in inspiration, constitutes a stab in the back for the 'mother' church in Constantinople. The fact that Patriarch Bartholomeos has supplanted Archbishop Christodoulos as the most popular personality in Greece (after the President of the Republic) indicates that Greek public opinion may have a basic understanding of these national considerations.

The Greek situation is perhaps most comparable with that of Israel and the Jewish diaspora. In both cases, religious freedom and state neutrality cannot be addressed simply as an internal question, confined to the borders of the state, and indifferent to coreligionists throughout the world. Moreover, the question impinges upon national security in both cases, since a religious minority inside the borders may be disloyal to the national state. In both cases, finally, a *siege* mentality is bred not only by the immediate security environment, but also by a historic consciousness of national uniqueness and solitude, which is grounded in a particular religion.

According to its architect Constantine Karamanlis, Greek membership of the EU in 1981 was supposed to terminate this 'secular solitude'. If the national identity of Modern Greece had been constructed exclusively or even primarily with reference to classical antiquity, bypassing Byzantium (as some had wished in the nineteenth century), it would be indeed quite secure today, in the context of both European integration and globalisation.

As it happened, however, this identity was constructed primarily with reference to Orthodoxy, that is, the Byzantine and Ottoman legacy. Consequently, membership in the EU (and NATO) where Greece is the only Orthodox country, has actually worked, on balance, in the opposite direction. Despite the manifold material benefits and changes, it has also exacerbated insecurity, and even alienation from the West. By 1985, the unlikely successor to Karamanlis as President of the Republic was to coin the term 'without siblings' (*anadelphon*) to define the existential status of the Greek nation. Now Archbishop Christodoulos can successfully promote the Orthodox Church as the only 'ark' of Greek national identity, threatened by European integration and globalisation.

The defence of national identity in terms of religion is perforce anachronistic and, in the case of Orthodoxy, exceptionally so. If it revives a siege mentality, the siege in question is that of Constantinople in 1204 (when the city fell to the so-called Fourth Crusade) rather than 1453 (when it finally fell to the Ottoman Turks). By 1453, hostility to the West was such that the Orthodox majority perceived the Ottoman Turks as a lesser evil than a reunion of the churches on the Pope's terms. As a Byzantine dignitary famously put it, it was 'preferable to see the turban of the Turk in the City than the mitre of the Latin'.[34]

Insofar as the Greek national consciousness has been shaped by Orthodoxy, it still carries the trauma of 1204 and the spirit of 1453. In the 1830s, for example, a Catholic king was considered more offensive than a Patriarch chosen by Muslims. Even today, and despite the recurrent tension between Greece and Turkey, no objections are ever heard in Greece, as in some Western countries, that Turkey has no place in Christian Europe. Religion is never invoked against Turkey, but it *is* invoked against NATO, for example. During the protracted crisis in what used to be Yugoslavia,

Greek public opinion was swayed by an explosion of unthinking and unconditional solidarity with Serbia as a 'sister' Orthodox nation (while at the same time a particularly sinister role was attributed to the Vatican). In this climate of opinion, and in the wake of its strident campaign against NATO, even the Communist Party (KKE) chose to include on its tickets (in 2000) notorious 'neo-Orthodox' nationalists – a novel type of 'fellow traveller'.

Even more significantly, following the Pope's various statements on the past responsibilities of the Catholic Church, what was expected of him during his long-delayed visit to Greece, in May 2001, was a full apology to Eastern Christianity as well, extending as far back as 1204 or even 1054. Despite the vocal protests of some fanatics, the visit turned out to be a success – and a personal triumph for Archbishop Christodoulos, who appeared to extract from the Pope precisely such an apology. It is highly doubtful, however, whether this was sufficient by itself to have a lasting impact on Greek Orthodox attitudes towards Catholicism and the West.

RELIGIOUS FREEDOM IN 'ENDANGERED' NATIONS

The Greek case demonstrates that religious freedom cannot be achieved simply as a matter of conformity to constitutional and international norms, as long as the linkage between a particular religion and a particular national identity remains active and vital for the latter's self-preservation, in the minds of those concerned.

In terms of models,[35] it would appear that, as long as an established church continues to be identified with an 'endangered' nation, change in the direction of pluralism is even less probable than an outright separation between church and state. Religious instruction in the Greek schools, for example, is defended nowadays solely on national grounds – and not on moral grounds, which could lead to education in 'consensual' religious values (as in Britain or Australia).

This situation, however, is by no means specific to the Orthodox Church (in Greece and elsewhere), as both Ireland and Israel demonstrate. Among Christian denominations, what may indeed be specific to Orthodoxy, in this respect, is a traumatic and defensive historical consciousness reaching into a far more distant past than even in Ireland. If Orthodoxy is uniquely anachronistic in this sense, this is no doubt also related to its plausible claim to constitute the *original* Christian Church, from which all other denominations subsequently broke away. Moreover, the anachronism is kept alive today by current sources of manifold insecurity – in Greece, but also elsewhere in the Orthodox world.

NOTES

1. A.D. Smith, 'Ethnic Election and National Destiny: Some Religious Origins of Nationalist Ideals', *Nations and Nationalism* 5/3 (1999), pp.331–55.
2. B. Anderson, *Imagined Communities: Reflections on the Origin and Spread of Nationalism* (London: Verso, rev. edn. 1991), p.144.
3. See, for example, C. Hayes, *Nationalism: A Religion* (New York: Macmillan 1960).
4. L. Greenfeld, *Nationalism: Five Roads to Modernity* (Cambridge, MA: Harvard University Press 1992), p.63.
5. S. Schama, *The Embarrassment of Riches* (London: Fontana Press 1988), p.59.
6. Y. Ktistakis, 'The European Protection of Religious Otherness', in D. Christopoulos (ed.), *Legal Issues of Religious Otherness in Greece* (Athens: Kritiki 1999, in Greek), pp.225–69.
7. *Eleftherotypia*, 9 Feb. 2000.
8. C. Tsitselikis, 'The Position of the Mufti in the Greek Legal Order', in Christopoulos (ed.), *Legal Issues of Religious Otherness in Greece*, pp.282–4 and 310–11.
9. *Eleftherotypia*, 12 July 2001.
10. *Eleftherotypia*, 6 Dec. 1997.
11. *Eleftherotypia*, 13 March 1999.
12. Ktistakis, 'The European Protection of Religious Otherness', p.258.
13. S.V. Monsma and J.C. Soper, *The Challenge of Pluralism: Church and State in Five Democracies* (Lanham: Rowman & Littlefield 1997).
14. Ktistakis, 'The European Protection of Religious Otherness', p.249.
15. S.P. Huntington, *The Clash of Civilizations and the Remaking of World Order* (London: Simon & Schuster 1997), p.70.
16. C.A. Frazee, *The Orthodox Church and Independent Greece 1821–1852* (Cambridge: Cambridge University Press 1969), p.188.
17. Ibid., pp.1–8.
18. K. Ware, 'The Church: A Time of Transition', in R. Clogg (ed.), *Greece in the 1980s* (London: Macmillan 1983), pp.209 and 212.
19. Ibid., p.210.
20. G.Th. Mavrogordatos, *Stillborn Republic: Social Coalitions and Party Strategies in Greece, 1922–1936* (Berkeley: University of California Press 1983), pp.268–71.
21. S. Troianos, *The Sources of Byzantine Law* (Athens: A.Sakkoulas, 2nd edn. 1999, in Greek), pp.177ff.
22. Frazee, *The Orthodox Church and Independent Greece 1821–1852*, p.33.
23. G. Karagiannis, *Church and State 1833–1997: Historic Overview of Their Relations* (Athens: Pontiki 1997, in Greek).
24. Ibid., pp.96–7.
25. P.M. Kitromilides, '"Imagined Communities" and the Origins of the National Question in the Balkans', *European History Quarterly* 19/2 (1989), p.159.
26. See, most recently, P. Matalas, *Nation and Orthodoxy* (Herakleion: University Press of Crete 2002, in Greek).
27. Frazee, *The Orthodox Church and Independent Greece 1821–1852*, pp.42–3, 50–51, 61, and 82–4. This has been precisely the attitude of most Protestants in Ireland towards a Republic dominated by the Catholics.
28. Mavrogordatos, *Stillborn Republic*, pp.252–3.
29. Cf. Ware, 'The Church: A Time of Transition', p.208.
30. See, for example, C.C. O'Brien, *Ancestral Voices: Religion and Nationalism in Ireland* (Chicago: University of Chicago Press 1995), and A. Michnik, *L'Église et la Gauche: Le dialogue polonais* (Paris: Seuil 1979), pp.34 and 135–7.

31. See Monsma and Soper, *The Challenge of Pluralism*.
32. Cf. S. Runciman, *The Great Church in Captivity* (Cambridge: Cambridge University Press 1968).
33. A. Alexandris, *The Greek Minority of Istanbul and Greek-Turkish Relations 1918–1974* (Athens: Centre for Asia Minor Studies 1992), pp.83–95.
34. R. Clogg, *A Short History of Modern Greece* (Cambridge: Cambridge University Press 1979), p.14.
35. See Monsma and Soper, *The Challenge of Pluralism*.

Catholicism and Democratic Consolidation in Spain and Poland

JOHN ANDERSON

The processes of democratisation evident in many parts of the globe since the mid-1970s have thrown up major challenges for religious institutions in general and the Roman Catholic Church in particular. For several centuries the latter institution had at best been sceptical about, and more commonly openly opposed, to democratic government, but during the post-war years the church came to favour and sometimes actively promote democratisation. In part this shift arose out of the post-war capitalist–communist confrontation which made democracy look the lesser evil, but it also stemmed from the intellectual and practical decisions emerging from the Second Vatican Council. In consequence, in Latin America, Europe, Africa, and Asia many (though not all) national hierarchies came to support movements for political liberalisation. Hence in Spain a new generation of bishops led by Archbishop Tarancón sought to distance themselves from the Franco regime and to criticise its social and human rights policies, whilst in communist Poland the Catholic Church provided a major space and voice for those critical of the communist system. However, once democratic governance had been achieved the two national churches faced new problems as they sought to define their role in rapidly changing polities and societies.

This article explores the efforts of two national hierarchies to develop their relationships with the new democratic orders, in particular during what political scientists describe as the 'consolidation' phase. The concept of 'transition' is generally used to refer to the process whereby the authoritarian regime is replaced by a new order enjoying democratic legitimacy. Yet in some ways the next task, that of consolidating democratic governance, is far more problematic insofar as it may involve changing the practice and attitudes of public and elites towards political power. Political leaders have to acquire the skills of bargaining and negotiation in a more open political setting, and be willing to abide by the democratic 'rules of the game'. Simultaneously the population also needs to be acclimatised to the new political structures, to accept them as legitimate and, ideally, acquire a democratic mentality characterised by tolerance of alternative viewpoints and commitment to change by peaceful means. Most political analysts accept that consolidation is a process rather than an end point and that few democracies in practice live up to the 'ideal type' model in the fullest sense, but still suggest the necessity of some development towards consolidation if a stable democratic order is to be achieved.[1]

In most countries the place of religion in these processes is relatively minor. Nonetheless it is arguable that religious institutions which enjoy the status of national church and that have contributed in some way to the process of political liberalisation do have the potential to contribute towards or undermine the prospects of successful democratic consolidation. For example, the statements and actions of religious elites may serve to strengthen or weaken the notion of democracy as the 'only game in town'. They might foster or hinder reconciliation where society is fundamentally divided over the changes that have occurred or over how best to come to terms with the past. The extent to which religious (and indeed all) elites play by the democratic rules of the game in pursuit of their own interests may impact upon their own and the new system's legitimacy. If they fail to act 'democratically' why should others? Equally their pronouncements and practices with regard to minority or individual rights may serve to strengthen or inhibit some of the values associated with pluralist democracies and thus impact upon the evolution of a democratic mentality amongst the wider public.

From the perspective of religious organisations consolidation throws up other questions, as they realise that democratisation may be a mixed blessing in terms of their social and political position, and ideological influence. In some cases they have to cope with what some writers refer to as the delayed and therefore speeded up processes of 'modernisation' (and secularisation) that have the capacity to undermine their position within the national community?[2] They also have to deal with elites who, though grateful for the churches' contributions to democratisation, have no desire to see excessive (non-elected) clerical intervention in public life. So the churches have to face up to the task of redefining their role in society and in political life? To what extent is it legitimate for them to intervene in the public sphere and by what means should they do so? What types of arguments might they be able to use in pursuing their public policy preferences and how might they reconcile absolutist ideals with a democratic political style rooted in bargaining and compromise? Can they claim any special privileges on the basis of their status as 'churches of the nation' or on the basis of their contribution towards democratisation? This essay cannot explore all these issues in depth, but asks about the political claims that the two churches made on the new democratic systems in the decade or so following the initiation of democratic transition. In particular it focuses on how they handled the question of their legal constitutional position in the new order and how they sought to exercise political influence.

FINDING A ROLE FOR THE CATHOLIC CHURCH IN THE NEW SPAIN

Historically the relationship of church and state in Spain had been strong and, despite mounting anticlericalism, the Concordat of 1851 had stressed the role of the Catholic Church as the religion of the nation and thus deserving of protection by the Crown.[3] This formal position was maintained in subsequent decades though periodic bursts of hostility to the church led to the destruction of religious property and occasional killings of priests and monks. These mounted under the Republican government of the early 1930s, and following Franco's revolt some 7,000 priests, monks, and nuns lost their lives. In such circumstances it was hardly surprising that many within the church welcomed the nationalists who promised to restore Christian civilisation and who once in power repealed republican legislation and restored many of the privileges taken by the previous administration. Many of these changes were reinforced in the Concordat of 1953, albeit at the expense of giving Franco a key role in the appointment of diocesan bishops.

Many within the church had hoped this new arrangement would create the conditions for a re-evangelisation of Spain, but in general they were disappointed, as much of the population remained indifferent to the church's doctrinal and moral claims. In consequence, as the civil war gradually receded in memory some religious activists began to adopt a position more critical of the regime. Partly under the influence of changing social conditions and partly in reaction to the theological innovations supported by Vatican II younger church leaders began to speak of the need to protect the vulnerable and ensure observance of human rights. Particularly influential here were Tarancón, by 1971 Cardinal Archbishop of Madrid, and a number of auxiliary bishops whose appointment Franco had no control over. With increasing urgency they began to support democratisation and develop links with opposition groups and after Franco's death openly expressed their support for the creation of a more pluralist political system.[4] Yet the emergence of democracy raised new problems for the church as it sought to define its role in the new political order. In particular, how should its formal position be defined and by what means should it exercise influence in the new polity. How it dealt with these questions was likely to have an impact not just on its own position, but also on public perceptions of, and loyalty towards, the church and thus on its subsequent influence in the public sphere.

Defining the Church's Legal Position

Addressing the congregation at the coronation mass of King Juan Carlos in November 1975 Cardinal Tarancón set out his vision of the relationship between church and state. Though noting with pride the historical connection between throne and altar, he made it clear that the church was not seeking any privileges in the new order or any recreation of the old ties.[5] Nonetheless, during subsequent months church spokesmen made clear their opposition to an American style separation of the two, and argued that the church needed to be taken seriously in a country where the vast majority of the population were Catholic. In Tarancón's words: 'the Church is a social reality ... and politics has to bear in mind and respect the real life of the people; it cannot ignore the fact that a large majority of the Spanish people belong to the Catholic Church.'[6]

Church leaders were particularly concerned when in November 1997 a leaked constitutional draft was found to make no explicit reference to the Catholic Church, instead simply stating that 'the Spanish state is not confessional'.[7] The church also had some reservations about the constitutional phrasing on issues such as religious education, divorce, and abortion. This unease was clearly reflected in a statement put out by the bishops in November 1977 which expressed support for constitutional guarantees of rights but argued that such rights could not be absolute or be used to justify giving offence to the religious sensibilities of the Catholic population. They also argued for a constitution providing a 'tutelage of public morality' to prevent a confusion of freedom and licence.[8]

In subsequent months the church continued to lobby hard on the question of constitutional recognition though it remained wary of making a public issue of confessionality. For that reason it preferred to argue its case within the corridors of power and proved willing to accept the first two clauses of the proposed Article 16 which guaranteed religious freedom to all and stated that no one should be obliged to declare their religious beliefs. It did, however, continue to argue for a formal recognition of the Catholic Church's special position to be inserted in the third clause, preventing the creation of a state church. In the political arena, the Conservative parties lined up behind the church, whilst the Socialists took a much more aggressive line, arguing for complete separation and an end of subsidies for religious schools. More surprising was the position of the Communists, with General Secretary Carillo describing his party as a 'spectator' on religious issues and stressing the need to avoid polarising society as had happened in the 1930s.[9] In consequence, his party joined the centre-right in finding a compromise formula which left the third clause of Article 16 reading: 'There shall be no state religion. The public powers shall take into account the religious beliefs of Spanish society and will maintain consequent relations of co-operation with the Catholic Church and other confessions.'[10]

This phrasing had the advantage of singling out the church of the majority without giving it any specific privileges, though arguably other documents discussed below do in fact favour the Catholic Church. The majority of the church leadership was content with this formulation, though not some of the other clauses which failed explicitly to promote Catholic values and left the door open for the introduction of divorce legislation. In consequence most advocated support for the constitution in the subsequent referendum, though nine bishops urged their flocks to reject the document. The leader of this group, Cardinal González Martin, defended his oppositional stance on the grounds that the new constitution made no mention of God or Catholic values, and represented an attempt to foist an agnostic constitution on 'a nation of the baptised'.[11] There was also a suggestion that the new Polish Pope John Paul II shared the views of the traditionalist Spanish bishops that the hierarchy should have fought harder for some reference to God and taken a tougher line on family issues.[12]

Whilst the constitution provided the most basic definition of the formal position of the Catholic Church in the new Spain, other texts and agreements served further to define its role in relation to both the state but also vis-à-vis religious minorities. For example, in 1976 and 1979 the Spanish state signed a series of agreements with the Vatican which replaced the Concordat of 1953. These guaranteed the legal status of the church, the right of parents to choose religious education for their children, the provision of chaplains in the armed forces, and some degree of state financial support for the church in the short term.[13] In consequence, it might be argued that the church received additional privileges via international treaty that were not possible for other religious communities. In part these agreements served to free the church from state control – notably removing the state's right to oversee episcopal appointments – but they also effectively provided guarantees for Catholic educational establishments and financial support that others did not receive. Whilst the Catholic Church was seeking to ensure its own position, it is worth noting that it did nothing to reinforce this by seeking the formal restriction of the rights of religious minorities, despite a long history of intolerance. The hierarchy fully supported the guarantees of religious liberty provided for in the constitution, and then fully supported the passage of a new Law on Religious Liberty in 1980s despite several older bishops arguing that to allow religious freedom would ultimately undermine the unity of the Spanish people. And though minor problems periodically surfaced – especially for new religious movements and for the Salvation Army which was refused permission to open a children's home in the Canary Islands because it was a 'destructive sect' – there has been no serious attempt to restrict minority rights since then.[14]

The Exercise of Political Influence

In his coronation sermon Cardinal Tarancón had argued that the church sought no special political influence, but in a later speech he stressed that this did not mean that the church would withdraw into the private sphere.[15] In practice under his leadership the church did attempt to avoid overt political involvement, most notably during elections and in relation to discussion about the possibility of creating a Christian Democratic Party. Though a number of leading centrist politicians supported by some bishops advocated this course, Tarancón remained opposed, arguing that anyone who used the names of the church or Christianity in the title of any organisation was 'blatantly usurping' them. In part this opposition stemmed from the church's own lack of organisational capacity and the fact that such a party would be outside the control of the church despite sometimes acting in its name. At the same time, under the early UCD governments there were no fundamental religious interests that required a political organisation (beyond the existing centrist and conservative parties) to defend the core values promoted by the church. In practice two small Christian Democratic parties were created in the mid-1970s, but in the 1977 elections the stronger of the two gained only 1.4 per cent of the vote, perhaps in part because of the lack of church support.[16]

Equally the leadership of the Catholic Church made only limited attempts to influence the voting behaviour of Catholic electors. Early on after the transition, Cardinal Tarancón stated:

The greatest service we can render to the Church and to the Spanish people is precisely this: to manifest clearly and publicly that we want to remain outside of all the vicissitudes of the struggle for power; and to recognise the liberty of Christians to confront temporal problems or their own accord according to the dictates of their consciences.[17]

Prior to the 1977 election the Church adopted a formal position of neutrality, though it was fairly obvious that much of the hierarchy hoped for the victory of Adolfo Suarez's UCD. Moreover, a letter from the Episcopal Conference on 'The Moral Responsibility of the Voter' called upon Catholics to assess party programmes in the light of their relationship to Catholic values. Individual bishops were more explicit, with one arguing that 'no Catholic can support the parties of the left because they are opposed to the Catholic creed'. Equally, despite formal neutrality, most bishops in the 1977 and subsequent election made clear their preference for parties of the centre-right.[18] Yet though subsequent episcopal appointments shifted the hierarchy in a more conservative direction, it became increasingly clear that only a minority of voters made their decision with reference to the church. During the late 1970s around 25 per cent of practising Catholics voted for the Socialists and by the 1990s most studies suggested the proportion voting for the Socialist party was only slightly lower than that voting for the right.[19]

Whilst abstaining from overt political involvement, the church had no intention of keeping silence on issues relating to core values or institutional interests, and on matters relating to abortion and divorce it was resolutely opposed to attempts at the liberalisation of public policies. Reluctantly, if still critically, it accepted the UCD's attempt to liberalise the divorce laws in the late 1970s, but resolutely – if ultimately unsuccessfully – opposed the partial decriminalisation of abortion under the PSOE government in the early 1980s.[20] In the sphere of education, tensions arose under the Socialist government when it sought to ensure that all private (that is, Catholic) schools followed the state curriculum in return for continuing state subsidies, but in practice these changes made little difference to the essentially pluralistic nature of Spanish education.[21]

Despite the heated nature of these and other debates, the striking feature of the emerging relationship between the church and the new order was its essentially consensual nature. More conservative bishops appointed by John Paul II were increasingly vocal about the moral failings of the new Spain, but few wanted to resurrect the polarisation that has caused such a major division within Spanish society in the past. The church increasingly recognised that it could not make the same claims on society and state in the new order as it had in the old. And larger questions sometimes emerged about the extent to which the church was engaged in legitimate lobbying to defend its own interests or whether it was seeking to maintain privileges that were no longer acceptable. More importantly, as Spain embarked upon a process of what some described as accelerated 'modernisation', the church found itself facing new challenges from secular ideas and consumerism that challenged both its hold on the flock and ability to influence their political and lifestyle choices. In such circumstances there was a growing emphasis on spiritual revitalisation at the grass roots, though this posed the danger of enhancing the very privatisation leading bishops were keen to avoid.

THE POLISH CATHOLIC CHURCH AND THE PURSUIT OF INFLUENCE

Though often seen as a deeply Catholic country, only in the twentieth century did the church come to adopt an uncompromisingly nationalist position, as the very future of the nation came under threat from Nazi and Soviet occupiers. During the early years of Communist rule, however, broader concerns took second place to the question of institutional survival as the doughty Cardinal Wyszynski struggled to maintain Catholic influence. Only in the early 1970s did the Catholic Church begin to move beyond self-defence and speak out more forcefully in defence of human rights. In consequence, by the end of the decade the church found itself in a tripartite alliance to resist oppression alongside the critical intelligentsia and the working class. All this was reinforced in 1978 by the election of Karol Wojtyla to the papal throne. During his first visit to Poland in June 1979 the new Polish Pope told one congregation that 'the future of Poland will depend upon how many people are mature enough to be nonconformists'.

One year later it turned out that more than enough Poles had the courage to support the emergent Solidarity movement and deliver a fundamental shock to the whole Communist bloc. Though the immediate causes of social unrest were economic, the workers quickly adopted religious symbols as their own whilst the church provided a moral basis to the struggle as well as encouraging the strikers to avoid excesses. The declaration of martial law one year later posed considerable problems for the church hierarchy, with Cardinal Glemp initially appearing to justify its imposition as the lesser evil, though many within the church sought to defend those rounded up by the military. As the decade progressed, the church's leadership became increasingly critical of the regime and in the years 1987–89 played a key role in assisting the transition to a new form of rule. Though only an observer at the Round Table Talks in April 1989, most sources suggest that its mediation was often crucial in overcoming difficulties, and the eventual outcome was the holding of a partially free election in June. The end of the Communist system, however, posed new dilemmas for the church as it sought to redefine its own position in relation to political influence and in adapting to the new pluralist mentality which treated the church as just one pressure group amongst many.

Defining the Church's Legal Position

The Catholic Church in Poland proved much more assertive than its Spanish counterpart during the transition period, making clear early on that its position needed to be respected and embodied in constitutional and legal forms. Perhaps ironically, given the speed of change, Poland was one of the last of the Central-East European states to adopt a completely new fundamental law. The provisional 'small constitution' adopted in October 1992 provided the basis for government in the early 1990s and the guarantees of religious rights here largely followed the Communist era constitution. At the same time, Article 82 maintained a commitment to the separation of church and state, neutral terminology the church's leadership viewed as smacking of the old order.[22] Nonetheless, the delay in formulating a full post-Communist constitution gave the hierarchy a chance to rethink what it might want from any future settlement.

Though there was some intermittent discussion of a final constitutional settlement immediately after the adoption of the 'small constitution', not until 1995 did the pace of debate quicken after seven drafts were put before the Constitutional Commission. Informally, the church supported the Solidarity-backed text that referred explicitly to the 1,000-year link of the people to Christianity and to 'the heritage of Christian faith and culture'. In addition it proposed support for the right to life from the moment of conception, and obliged the state to provide for the teaching of 'legally recognised religious beliefs at public schools'. Other versions appearing to lean in the direction of the church included that of the Senate, which started with an invocation to God, and that proposed by the Confederation of Independent Poland which argued for granting the Roman Catholic Church 'a leading position amongst denominations of equal rights'.[23]

During the course of the debate, church spokesmen focused repeatedly on three issues: the need to avoid the word separation in defining the relationship of church and state, the inclusion of some reference to God and Christian values, and to the protection of unborn life. Bishop Tadeusz

Pieronek, Secretary of the Bishops's Conference, accepted that the two should be separate but argued that in a strongly Catholic nation there was no need to make formal statements about this.[24] A similar argument was made by liberal Catholic and former Prime Minister Tadeusz Mazowiecki, who suggested that the church was a part of the national furniture that could not simply be shunted aside.[25] Lech Walesa, in his typically blunt way, reminded Poles that 'communist bandits ran the country for fifty years, but the Church for 1,000 years' and argued that it would therefore be improper not to give this constitutional recognition.[26] In contrary vein, minority representatives argued very strongly for a formal separation, fearing the potential restoration of a state-backed national Catholicism.[27]

The debate reached the floor of the Sejm in early 1997 where Solidarity leader Marian Krzaklewski made a passionate appeal for an explicit reference to religious values in the constitution's preamble. Eventually the Constitutional Commission opted for Tadaeusz Mazowiecki's rather awkward wording, which spoke of the constitution being adopted by 'all Polish citizens, both those who believe in God, who is the source of truth, justice, goodness and mercy, as well as those who do not share this faith and derive the values they recognise from other sources'. It then went on to speak of a culture rooted in 'a Christian heritage and universal human values' and recognised the people's responsibility 'before God or one's conscience'. With regard to the question of church and state the text spoke of relations being based upon the principles of respect for the autonomy and mutual independence of each. Despite this, special recognition was given the Catholic Church in a clause stating that its relationship with the state would be further defined by an international treaty with the Holy See.[28]

Not all in the church were happy with this formulation, which Cardinal Glemp described as failing to meet the expectations of the majority of the population. Others were more forthright, with one bishop describing the document as morally unsound and several openly calling upon their flock to vote no in the constitutional referendum. In the event, only 40 per cent of the population turned up to vote and a small majority of these approved the offered text.[29] In consequence, though still unhappy, church leaders turned their attention to persuading the authorities to ratify the long delayed Concordat with the Vatican. Agreed in 1993, parliamentary approval has been prevented as a result of liberal and socialist suspicions about some of the privileges it appeared to grant the church. For example, Catholic marriages were made legally binding, certain religious feast days made public holidays, subsidies were granted to some Catholic educational establishments, and priests given access to public institutions. Religious minorities and liberal critics argued that such an institutionalisation of the church's position could only be detrimental to non-believers, especially with regard to religious education and in the provision of parish cemeteries whose priests might refuse to bury the dead. The church countered that the terms of the agreement simply gave it freedom to carry out its true mission and entailed no privilege or discrimination. In early 1988 the Sejm finally adopted the Concordat and in so doing perhaps took the sting out of debates over the formal place of religion in the new Polish society.[30]

Religious minorities remained uneasy about some of the provisions of the Concordat, as well as the practical activities of Catholic authorities in parts of the country, but they faced little in the way of co-ordinated hostility from the church hierarchy. Though some Catholic bishops appeared committed to restoring something resembling a national Catholic state,[31] the commitment of the international church and the Pope himself to human rights preventing the institution from taking positions that could be seen as opposing minority rights. Legally, a 1989 Statute on Guarantees of Freedom of Conscience and Creed provided all religious communities with a relatively open regulatory framework, whilst Article 53 of the Constitution committed the state to defend religious rights. Occasionally problems surfaced in rural areas where clerical influences sometimes led to expressions of hostility towards minority groups, whilst in the east of the country some local and church authorities acted in ways that discriminated against the sizeable Orthodox minority. Problems also continued into the new century over issues of property ownership as Catholic parishes sought to reclaim church buildings previously handed over to other communities. And towards the end of the 1990s elements within the church and the administration argued for tighter control of the 'sects'.[32] For all this, there have been no major infringements on religious liberty promoted by the authorities or the church, and in this sense one might argue that the institution has been supportive of attempts to create the more pluralistic atmosphere that is often seen as conducive to a consolidating democracy.

The Exercise of Political Influence

As in Spain, the Catholic Church denied any intent to seek a political role, but in practice the hierarchy was far less restrained than its Spanish counterpart in seeking to influence the political process. True, it made no concerted efforts to form a Christian Democratic Party, but it consistently offered backing to those seeking to create parties supportive of church interests and values. In the first instance, immediately following the fall of

Communism, this meant backing the Solidarity coalition in the 1989 elections. Church leaders played some role in initiating Solidarity electoral committees which in many cases held their meetings on church properties. Pulpits were used to back some candidates or denounce others, as in the case of a doctor who had performed abortions, and ostensibly neutral advice was offered to a citizenry voting in free elections for the first time.[33] And whilst officially the church supported no party, in 1990 Cardinal Glemp held well publicised meetings with the leaders of the Christian National Union and the Christian Democratic Labour Party.[34] Subsequent elections followed a similar pattern as church leaders tried to encourage rightist parties to form broad electoral coalitions capable of taking on the revitalised Socialist Party. Thus in the 1993 parliamentary elections the Archbishop of Gdansk brokered an agreement amongst the fragmenting Conservative parties to form a Catholic Election Committee, Fatherland. Yet in the event the bloc and its constituent parties did badly, in part because of divisions between those of a more Christian Democratic orientation and those inclined to a more radical neo-liberalism. In consequence, the religious constituency was left largely under-represented in the new political order.[35]

The church leadership was far more outspoken during the 1995 presidential elections, combining a formal commitment to neutrality with a call to voters not to support the 'candidates who participated in the exercise of power at the highest party and government levels under totalitarian rule'.[36] In practice this represented a scarcely disguised call to vote against the Socialist candidate Alexander Kwasniewski. This became more overt after the first round of the voting when Gdansk Archbishop Tadeusz Goclowski called for a large turnout in the second ballot to preserve freedom and Christian values. In similar vein, the Archbishop of Lublin advised his flock only to vote for a Catholic and Cardinal Glemp stated that the two candidates presented voters with a choice between 'Christian values and a system of neo-pagan values'.[37] Given that the voters rejected this advice, one needs to be wary of overstating the political influence of the church. Nonetheless, Kenneth Chan's study of voting behaviour during the 1990s does indicate a much closer relationship between religious identity and political choice than can be found in Spain or other strongly Catholic countries. Broadly speaking, the church has promoted a rightist outlook over the last decade or more, and studies of voting behaviour during the elections of the early 1990s do show a broad distinction between religious-traditionalist and secularist blocs of voters. Moreover, in the 1995 presidential elections religiosity was a better predictor of choice than other variables.[38] Today, however, it appears that this factor may be declining in significance, with the majority of voters focusing heavily on what parties might be able to deliver in the economic and welfare areas.

On issues of public policy the Polish hierarchy tended to be more outspoken than was the Spanish church during the first decade of the transition process, though the extent to which it went beyond legitimate lobbying to the pursuit of privilege remains open to debate. Almost immediately after the collapse of the old system, the church called for a restoration of religious education in schools and in June 1990 the bishops suggested that this should be compulsory so as to combat the distorted view of religion promoted by the old regime.[39] During the course of the 1990/91 school year a growing number of school authorities did in fact introduce religion and ethics classes, though in theory parents were permitted to withdraw their children. In early 1993 parliamentary ombudsman challenged the practice of giving grades for religion classes and the state financing of the clergy involved in giving lessons.[40] Following subsequent debates in the Constitutional Tribunal, it was decided that religious education in schools was permissible but children would be offered the choice of Catholic, other religious or ethics classes. In practice, however, few schools had the resources to meet these objectives, and in rural areas there were considerable pressures on all parents to permit their children to take Catholic-run classes.[41]

During the same period there was also considerable discussion about the role of the media in the new Poland, with the bishops expressing considerable unease about its perceived permissiveness and poor moral tone. During parliamentary debates over a new media bill during the winter of 1992/93 the bishops suggested including a clause requiring the media to respect Christian values and not to promote activities that conflicted with morality and the public good. At the same time, the law created a National Council to monitor the media, some 25 per cent of whose membership was to be made up of church representatives. Many within parliament opposed this clause, arguing that it gave the church too much power, and the head of national television suggested that in practice it might be hard to define what Christian values meant in practical terms.[42] Minority representatives were also unhappy with what they saw as unequal treatment in the media, with weekly broadcasting of masses and the creation of Catholic radio stations seen as evidence of 'creeping establishment'.[43]

Perhaps inevitably, however, it was the issue of abortion that provided the major focus for religious interventions in the public arena during the 1990s. Here the church, backed up by the Pope, adopted an uncompromising position and in October 1990 supported a parliamentary bill that would have prohibited the practice in virtually all circumstances. During mid-1991 fierce debates took place in the Sejm as both sides fought bitterly to promote their position, whilst liberals within Solidarity's ranks sought a compromise position. Though the bill fell, the church made clear that it would return to the question following the next parliamentary elections. With a new parliament in place the issue was brought before parliament at the end of 1992. Parliament did indeed approve more restrictive legislation, and though Cardinal Glemp saw this as a step forward it was still not seen as sufficiently restrictive by the church.[44] Moreover, the return of the Socialists to power in 1995 brought a partial re-liberalisation of the law, much to the dismay of the church leadership, and the issue looked set to remain a political football for the rest of the decade. In consequence of this, the church sought guarantees for the right to life in the constitution being debated during the mid-1990s, though the eventual phrasing remained ambiguous with regard to abortion and the hierarchy remains far from satisfied.[45]

CONCLUSIONS

In some respects the process of transition was very similar in Spain and Poland. In both cases democratisation emerged out of a process of negotiation and argument around the table, rather than from violent protest or imperial collapse. In both cases the Catholic Church had played a key role in the 'return of civil society' and had publicly expressed support for the process of democratisation. Yet there were also differences in that one transition led to the displacement of a regime ostensibly committed to a religious vision of the nation, whilst the other saw the removal of a system seemingly promoting an anti-religious ideology which restricted religion to the private sphere. They also took place at different points in Catholic 'history'. The first occurred at the end of a period of Catholic liberalisation and under the gaze of a newly appointed pontiff still finding his feet. The second took place at a time when John Paul II had stamped his own mark on the wider church and had every intention of ensuring that his Polish colleagues provided an adequate defence of Catholic values and interests.

These similarities and difference undoubtedly played a considerable role in shaping the ways in which the two hierarchies handled the process of democratisation, though in each case it is problematic to speak of the church as an actor with a single voice. Broadly speaking the Spanish church had a more 'centrist' or 'liberal' orientation in the late 1970s than its Polish counterpart 15 years later, though in each institution there were highly conservative voices arguing for resistance to 'the spirit of the age'. Both, however, were influenced by the post-Vatican Council's emphasis on human rights and religious liberty. In consequence, each publicly supported the creation of democratic orders and neither put forward serious arguments for the restriction of minority rights, unlike their Orthodox counterparts in Greece, Bulgaria, and Russia.[46] Each also shared certain assumptions about the limitations of democracy, arguing that majority decision could not decide moral and ethical issues. In consequence, each stated quite clearly from the outset that they opposed the use of voting on questions such as divorce and abortion, for these were issues where God and natural law laid down absolute standards that could not be transgressed by any healthy society. Equally, both national churches were concerned to ensure that the new states gave legal or constitutional recognition to the historical connections between the nation and its religious institutions. Yet in defending the latter position they did tend to resort to demographic majoritarianism, arguing that in this case recognition was essential because most of the population formally adhered to the Catholic Church.

Yet in practice, despite shared objectives, they were operating in different contexts and often opted for different strategies in seeking to pursue these objectives. Hence the Spanish hierarchy was extremely concerned to avoid any revitalisation of the religious-secularist tensions that had cost Spain so dear in the 1930s, and joined other political actors in seeking consensual solutions to the constitutional debates. Though outspoken in opposition to divorce and, more especially, abortion, its language always left the door open for discussion – occasionally to the dismay of the Vatican. By way of contrast, the Polish bishops tended to adopt a more strident tone, arguing for very explicit public recognition of Christianity and the church in the constitutional text, and pursuing an absolute ban on abortion during the early 1990s. Whether either strategy was successful remains open to discussion, for both Spain and Poland now permit divorce, whilst within certain limits abortion is also possible.[47] On the other hand both succeeded in getting some recognition of the church's national status written into the constitutional texts, albeit rather 'softly' in the Spanish case.

More important for us, however, is the question of whether the positions adopted by the Catholic hierarchy served to ease or hinder the process of democratic consolidation. These were bodies with significant public support, though not necessarily major influences on political life, and the positions they took might have given backing to the democratisation process in two ways. They could do this firstly by encouraging some of the values that one associates with democratic governance such as tolerance and acceptance of others. Here the picture is mixed. As already noted, they did support pluralism in 'their own patch' by offering few objections to the legal and practical realisation of religious liberty – albeit with little enthusiasm in some cases. Though Cardinal Glemp in Poland and some of the older hierarchs in Spain had some sympathy for the 'error has no rights' approach which dominated pre-Vatican II thinking, they recognised that the world had changed. Equally importantly, though the Pope might attack sectarian 'ravening wolves' who sought to steal flocks in Latin America, he did not generally support attempts at physical or legal restriction of their rights, rather preferring to focus on counter-proselytising strategies that reinforced the faith of the Catholic community. Hence the official commitment of the international body to ideas about individual rights helped at some level to reinforce pluralist values in some areas of society.

The second way in which the church might have reinforced or undermined democratic consolidation relates to its promotion of the democratic rules of the game or the notion of democracy as the 'only game in town'. Here the tensions were more basic because of the very nature of the church. Traditionally it had seen the forms of rule as less important than the nature of that rule, that is whether it promoted a Catholic understanding of the common good. Democracy had in the second half of the twentieth century come to be seen as better than most other forms of rule, but where majorities promoted policies or values at odds with those of the church it too must face criticism. This dilemma was particularly acute for the Polish church because it had acquired influence by developing an ethical critique of the Communist system, by proclaiming divine and absolute truths against a system perceived as godless. Whilst all very well in the past, this division of the world into good and evil was hard to maintain into a democratic political system which is rooted in concepts of uncertainty, compromise, bargaining, and negotiation. Or, as Stepan and Linz suggest, an ethical notion of civil society that was useful in combating authoritarianism may prove 'dysfunctional' for political society in a consolidated democracy.[48]

The dilemma facing these churches was how to lobby for their own interests and values but to do so in ways that did not appear to representing special pleading for advantage or privilege. With regard to constitutional recognition, both utilised the language of democracy to argue that their status as majority churches demanded a formal recognition that in no way entailed any restriction on minority rights. It simply recognised a 'sociological fact'. More problematic was arguing their case for certain areas to be effectively excluded from this majoritarian approach, by using what some have described as 'private' arguments. That is, by claiming that certain areas were out of bounds for electorates and legislators they were utilising arguments that could not be contested and basing them on grounds that could not be shared by the whole society. And, as several writers have suggested, if one group claims certain areas as beyond the ken of public debate or voting in a democracy, why should others not do likewise.[49] This is not to say that religious organisations should simply deny their religious and theological inheritance or disguise it behind bland liberal sentiment – along the lines of an archbishop defending lenten fasting as a means of dieting. Rather they should find arguments that, whilst open about their religious origins, are also expressed in ways that do not simply rely on a 'God told me' approach which is essentially not contestable. Whether this will always be possible remains unclear and it is likely that tensions will resurface as absolute values come into conflict with the 'clash of interests' which lie at the heart of democratic politics. But in our cases it does seem that the Spanish Catholic Church has come to terms with this dilemma, as its leaders have come to focus primarily on revitalisation of their faith communities with only occasional forays into the public square.[50] For the Polish church this change has proved more problematic, though since the adoption of the constitution in 1997 its political interventions as an institution have been less public and confrontational. In particular, and like its Spanish counterpart, it has had to concentrate its attentions on dealing with the consequences of delayed modernisation in the form of a Western-style consumerism that offers alternative possibilities to those provided by the men in black. In that sense, both churches have been forced to take the road of backing freedom for all, not just for believers, and in that sense, however reluctantly in some cases, to adapt to democratic consolidation with all its uncertainties and occasionally undesirable side effects.

More generally, these case studies suggest that the relationship of the churches to democratisation is shaped by no single factor. In both cases, historical experience was important, though arguably the Spanish hierarchy appreciated the inheritance better than its Polish counterpart in making relatively modest claims on the new system for fear of re-awakening the old secular-clerical divisions that had torn Spain apart in the past. By way of contrast, the Polish church, used to battling against a hostile political system, appeared to believe that its past role in protecting civil society rendered it deserving of special consideration. This led it to adopt the same robust attitude to democratic authorities as it had done with their Communist predecessors. Equally, it may well be that the Spanish church more quickly realised the likely impact of delayed modernisation on their hold over the flock, and the probable secularising implications of the new social and political order. In both cases the religious institution enjoyed the support of the majority of the population but faced the evaporation of this support if religious leaders made what were seen as excessive claims on the political order. It might be argued that both sought legal protection for their interests and values in order to prevent competition, but because this came from moral pluralism rather than religious alternatives, most of their campaigning focused on moral issues rather than curbing minority rights. Above all, however, it seems that the relationship of the churches to democratisation is shaped by their particular historical relationship with the political order, their perception (or mis-perception) of their political capital, and, in the Catholic case, of the broader attitude to political order, political influence, and minority rights of the international institution at the point of transition.

NOTES

1. A useful introduction to this distinction can be found in J. Linz and A. Stepan, *Problems of Democratic Transition and Consolidation* (Baltimore and London: John Hopkins University Press 1996).
2. See the discussion in J. Casanova, *Public Religions in the Modern World* (Chicago: University of Chicago Press 1994), pp.11–39; G. Davie, *Religion in Modern Europe: A Memory Mutates* (Oxford: OUP 2000), pp.28–9.
3. D. Nichols, 'Religious Liberty in Spain', *Iberian Studies* 1/1 (1972), p.5.
4. Cf. F. Lannon, *Privilege, Persecution and Prophecy: The Catholic Church in Spain, 1875–1975* (Oxford: Clarendon Press 1987); A. Brassloff, *Religion and Politics in Spain: The Spanish Church in Transition, 1962–96* (London: Macmillan 1998).
5. R. Graham, *Spain: Change of a Nation* (London: Michael Joseph 1984), p.214.
6. Quoted in Brasslof, *Religion and Politics in Spain*, p.95.
7. William J. Callahan, *The Catholic Church in Spain, 1987–1998* (Washington DC: Catholic University of America Press 2000), p.567.
8. Ibid., p.566.
9. R. Gunther, G. Sani and G. Shabad, *Spain after Franco: The Making of a Competitive Party System* (Berkeley: University of California Press 1998), p.221.
10. W. Callahan, 'Church and State in Spain, 1975–91', *Journal of Church and State* 34/3 (1992), p.507.
11. *The Tablet*, 9 Dec. 1978.
12. Brassloff, *Religion and Politics in Spain*, pp.97–8.
13. J. Hughey, 'Church, State and Religious Liberty in Spain', *Journal of Church and State* 23/3 (1981), pp.100–101; this financial support remains extensive, with a subsidy estimated at around $10m in 2000.
14. On the current legal position, see G. Moran, 'The Legal Status of Religious Minorities in Spain', *Journal of Church and State* 36/3 (1994), pp.579–95; US State Department, *International Religious Freedom Report, 2001*.
15. Brassloff, *Religion and Politics in Spain*, pp.86–7.

16. Cf. Graham, *Spain*, p.225; V. Perez-Diaz, *The Rebirth of Civil Society* (London: Harvard University Press 1993), p.170; L. Edles, *Symbol and Ritual in the New Spain* (Cambridge: Cambridge University Press 1998), p.69.
17. R. Gunther and R. Blough, 'Religious Conflict and Consensus in Spain: A Tale of Two Constitutions', *World Affairs* 43/4 (1981), p.383.
18. Gunther *et al.*, *Spain after Franco*, p.228.
19. J. Montero and K. Calvo, 'Religiosity and Party Choice in Spain', in D. Broughton and H.-M. ten Napel (eds.), *Religion and Mass Electoral Behaviour in Europe* (London: Routledge 2000), pp.118–39.
20. *The Tablet*, 21 Feb. 1981; Brassloff, *Religion and Politics in Spain*, pp.123–24.
21. J. McNair, *Education for a Changing Spain* (Manchester: MUP 1984), pp.139–50.
22. M. Brzezinski, *The Struggle for Constitutionalism in Poland* (London: Macmillan 1998), pp.106–10.
23. *BBC Summary of World Broadcasts* EE/2055, 23 July 1994; J. Karpinski, 'The Constitutional Mosaic', *Transition* (Aug. 1995), p.9.
24. *BBC SWB* EE1684, B/5, 10 May 1993.
25. Brzezinski, *The Struggle for Constitutionalism in Poland*, p.122.
26. *BBC SWB* EE/2258, A/6, 25 March 1995.
27. S.P. Ramet, *Whose Democracy? Nationalism, Religion and the Doctrine of Collective Rights in Post-1989 Eastern Europe* (Oxford: Rowman & Littlefield, 1997), p.105.
28. *BBC SWB*, EE/2970, C/4, 18 March 1997.
29. Cf. *BBC SWB* EE/2902, C/5-6, 25 April 1997 and EE/2910, C/9-10, 5 May 1997.
30. Cf. *The Warsaw Voice*, 2 June 1996; *Catholic World News*, 9 Jan. 1998.
31. Cardinal Glemp amongst others initially appeared to have some sympathy for the pre-Vatican II position that error has no rights, and to have explicitly advocated the creation of a national Catholic state. Casanova, *Public Religions in the Modern World*, pp.110–11.
32. These religious liberty issues are explored in more in my forthcoming book on religion and politics in transitional societies (CUP, 2003).
33. K. Kosela, 'The Polish Catholic Church and the Elections of 1989', *Religion in Communist Lands* 18/2 (1990), pp.124–37.
34. A. Sabbat-Swidlicka, 'Polish Bishops Discuss Current Issues', *Report on Eastern Europe*, 20 April 1990, pp.25–8.
35. F. Millard, 'The Shaping of the Polish Party System, 1989–93', *East European Politics and Society*, 8/3 (1994), pp.467–94.
36. *Open Media Resources Institute (OMRI)*, 205, 20 Oct. 1995.
37. Cf. *BBC SWB* EE/2460, C/5; EE/2461, C/15 and EE2465, S1/0 on 14, 15 and 20 Nov. respectively
38. K. Chan, 'The Religious Base of Politics in Post-Communist Poland', in Broughton and ten Napel (eds.), *Religion and Mass Electoral Behaviour in Europe*, pp.189–90.
39. *Keston News Service* 12 July 1990, 14 and 25 Oct. 1990.
40. M. Ebolz, 'The Roman Catholic Church and Democracy in Poland', *Europe-Asia Studies* 50/5 (1998), p.821.
41. A. Sabbat-Swidlicka, 'Polish Ombudsman Over-ruled on Religious Instruction', *RFE/RL Research Report* 2/28, 9 July 1993; Brzezinski, *The Struggle for Constitutionalism in Poland*, pp.178–82; Ramet, *Whose Democracy?* p.101.
42. *BBC, SWB* EE/1576, B/11, 1 January 1993 and EE/1629, B/5, 5 March 1993; A. Sabbat-Swidlicka, 'Church and State in Poland', *RFE/RL Research Report* 2/14, 2 April 1993.
43. *Annual Report on International Religious Freedom for 1999: Poland* (Washington DC: US State Department 1999), Section 1.
44. *The Independent*. 17 and 18 May 1991, and 27 Nov. 1991; Sabbat-Widlicka, 'Church and State in Poland', pp.47–8.
45. *OMRI* 168, 29 Aug. 1996; J. Karpinski, 'Poles Divided over Church's Renewed Role', *Transition*, 5 April 1996, pp.11–13.
46. J. Anderson, 'The Treatment of Religious Minorities in South-Eastern Europe: Greece and Bulgaria Compared', *Religion, State and Society* 30/1 (2002), pp.9–31.
47. Speaking off the record, an experienced Vatican diplomat suggested to me that the absolutist

positions adopted by the Polish hierarchy could often be counter-productive both in terms of achieving goals and in engendering public support.

48. Stepan and Linz, *Problems of Democratic Transition and Consolidation*, p.272.

49. This argument is made in relation to Latin America in M. Fleet and B. Smith, *The Catholic Church and Democracy in Chile and Peru* (Notre Dame: Unviersity of Notre Dame Press 1997), p.179. Or, as Casanova suggests, so long as the church's argument are made in the public sphere of civil society, they are legitimate and likely to be more effective, whilst when they appeal for state sanction and claim privileged knowledge they are likely to be rejected by democratic polities. Casanova, *Public Religions in the Modern World*, p.223.

50. Cf. Davie, *Religion in Modern Europe*, pp.152–4; Callahan, *The Catholic Church in Spain*, Chapters 23–4.

The Contested Politics of Positive Neutrality in Hungary

ZSOLT ENYEDI

On one view the relevance and urgency of debates concerning the freedom and equality of churches in Europe seem to have faded over the past century. The tensions that existed among churches and between religious movements and 'humanist' circles appear to have ceased to be the cause of major political conflicts. Social and political developments, such as secularisation and the embracing of liberal democratic principles by the Second Vatican Council, have taken the steam out of the old conflicts. And the creation of Europe-wide legal standards has lowered the stakes by increasing uniformity across the continent.

Yet the issue of religious equality is back on the European agenda. The continent-wide campaign against 'dangerous cults', accelerated flows of immigration resulting in growing levels of multiculturalism, the increased political influence of churches and the reconstruction of national identities along religious lines in ex-Communist Eastern Europe have refocused attention on issues surrounding state neutrality. The pressure towards European uniformity has in itself highlighted the historically shaped differences between the nation states. The process of the establishment of new European norms has mobilised the churches, especially the Roman Catholic church.

The issue of religious equality is particularly relevant to Eastern Europe, because there the role of religion in social, private, and political life is being re-defined in a period when governments are struggling with a lack of popular legitimacy. Understandably, many politicians see in churches the potential providers of this legitimacy. And since most nations are religiously heterogeneous, the result is the rise of new political conflicts. Not only do these nations comprise various denominations, but they also contain die-hard atheists and anti-clericals, followers of new cults, and, last but not least, the members of the traditional churches. The latter group, whose members were second-class citizens for decades, now hope to return to the pre-communist *status quo*. But in virtually all countries this *status quo* meant a hierarchy of ecclesiastical organisations. Accordingly, a return to that pattern threatens the interests of several groups, for example, the classical pariah churches, the atheists, and the new, typically neo-Protestant, religious communities.

It is a widely shared insight within the literature of transitology that the fall of Communism did not present the respective countries with a *tabula rasa*.[1] In other words, the Eastern European 'Founding Fathers' did not act in a vacuum. Historical, geographical, economic, cultural, and international constraints shaped their decisions. Yet the *tabula rasa* metaphor should not be discarded in all its aspects. The Founding Fathers were confronted with a large number of alternatives whether they surveyed the West European models or their own historical traditions. As a result, the rules governing the exercise of religion or the role of churches in public life differ from country to country, and often from government to government. While the final settlements may very well be under the influence of various deeply historical factors, the initial regulatory solutions adopted were typically the products of rational deliberation and strategic bickering, in the course of which a range of different interests and values have been articulated and confronted.

HISTORICAL DIFFERENCES AMONG THE CHURCHES IN HUNGARY

Hungary belongs to that group of eastern European countries (together with Latvia, Bosnia-Herzegovina, Macedonia, and so on) where the denominational landscape is deeply fragmented. Three churches had a continuous national relevance throughout the centuries: the (mainly Roman) Catholics, the Calvinists (Reformed church) and the Lutherans (Evangelical church). Minor protestant churches and the Jewish community also played a culturally and politically essential role. Today there are around 100 churches functioning in the country. There is a general awareness that after the collapse of Communism a wave of American and Far Eastern religious movements reached the country, and indeed every year five or six new churches register. But these groups make up no more than two or three per cent of the population.[2]

Tensions between Catholics and Protestants were central to political conflict between the sixteenth and nineteenth centuries, although they were often combined and overshadowed by other allegiances, such as pro- and anti-Habsburg loyalties. The tradition of tolerance was also present, particularly in the politics of the Transylvanian Principality and the liberal revolution of 1848 served as another major historical source of the legitimacy of religious toleration. Yet the normal state of affairs in Hungary, as everywhere else, was that religious communities continuously differed in the amount of power, privilege, and prestige they enjoyed, and many of them were treated by the state as politically and socially subversive actors.

As a consequence of the evolution of customary law and of independent executive actions, three clusters of churches had emerged by the nineteenth century: co-opted, registered, and tolerated. No explicit legal definitions were attached to these labels, but according to ministerial interpretations they referred to the level of legal state protection.[3] The co-opted churches received administrative assistance for church tax collection, and the government gave subsidies and covered part of the clergy's salaries. In the first part of the nineteenth century the Catholic, Lutheran, Calvinist, and (since 1790) Orthodox churches were considered co-opted. There existed some room for movement in the hierarchy of churches: the Unitarians became co-opted in 1848, and the Jews were registered in 1874 and then co-opted in 1895. In 1905 the Baptist church, and in 1916 the Islamic religion, were accepted as registered.

Today, the main dividing line runs between 'historical' and non-historical churches, but which churches count as 'historical' is not entirely clear. The Roman Catholics, the Calvinists, the Lutherans, and the Israelite church (Jewish community) form at the moment the core of this group. There is considerable uncertainty about the status of minor churches that had a continuous presence in the last centuries, like the Unitarians, the Greek Catholics, and the Orthodox churches. Depending on the particular aspect of church–state relations, these churches are either included or not into the 'historical' group

Since the Counter-Reformation, the Catholic church has had an unquestionable numerical and political primacy over the other denominations. Yet it was a primacy in opposition to the liberal governments of the nineteenth century. These governments, backed by the Protestant churches which were more thoroughly impregnated by the spirit of nationalism and liberalism, proved successful in curtailing the Catholic church's privileges and in moving the country closer to the separation of church and state. The anti-liberal turn in Hungarian politics at the end of the nineteenth century, and particularly after 1918, brought the major churches and the state into a closer union however, in both symbolic and financial terms.

Communism destroyed the historical church–state regime. The churches, not so much *de jure* but *de facto*, lost their autonomy. Their infrastructure was also almost completely destroyed. Violent anti-clericalism and anti-religiosity were distinguishing features of the Communist dictatorship under Rákosi. The Kádár regime that followed the defeat of the 1956 revolution continued to employ repressive measures at least until the 1970s, but it also made some significant symbolic concessions. Yet social modernisation, together with ongoing anti-religious propaganda, pushed the churches to the margins of Hungarian social life.

During the Communist period the churches embodied a fundamental challenge to the official world view. This challenge became less political in nature as the church leaders found a *modus vivendi* with the Communist government. Opposition movements could not derive support from the higher clergy; a number of whom had even become members of the Communist parliament. Those religious communities, both within and outside the mainstream denominations, which supported the conscientious objectors or provoked the suspicion of the authorities by simply being too active in their religious or social duties, were soon disciplined by the church elite. The Catholic church publicly condemned those members who refused to serve in the army. The political opposition within the churches was crushed by the clergy, while the religious opposition to the clergy was intimidated by the state.[4] The close co-operation between bishops and the infamous Office for Church Affairs provided the condition for a seemingly peaceful coexistence of church and state – at least at the elite level.

The various churches were not all equal targets of the Communist government. The Catholic church was undoubtedly the principal public enemy in the 1950s. But in the Kádár period opposition to the regime was found more in the minor communities. Conscientious objection to military service was a particularly sensitive issue in those years. Finally, one of the most affected communities, the Nazarenes, was officially recognised by the state in 1977, and its members were allowed to serve as unarmed soldiers. (This 'sect' first applied for recognition in 1876, that is, 100 years before they were finally accepted.) The Communist authorities registered a second small church in 1981, after a split among the Methodists, largely concerning the issue of co-operation with the authorities. In spite of these concessions, the government typically sided with the mainstream churches in conflict situations.[5] To put it differently, the religious market was under state control, and this control protected the oligopolistic position of the established players.

THE INSTITUTIONAL FRAMEWORK

The transition to democracy in 1989 fundamentally changed both the religious and the political environment of the Hungarian churches. Artificial barriers to entry into the religious market disappeared. While this change brought many potential risks for the existing churches, they found themselves in a position to actively shape the pattern of church–state relationships. Yet the most important pieces of legislation, the amendment of the Constitution and the Law on Religious Freedom (Act 4/1990), were drafted without their direct participation. The Round Table negotiations, which determined the institutional set-up of a democratic Hungary, were conducted among political elites, many of them not having a particularly high opinion of the clergy. But the prevailing spirit was not anti-clerical, and especially not anti-religious. There was a widespread consensus among the various parties that religion and the churches are functional elements in a healthy civil society. To put it differently, the major intellectual current which dominated in those days in Hungary, and which left its mark on the legislation concerning churches, was a secular, but pro-religious liberalism. Accordingly, the new institutional patterns incorporated the following building blocks: state neutrality, uncompromising freedom of religion, and church autonomy.

By accepting the principles of equality and state neutrality, the makers of the constitution have severely limited the scope for state discrimination or even differentiation between churches, but did not foreclose on it completely. In defining the relevant norms, the Constitutional Court had a particularly prominent role. According to the Court's decision (4/1993) the state should be neutral, but the differential treatment of churches, taking into account social and historical reality, need not constitute a breach of neutrality. Therefore, it is not unconstitutional, for example, to guarantee to the four historical churches special access to such institutions as public TV and radio boards, army chaplaincy, or governmental committees on church–state relationships.

The Constitutional Court has endorsed the idea of active neutrality: the state has the duty to provide the churches with the means that are necessary for their operation. The state is responsible for the protection of the freedom of religion. It must ensure an environment suitable for the formation and development of individual belief. In other words, freedom of religion presupposes an active, positive attitude on behalf of the state.[6]

Among the political elites there exist three major approaches to church–state relations. The first advocates a 'closed club' model. This approach is motivated by philosophical conservatism and attitudinal conformism; it sees the new religious groups as a danger to the established churches. It does not, however, call for the establishment of state religion, but regards the Catholic and mainstream Protestant interests as being identical with Hungarian interests and, from time to time, raises the possibility of the establishment of a second chamber where the so-called historical churches would be represented. The centrist, 'gradual acceptance' model calls for consumer-protection in the religious market. According to this model, it is the task of the new religious movements to prove that they deserve the same privileges as the old ones. As they grow in size and as their deeds testify to their social utility, the state should gradually grant them the rights enjoyed by established churches. This approach accepts the norm of state neutrality but emphasises that the passivity of the state in these matters favours those who have no religious needs.[7] The third, 'strict neutrality', approach is vehemently opposed to the establishment of any hierarchy among the churches, but is willing to elevate churches from among the private institutions. The most 'anti-clerical' circles would like to see churches having no different legal status than other voluntary associations, but this view does not receive significant political backing.

The practice of church–state relations reflects a commitment to the consensual value of positive neutrality, but oscillates between the 'closed club', 'gradual acceptance', and 'strict neutrality' models. In accordance with the positive neutrality principle, churches are exempted from local taxes and dues, have access to a set of further tax exemptions, and the church schools, hospitals, and so on are provided state support. Church schools are therefore distinguished from private schools, which are also entitled in principle to state support, but a lower level is guaranteed to them.

While churches are privileged over civic organisations, the exact level of privilege changes according to election outcomes. Examples abound. The 1990–94 MDF-led government introduced state salaries for religious instructors; the 1994–98 Socialist-Liberal government abolished them; while the third, Fidesz–MPP-led government reintroduced them. The church schools were not given exactly the same amount of financial support as state schools during the Socialist-Liberal government (1990–94), but the Fidesz–MPP government (1998–2002) placed them on an equal footing.

The amount of direct financial support given to particular churches was left initially to parliamentary and governmental deliberations too, leading to the politicisation of the issue. The decisions taken in the early post-Communist years dissatisfied the right and the left alike. The most controversial of these decisions concerned four minor churches which were denied state support in 1993 because the MPs found them to be 'subversive'. This decision, together with the question of religious teaching in state schools, sparked heated arguments among the parties concerning the neutrality of the state in church affairs.

Since 1996, churches have been principally financed by taxation in order to make them more independent from party politics. Citizens can offer one per cent of their income tax to one of the churches. The number of those who do so increases year by year, although it has still not reached one-fifth of all taxpayers. The churches have almost absolute autonomy in financial issues: the state may not control the management of the churches' funds. However, the churches are not autonomous in the sense of being self-sustaining. The mainstream churches receive half of their finances from the state and less than a quarter from their members (the other sources include services provided by the churches for fees, foreign donations, etc.). In 2001 the Catholic church had a yearly budget of 34 billion, out of which 21,5 billion came from the state.[8] If one counts all the educational, social, etc. institutions that belong to churches, then state finance contributes three quarters of the overall budgets.[9]

POLITICISATION OF CLERICAL STRUCTURES

Next to factors such as size and historic relevance, the relative status of specific churches is strongly dependent on their relationship with political actors and on their own political actions. Three churches seem to be particularly politicised in Hungary: the Roman Catholic church, the Calvinist church, and the Congregation of Faith. The Catholic church has the most institutionalised relations with the state and the political elite. The secretary of the Council of Bishops meets four times a year with the representatives of the parliamentary parties.[10] The charismatic, evangelical Pentecostal Faith church actively supports the Alliance of Free Democrats (SZDSZ) and, according to some observers, at a certain point it was able to influence the leadership selection and the programme formation within the party.[11]

Churches can become politicised in two ways. They can make a conscious decision to become players in the political field or they can simply allow politics to penetrate their own sphere, becoming factionalised according to political sympathies.

Politics Penetrating Churches

Since they cannot be party members or active politicians, Catholic officials, in general, are less vulnerable to party politicisation, while Lutheran pastors must suspend their clerical office while working as MPs. Until recently, there was no such limitation in the Reformed church by contrast, and this state of affairs probably contributed to the particularly strong political conflicts within this church.

There are three major political phenomena that can lead to tensions within the Hungarian churches: liberalism, anti-Communism, and nationalism. The first of these is the least significant one. The liberal wings of the Hungarian churches are weak. Liberal movements are most visible among the Catholics, but within the church they are isolated. For example, the liberal Catholic journal *Egyházfórum* ('Church Forum') is not accepted by the Hungarian Catholic Publishers Society, and has no right to use the Catholic label.

Within the majority of churches there are more serious tensions concerning co-operation with the Communist authorities in the past. Interestingly, it is the liberal and the extreme-right politicians who urge the purging of the clergy. In 1990 a separate parliamentary committee was set up to investigate state–church relations under Communism, but it was soon dissolved. According to rumours, the Prime Minister was shocked by the long list of priests who reported to the secret police on their colleagues. While some of the MPs on both government and opposition sides were in favour of making the respective documents public, the majority decided to close down the investigation. According to a right-wing MP, 'Only freemasons and atheists would benefit from this process'.[12] The main official argument was that the autonomy of churches should be respected and the churches should be allowed to renew themselves from inside.

Finally, the attitude towards nationalism and the extreme right has divided the mainstream churches, particularly the Reformed church. Bishop Hegedűs and his diocese actively support the Party of Hungarian Life and Justice (MIÉP), a nationalistic and anti-Semitic party. His son, also a Calvinist pastor, is the Vice-Chairman of that party. This intensive co-operation between Calvinists and the extreme right became more and more embarrassing for the moderate leaders of the church, who are either non-political or stay close to the moderate right, that is Fidesz–MPP. When Hegedűs junior was indicted in 2001 by the state prosecutor for publishing an article in which he explicitly asked for the 'exclusion of Jews', the church had no choice but to act. The national synod of Hungarian Calvinists condemned the article, forbade pastors to be party members, and asked for the removal of all party-related organisations from their church buildings. The last measure was aimed at removing an extreme right radio studio from one of the Budapest Calvinist churches. Since then, pastors who run for office have had to suspend their appointments in the church. Nevertheless, a number of pastors decided to disobey the decisions of the synod and to run as MIÉP candidates for the 2002 parliamentary elections.[13]

Churches in the Political Arena

The active involvement of churches in politics typically happens along three fronts: when their immediate organisational interests are at stake, when freedom of religion is threatened, and when faith-related moral issues are on the political agenda. As far as the first situation is concerned, Hungarian churches proved to be outspoken defenders of their organisational interests. For example, in 1991 mainstream churches and MPs fought together to remove the head of the public radio channel, who refused to allocate appropriate time for religious programmes.

As far as issues related to freedom of religion are concerned, Hungarian churches left the battles largely to politicians close to them. The 1990 law, as mentioned above, was prepared by the party elites. And later, when the threshold for achieving church status became a political issue, large churches had again a modest public role in the debates. Only minor churches, feeling that they were the real targets of the planned restrictions, participated openly in the related political campaigns.

Finally, in terms of the debates concerning public morality, the Hungarian churches are relatively active, but place the emphasis on different issues than most Western churches. One example can be cited from 2001 when one of the most important political debates concerned a so-called status law, a law that provided Hungarians living in the neighbouring countries with a special Hungarian ID card and a number of privileges (free travel and medical treatment in Hungary, support for Hungarian education for their children and so on). In order to persuade the Romanian government to accept this law, the Hungarian government made a concession extending the right to possess a Hungarian work permit to all Romanian citizens, and made some further modifications in the way the 'status law' should be implemented. The Free Democrats were opposed to the law from the outset. The Socialists supported the law itself, but objected to the amendments. Public opinion seemed to be on the side of the opposition: the popularity of the main government party suddenly dropped. At this point the three historic churches, Roman Catholic, Calvinist, and Lutheran, issued a declaration criticising the attacks on the government. The churches regarded it as their fundamental duty publicly to support a government trying to reintegrate the Hungarians living in the 'lost territories'.

On other moral issues the churches have been less assertive. In spite of the fact that the present Pope is particularly outspoken about anti-Semitism, the Hungarian historical churches do not want to play a major role on this particularly sensitive issue. They have usually been unwilling to condemn unequivocally particular examples of anti-Semitic or xenophobic rhetoric, with the notable exception of the case of Hegedüs junior. In 2001, a group of intellectuals claiming to be members of the mainstream Christian churches publicly asked the clergy to come out against racism and anti-Semitism. The Catholic church decided to ignore the letter, while the Reformed and Lutheran churches explicitly rejected the attempt to influence them 'from outside'.

The real possibility, or danger, of church politicisation comes during the time of the electoral campaigns. In Hungary before the parliamentary elections the mainstream churches issue circulars. These circulars contain, next to a general call for participation, a list of points believers should rely upon when voting. For example, in the Catholic circular published on 16 March 2002, the issue of demographic decline, the classic issue of the Hungarian right, was singled out as one of the crucial criteria. The believers were also asked to vote for those who 'help the development of a healthy national conscience, [and] make sacrifices for Hungarians abroad'.[14] Both the Catholic and the Calvinist circulars emphasised that one should decide on the basis of performance, not promises, which happened to be one of the main slogans of the right-wing government parties. The Catholic church has also reminded the flock in 1998 and in 2002 not to waste votes on small parties. This reminder was supposed to help the largest right-wing party, Fidesz–MPP. In 2002, the Calvinist church called on its members to vote for the parties representing 'Christian-national' values and not to let themselves be intimidated. After the first round, won by the Socialists, the Reformed church issued a second circular, reminding the voters that 'the balance of power among the parliamentary parties may change' in the second round.

In 2002 the most politically active Catholic bishop, Endre Gyulay, ordered the parishes in his diocese to conduct prayers for the success of the elections every Sunday for almost half a year. He has also suggested a number of texts to be used in these prayers. These texts avoided references to such political issues as racism or nationalism, but included the following sentence 'Save the nation from selfish, extreme, liberal ways of thinking!'

While the churches themselves exercise some degree of restraint, many individual clergymen, journals,[15] and lay organisations actively campaign on behalf of the right. In 2002 a number of priests produced leaflets and distributed them after mass, explaining why voting for the opposition is contrary to Christian interests. One parish priest suggested that those believers who voted for the Socialists or the Liberals ask for forgiveness.[16] In some church schools the teachers wrote letters to the parents warning them that a left-wing victory could make the very future of the school uncertain. The Christian Intellectuals' Society organised a pilgrimage in March 2002 'for the victory of the right'.

This society had a conspicuous role in another affair as well. In 2002, the Socialist ex-Prime Minister wrote an open letter to the Catholic church asking it not to interfere in the electoral campaign. The letter also accused priests of actively campaigning in favour of the government parties, even during confession. The churches took the letter as an insult. The outcry among clerical circles turned out to be even greater when a Socialist youth organisation announced that it would record the priests' political statements during sermons. Although this initiative was soon dropped,[17] a large-scale protest developed. The Vice-Secretary of the Ministry of Culture repeatedly compared it to the practices of Hitler's Germany. A Fidesz–MPP MP labelled it intellectual terrorism, reminding the public that the extermination of people begins usually with this sort of 'intellectual extermination'.[18] The Christian Intellectuals' Society was particularly industrious in keeping the issue on the agenda, organising large-scale demonstrations in front of the Socialists' headquarters.

THE CLERICALISATION OF POLITICAL STRUCTURES

In Hungary there has never been much doubt about which political camp is on the side of mainstream churches and which is not. When the Socialist PM signed the agreement with the Vatican, for a moment it seemed that the Socialists were making peace with the largest church.[19] But very soon the pattern of clerical vs. anti-clerical camps was re-established. This fundamental division is mirrored in the programmes of the governments. The Socialist-Liberal (1994–98) government programme[20] emphasised the need to strengthen the separation between church and state. The manifesto stated that 'In the long run the government prefers the churches to be maintained by their members', although it has also added that 'It accepts, at the same time, that at this point churches still need state support'.

The programme lacked references to the category of 'historic churches' and it expressed an explicit sympathy for the cause of the small churches.

> In the spirit of freedom of conscience and equality before the law, the government respects the rights of smaller religious communities that lack historical traditions. It finds the propaganda against religious minorities or the idea that any religious community should be stigmatised by a legislative act on the basis of rumours unacceptable.[21]

In contrast to the Socialists, the Fidesz–MPP-led government (1998–2002), started with the assumption that the separation of church and state was complete, and that the task of the new government was to establish new forms of co-operation. The new government programme[22] stated:

> The government acknowledges with respect the work of the historic churches in the life of the nation, and counts on their service in the spiritual, intellectual, cultural, educational, and social fields. Therefore it regards as its task to ensure the freedom of churches in a legal and material sense as well. Churches can be free only if their material independence, their capacity to function properly is guaranteed.

According to the government manifesto, the existing financing regime places the 'real churches' in a 'derogatory' light, by placing them on an equal footing with various dubious enterprises. The government asserted that only actual social support or historical record could justify state subsidies.

This new government programme also pointed out that churches were hitherto discriminated against since their educational and welfare activities received less support than the activities of institutions run directly by the state or by the local governments. This amounted to an unconstitutional discrimination 'between children, patients, and citizens on the basis of religion' and to the 'double taxation of the religious population'.

The leading party of this government, Fidesz–MPP, is now an integral part of the clerical camp in spite of the fact that it was seen in the early 1990s as being explicitly anti-clerical. The views of the party on church–state matters changed radically, in parallel with the sharp right-wing turn in 1993. Already by 1996 the party was criticising 'extreme liberal' opinion which expects the state to support all churches equally, arguing instead for a differentiation according to the churches' behaviour and values.

Fidesz–MPP adopted these views from the right-wing parties. The new orientation was strengthened by the joining of many ex-Christian Democrats after the collapse of their party. One of them, Zsolt Semjén, became the head of the government administration that regulates church–state matters. In this capacity he reiterated his well-known opinion:

> It is not the government that makes a difference between churches, but the history and the society. Everybody can understand this: a religious experiment invented yesterday is not the same as the Catholic or the Calvinist church. Let me cite an analogy: an airplane and a bicycle are both vehicles, but one cannot apply the same traffic rules to both of them.[23]

Proposals submitted in 1993 and 1998 by right-wing MPs to raise the threshold for church registration were resurrected under the Fidesz–MPP-led government. These proposals requested as a condition of registration 100 years of existence in Hungary and a minimum of 10,000 members.[24] Since the Socialists rejected these ideas unequivocally, and since their support was necessary for the amendment of the law, the government experimented with different kinds of thresholds. Finally, it submitted a proposal that granted the authority to register religious communities to a specialised court. The proposal also required the submission of theological dogmas to be examined by the court to determine whether they violated public morality and whether they were truly religious; that is, whether they are universal and refer to the supernatural. If an applicant was found to concentrate its activity mainly on business, parapsychology, political representation, alternative medicine, dissemination of humanist tenets, or magic, then the application was to be rejected.

The Socialists expressed their conditional support for the government proposals. They asked for minor amendments, but agreed with the general thrust of the law, that of reducing the potential for the abuse of religious freedoms. In spite of this relative consensus between the major parties, the vote in the parliament was preceded by intensive campaigns in favour and against the new law. Petitions and demonstrations were organised by both sides. In the midst of the parliamentary debate, the Fidesz–MPP invited 14 small churches to a special meeting in the parliament in order to demonstrate that the intention of the law was not to discriminate between churches according to their size.[25]

In the end, the Socialists withdrew their support for the amendment, partly because some of their own proposals were rejected, and partly because the government in parallel introduced some new regulations (see below), which did discriminate against small religious communities. Some government MPs threatened the opposition with organising a referendum on the issue, but no real action followed.

Although this crucial piece of legislation has been frustrated, the government, during its four-year term, has availed itself of many other opportunities to implement its programme. These measures increased the volume of government subsidies to churches, elevated mainstream Christianity to the status of a state philosophy, and strengthened the hierarchy that exists among the churches. Many of the new measures did not reach parliament. For example, competitions for grants organised by ministries were often open to mainstream churches only.

In 1998 the incoming Fidesz–MPP government swiftly introduced state financing of religion teachers and finalised the list of properties to be restored to the churches and the timing of their return. The Prime Minister has expressed his intention to involve the state in providing pensions for the clerical employees. Church subsidies were increased from the yearly 16 to 31 billion Forints. The government invested a large amount of money in financing religious tourism, building a new Catholic university and reconstructing religious buildings.

Most new subsidies and exemptions have been given to a selected group of churches. The Fidesz–MPP government has decided to supplement the salary of priests from the four historical churches who work in small settlements. In 2002, this new form of subsidy was extended to another five churches, but no guidelines were issued to the public concerning the criteria of selection.[26] The government has also exempted some of the churches from paying VAT; the law did not specify which churches are to be exempted but simply referred to churches that have an agreement on the matter with the government.

The government further differentiated among the churches in its introduction of tax-deductible donations. From 2000, churches wishing to receive donations that make the donors eligible for tax return must satisfy one of the following three criteria: 100 years of existence or 30 years of institutional existence on the territory of Hungary or tax offers received from more than one per cent of all eligible taxpayers. The criteria are more restrictive then they look at first sight, because when calculating the 30-year-long institutional existence the period between 1948 and 1990 does not count. That is, at the moment only churches whose existence dates back to 1928 are eligible.[27] One per cent of all taxpayers is also a high threshold, since the large majority of taxpayers do not offer a portion of their taxes to churches. In 1999, for example, 89 churches received donations, but out of these churches only two were supported by more than one per cent of all taxpayers (4.3 million people): the Roman Catholics received support from 7.5 per cent of taxpayers and the Calvinists from 2.4. The documentation of historical existence was less stringent: old newspaper articles indicating the persecution of members of a church were, for example, accepted as proof of institutional existence. Because of this, one of the most controversial communities, the Jehovah's Witnesses became eligible for tax funding.

Since 1997, direct subsidies to the churches have been based on one per cent of tax assessments, which was then supplemented by the government by up to 0.5 per cent of the income tax revenue. The Fidesz–MPP government has increased the target level to 0.8 per cent and allowed the ratio of supplements to be determined not by the ratio of tax dedications, but by the census figures. This proved to be a controversial change since some of the churches, most conspicuously the Roman Catholic church, actively campaigned during the 2000 census for people to register their denominational affiliation, while others, marginal movements and cults, asked their members not to declare their membership. At the time of the 2000 census it was not yet public that the information submitted would be used for financial purposes.

The Free Democrats labelled these moves as a 'financial religious war'. But the government was fighting a symbolic war as well. Public TV and Radio more than doubled the amount of time devoted to mainstream religious programmes during the government's four years in office. All Saint's Day (1 November) was declared a public holiday, and the Prime Minister promised that the Feast of the Assumption of the Blessed Virgin Mary (15 August) would soon become a public holiday too. Even more symbolic was the proposal of the Fidesz–MPP to give state acknowledgement to church marriages. The proposal was criticised, among other reasons, because of the threat of further discrimination, the intention of the government being to give this right to churches that have the 'appropriate institutional background'.[28]

These various regulations on different aspects of church–state relations constitute a specifically Hungarian model in the eyes of the government officials who argue that:

> The model compensates for the damages caused by the decades of the fallen regime that persecuted the church, and, on the other hand, avoids those deadlocks where, led by the secular myths of the past century, the church policy of some of the western nations ended up … The Hungarian model of church policy is faithful to the spiritual legacy of our first king Saint Stephen (997–1038), which proclaims: whatever is beneficial to the church is also beneficial to the nation, and whatever is beneficial to the nation is also beneficial to the church.[29]

Examples of gestures of friendship between church and state under the Fidesz–MPP government abound. Government ministers have repeatedly pointed out the strong organic ties between the Hungarian state and Christianity. The turn of the Millennium gave plenty of opportunities to remind citizens that the birth of the Hungarian state was promoted and blessed by the Pope in 1000 AD. The co-ordinator of the millennial celebrations proposed that the separation of church and state should be symbolically suspended during the commemorations. Even the government saw this proposal as going too far.

Fidesz–MPP Prime Minister Orbán, in spite of being a Calvinist, spoke of the Pope (whom he visited twice during his four years in office) as 'the Holy Father' and even stated once that the Hungarian government 'has voted for Catholic values'. Orbán has often participated in Catholic masses and processions. The church holiday that was made public by him, and the one he promised to make public, are both Catholic feast days, and were chosen against more ecumenical days. According to some interpretations, these pro-Catholic gestures are not only a conscious recognition of the larger size of the Catholic Church in comparison to other denominations, but are also because Catholic rituals are more suitable for community- and leadership-building than Protestant ones.[30] After the elections thousands attended the mass dedicated to Orbán and his family in Saint Stephan Basilica, the largest Catholic church in Budapest.

There are many signs that the Prime Minister's policies cannot be understood in terms of a simple *quid pro quo*, where the secular government pays the necessary price for the spiritual support of the churches. Most pro-clerical initiatives did not come from the churches but from the Prime Minister. It was he, for example, and not the Catholic church, who announced that it is a long-standing grievance of Catholics that 15 August is not a work holiday.[31] It was he, and not the churches, who proposed that the state should supplement the salaries and pensions of the priests.

The respective churches did not object to these measures, but in some cases they seemed to be stunned by the pace of developments. When the Fidesz–MPP announced the plan to place church marriage on a par with civil ones, the first reactions of the clergy were mixed. The head of the Calvinist synod, bishop Bölcskei, confessed: 'I don't see at this point what would be the advantage of this change.'[32]

The role of 'ally of churches' is seen as attractive for most politicians. But the left participates half-heartedly in this symbolic competition, being constantly reminded that it has no chance to capture this particular stronghold, while the right has good reason to be confident that it can. Right-wing politicians regularly claim that the contending political alternatives differ, most of all in their attitudes towards nation and religion, and the gestures of church leaders substantiate this interpretation.

CONCLUSION

In Hungary religion has become truly de-privatised during the last decade. Following Casanova's terminology,[33] public religions are not only present in civil society, but also have a presence in political society and in the state. In strictly formal, institutional terms the Hungarian state is religiously neutral and the country does not have established churches. Indeed, the Hungarian Constitution and the Law on Religious Freedom provides for a framework that is more strictly neutral than most of the Western European ones. Hence, the stereotype that in Eastern Europe there is necessarily more discrimination against marginal churches simply does not hold. One observer goes even so far as to say that 'Freedom of religion for members of minority faiths could end up being limited in the new societies of eastern Europe and the former Soviet Union *because* of the growing ties with European institutions, not in spite of these developing connections.'[34]

This institutional set-up is, however, at odds with the role played by religion and by churches in legitimising the new political actors. The symbiosis between the mainstream churches and the Hungarian right (and less relevantly, between marginal religious communities, atheists, and the Hungarian left), together with the alliance of the historic churches against the newcomers, has inevitably led to the development of a political hierarchy among churches. The result is a partial,[35] multiple, and fragile establishment. The outcome is not that different from what we find in Western European countries. But in Hungary the direction of these processes is diametrically opposed to that in much of Western Europe, where the churches have gradually cut most of their links to party politics during the last half a century.

The findings presented in this article seem to confirm the thesis that churches are given privileges by the state in accordance with the legitimacy they can provide to the political elite.[36] But the Hungarian example draws attention to the structured nature of the political elite; some factions are able to benefit from co-operation with churches, others are not. It also makes the point that the legitimacy provided by churches is mainly a product of the actions of the politicians themselves. The Hungarian right's project involves two steps. In step one, Hungarian nationhood is conceptualised as being interwoven with loyalty towards the historical churches. In step two, the support of these churches is interpreted as a sign of the respective parties' true Hungarian-ness.

The Hungarian case seems to be a good illustration of the fact that a high level of state support provides ample opportunity to rank the churches according to their political utility. But it would be a mistake to regard discrimination itself as the real purpose of state activity in this field. Support often goes to churches not preferred by the regime. In fact, Hungarian government officials have at times tried to deliver state subsidies to minor churches that are opposed in principle to state authority, and any state support. The roots of the activist role of the state can be found as much in general expectations about state responsibilities as in the particular sympathies between political factions and particular churches. This general systemic feature is well illustrated by the fact that the state in Hungary, as in a large part of continental Europe, is the main subsidiser of political parties as well. The difference is that in the case of parties there is the common principle that electoral results guide the amount of state support. Until state support of religious life lacks a similar consensual standard, and until there exists sharply opposing expectations regarding the role of the government in the provision of religious freedom, state support and discrimination will remain inextricably interwoven.

Unfortunately, by adopting the norm of state inaction, one cannot completely escape this danger either. The state has grown to such a level in modern societies, that it is difficult to see how the principle of non-interference can be sustained.[37] A wide variety of symbolic gestures, informal actions, and lack of action, as well as overt financial and legal discrimination, constitutes the political hierarchy of churches. The Hungarian case serves as a powerful reminder of the necessity of considering church–state regimes in their wider political context in order to evaluate the perils of state (in)action for religious equality and freedom.

NOTES

1. See H. Kitschelt, 'The Formation of Party Cleavages in Post-Communist Democracies: Theoretical Propositions', *Party Politics* 1 (1995), pp.447–72.
2. A. Máté-Tóth, 'Szektablabla'['Sect-yack'], *Népszabadság*, 15 Jan. 2001.
3. L. Péter, 'Hungarian Liberals and Church–State Relations (1867–1900)', in Gy. Ránki (ed.), *Hungary and European Civilization* (Budapest: Akadémiai Kiadó 1989), pp.79–139.
4. T. Ruff, 'Átvilágítatlanul'[Not lustrated], *Beszélő* 2/7 (July 1997), pp.40–45.
5. Richardson claims that small groups, because of their insignificance, have escaped the attention of the oppressive state apparatus. See J.T. Richardson, 'New Religions and Religious Freedom in Eastern and Central Europe, with Special Focus on Hungary', in A. Sajo and S. Avineri (eds.), *The Law of Religious Identity: Models for Post-Communism* (The Hague: Kluwer Law International 1999), p.207. While this might have been the case with some minor, inward-looking communities, many of the 'sects' have been aggressively targeted by the Communist secret police.
6. See Decision 4/1993 of the Constitutional Court. See also P. Erdő, and B. Schanda, 'Church and State in Hungary: An Overview of Legal Questions', *European Journal for Church and State Research* 6 (1999), pp.220–31; and B. Schanda, 'The Relationship between State and Church in Hungary: The Financing of the Church', in Sajo and Avineri (eds.), *The Law of Religious Identity*, pp.175–94.

7. B. Schanda, 'Constitutional Litigation Concerning Religious Freedom in Hungary', *Interights Bulletin* 11 (1997), pp.125–8.
8. *Népszabadság*, 18 Oct. 2001.
9. See B. Farkas, 'Az egyházak gazdálkodása Magyarországon' [Church Finance in Hungary], *Egyházfórum* 2 (2001), pp.3–7 and 3 (2001), pp.3–7; and B. Schanda, 'Relationship Between State and Church'.
10. *Népszabadság*, 23 Feb. 2002.
11. Concerning the controversies surrounding the Faith church see Zs. Enyedi, 'Finding a New Pattern: Church-State Relations in Post-Communist Hungary', Paper presented to the Workshop 'Church and State in Europe' ECPR Joint Sessions, Copenhagen, 14–19 April 2000.
12. S. Varró, 'Pártállam és egyház' [Party-State and Church], *Magyar Narancs*, http://www.mancs.hu.
13. The party failed to surpass the five per cent threshold at this election, and therefore the candidates did not have to choose between their political and clerical carriers.
14. When asked in an interview, the secretary of the Conference of Bishops did not deny that the listed points of view indicate a particular political party.
15. *HVG*, 5 April 2002.
16. *Népszabadság*, 29 March 2002.
17. Even the ombudsman found it unconstitutional, claiming that the sermons are not public events.
18. *Hetek*, 25 Jan. 2002.
19. The Socialist-Liberal government was deeply divided on the issue of the agreement, the Free Democrats protesting against it.
20. See at http://www.katolikus.hu/horn.html.
21. This sympathy towards small churches was reflected in the fact that the Socialist-Liberal government made it easier for communities which possessed no properties before communism to receive state support.
22. See at http://www.katolikus.hu/orban.html.
23. http://www.nkom.hu/kronikas/20001/vallasszab.shtml
24. At the moment 100 signatures suffice and religious organisations need official recognition only if they wish legal personality.
25. However, none of the churches known to be against the amendment were invited.
26. The salaries are not paid directly to the priests, but to the central administration of the churches.
27. Recent splinter groups are not eligible, with the exception of the Evangelical Brotherhood of Love. The split of this church from the Methodists was considered to be caused by external forces, i.e. by the Communist government
28. *Népszabadság*, 23 May 2001.
29. Z. Semjén, 'The Hungarian Model of Church-State Relations', in B. Schanda (ed.), *Legislation on Church-State Relations in Hungary* (Budapest: Ministry of Cultural Heritage 2002), pp.7 and 9.
30. M.G. Tamás, 'Katolikus értékek' [Catholic values], *Magyar Hírlap*, 20 Nov. 2000.
31. One of the leaders of the liberal Pax Romana commented in an interview that she was not aware of any expectations within the Catholic church that the Assumption of Mary should be celebrated by the state. She noted that these suggestions came from politicians who are Christians 'for a living', and who have no idea what Christianity is really about. *Magyar Narancs*, 'A nyáj lent, a lábai alatt.' [The flock down, under his legs], http://www.mancs.hu.
32. *Népszabadság*, 17 May 2001.
33. J. Casanova, *Public religions in the modern world* (Chicago: Chicago Press 1994).
34. Richardson, 'New religions and religious freedom', p.202 (italics in original).
35. R. Teitel, 'Partial Establishments of Religion in Post-Communist Transition', in Sajo and Avineri (eds.), *The Law of Religious Identity*, pp.103–16.
36. See R. Stark and W.S. Bainbridge, *A Theory of Religion* (New York: Peter Lang Publishing 1987); R. Finke, 'Religious Deregulation: Origins and Consequences', *Journal of Church and State* 32/3 (1990), pp.609–26; R. Finke, 'The Consequences of Religious Competition:

Supply-Side Explanations for Religious Change', in L.A. Young (ed.), *Rational Choice Theory and Religion* (New York: Routledge 1997), pp.45–64; A. Gill, *Rendering unto Caesar: The Catholic Church and the State in Latin America* (Chicago: University of Chicago Press 1998), A. Gill, 'The Politics of Regulating Religion in Mexico: The 1992 Constitutional Reforms in Historical Context' *Journal of Church and State* 41 (1999), pp.761–94.

37. K. Daniel and W.C. Durham, 'Religious Identity as a Component of National Identity: Implications for Emerging Church–State in the Former Socialist Bloc', in Sajo and Avineri (eds.), *The Law of Religious Identity*, pp.117–52.

The Catholic Church and Civil Society: Democratic Options in the Post-Communist Czech Republic

JOAN O'MAHONY

The presence or absence of civil society is increasingly regarded as an indicator of the strength of democracy in the post-Communist regimes of Eastern Europe. As the space denoting the realm of engaged autonomous citizenry, civil society is a welcome antidote to the traditional reliance on fair elections and free speech as democracy's constitutive features. Nevertheless, studies of democratisation that have taken this recent 'civic turn' often fail to tell us much about the strength of those organisations which are part of the so-called 'third sector'. As a typical example of an organisation in civil society, churches suffer from this lack of attention to the precise attributes of their new-found civic freedoms.[1] One reason for this is the tendency to place a stress on the *quantity* of associations as an adequate measurement or indicator of civil society. For example, the American institution Freedom House provides much useful comparative data on organisations in Eastern Europe but because of its generalising aims does not set out to study particular organisations in any detail.

Certainly, many approaches go beyond the quantitative and emphasise instead what many regard as the *sine qua non* of civil society – independence from the state. In these accounts civil society is regarded as present when organisations are free, or liberated, from state interference.[2] Yet the problem with this focus on independence is that while it captures one important aspect or condition of freedom – freedom from domination – it fails to capture freedom's other dimension – autonomy – the power of self-government, or the ability, as Arendt argued, to do, to create, and to act.[3] These two entwined and complementary aspects of freedom are implicitly recognised in the model of civil society advanced by Eisenstadt, who emphasises not only the independence of associations from the state but also 'the access of different sectors of society to the agencies of the state'.[4]

Studies of the realignment of churches and religious organisations in the emergent civil societies of Eastern Europe would benefit from a concern with both these features, drawing our attention not only to the weakening of state controls over church life but also to the expansion of genuine opportunities for autonomous religious action. These developments in the Czech Republic form an especially instructive case. Czechoslovakia's inter-war experiences of democracy inspired much anticipation of a rapid advance in the institutionalisation of post-Communist democracy. Yet with regard to civil society, and in comparison to Hungary, Poland, and Slovakia, the Republic has a poor record in establishing those conditions that would protect and consolidate the opportunities for sustained civic engagement.

CHURCH AND CIVIL SOCIETY IN THE CZECH REPUBLIC

The Czech Constitution adopted on 16 December 1992 declares that 'Democratic values constitute the foundation of the State, so that it may not be bound either by an exclusive ideology or by a particular religious faith'.[5] While the Constitution clearly favours a state strategy that is neutral and non-partisan towards religious organisations, it nevertheless leaves open to question what the content or details of the arrangement between state and church should be. In practice, state–church neutrality has been open to a variety of interpretations. In the United States neutrality is understood to demand the equal consignment of all religions to the private sphere, while in the Netherlands the state strives to ensure that religious organisations have equal opportunities to act in public.[6] Yet, even among those countries where church–state neutrality is understood as compatible with a public role for religion, questions about the nature of that public role, its protection, its limits, and its financing have found diverse solutions.

In the Czech Republic these substantive questions about the role of churches have arisen within the context of a broader debate about the nature of post-Communist democracy. Hadjiisky describes the two main and opposing views of democracy that have emerged in the Czech Republic as 'participatory' and 'majoritarian'.[7] The participatory model, dominant in the 1989–92 Government of Civic Forum, aims to place 'the citizen at the centre of political life by promoting various kinds of civic participation in public affairs'.[8] This model was displaced by an elite, Schumpeterian, 'winner take all' approach of the Civic Democratic Party (ODS), the main party in government from 1992 to 1997, a party firmly committed to a 'a delegative conception of democracy in which the relation between the citizen and the state is expressed through the mere act of voting'.[9] The outcome of the 1998 elections brought predictions for a more inclusive, less magisterial style of government. These expectations were modified substantially when the Social Democrats (CSSD), short of a ruling majority, signed an opposition agreement with the ODS. 'Thanks to this agreement, and despite its electoral defeat, the ODS has retained a major and very direct influence on parliamentary debates and on the government's policy.'[10]

This chapter seeks to establish and explain the extent to which the status of the Czech Catholic Church is the product of continuing attempts to institutionalise a post-Communist democratic society. In both its versions, participatory and elite, Czech democracy is resolutely liberal in its commitment to the rights-bearing citizen exercising his or her freedom in a sphere of activity, habitually referred to since the collapse of Communism, as civil society. But in the elite view, this civil society is an organised set of individual and private interests where the freedom of the citizen is wholly secured through legislation that minimises, as far as possible, the intrusions of the state. This perspective has been critically modified by the participatory approach which argues that individual freedoms are best produced when supplemented with the recognition and protection of those groups and organisations through which the individual acts. Moreover, the participationists maintain that, far from being matters of private concern, the activities of these groups are more appropriately described as public, albeit a public lying outside the state and the realm of formal government.[11]

These diverging perspectives on the conditions of freedom have important policy implications. Participationists typically argue that proper recognition of groups and associations requires the creation and preservation of the resources that allow groups to govern themselves. This can involve directing public monies away from the state and towards various publics in civil society, and can also include the involvement of civic organisations in broader public debates that concern their way of life. Democratic elitists disagree. They argue that freedom is best protected by leaving public decisions to elected representatives. Indeed, ordered and stable decision-making is only possible if these representatives are 'shielded from too much participation by the population: Citizens must, as it were, accept the division of labour between themselves and the politicians they elect'.[12]

CIVIL SOCIETY AND RELIGIOUS INDEPENDENCE

To what extent does the contemporary Czech Catholic Church fit the first of civil society's ideal typical features: independence from the state? The most immediate point of comparison is with the position of the church under Communism, and in this respect there has been much space for an expansion in religious freedom.

We have taken the Bishops' land, We have taken their press. I have put commissioners into every consistory. I have closed all the church schools. Now we are gradually taking away their churches. We are imprisoning priests. And now ... another important measure – a new wage law for priests ... We will decide who will get paid and under what conditions.[13]

This announcement in September 1949 by the General Secretary of the Czechoslovakian Communist Party, Rudolph Slansky, illustrates the conditions under which religious organisations existed until the collapse of Soviet power some 40 years later. With the exception of Albania and Russia, the Catholic Church in Czechoslovakia suffered the greatest degree of repression in the Soviet Union and Eastern Europe. While not officially banned under Communism, the churches' subjugation by the authorities was so wholly efficient as to render the church virtually obsolete. Monasteries, convents, churches, and church land were nationalised by the state. Church schools were closed and Catholics in the education system and in the workplace were discriminated against. More than 15,000 members of the religious orders were sent to prisons or camps. Bishops and priests were required to apply for state permission to practice. This was regularly refused. The church had no economic independence, and all wages to priests and bishops were paid by the state. The majority of Bishoprics remained empty and it was virtually impossible to get a place in a seminary.[14]

The revolutionary events of 1989 brought an immediate increase in religious independence. In addition to the individual rights to belief and practice guaranteed in the Constitution, Act Nr. 308 was introduced in 1991, setting out the position of the churches and religious organisations. This act ensured the extrication of the state from many of the day-to-day affairs of the church. It abolished the State Office for Religious Affairs, which was established in 1949 to supervise the activities of religious organisations. In its place, the Act guaranteed that 'Churches and religious societies administer their own affairs, in particular they establish their bodies, appoint their priests, and establish religious orders and other church institutions, independent from the organs of the state'. The law entitled churches to 'have their own press and publishing houses and printing offices' and to 'set up and operate their own health-care facilities, social care facilities and also participate in the provision of such services in the government run facilities'. Finally, the law allowed for the establishment of church schools, the right, with parental agreement, to teach religion in state schools, and the right to provide services to the religious in military establishments.[15] The

1991 Law has recently been replaced by Law Nr. 3/2002 with the intention of liberalising the process of registration for churches and consolidating the provisions in the earlier act.[16]

Outstanding Issues of Church Independence

While these changes have dramatically increased church independence, the significance of the increase is diminished by the continuing failure of successive governments to reform the economic relationship between church and state. This relationship remains governed by the Communist 1949 law which placed in the hands of the state the management of the church economy. Under this law, priests and bishops are effectively regarded as civil servants, and receive their salary from the state. Both church and government agree on the need to reform the relationship, but the matter is complicated by an agreement that the ending of direct state financing should happen in tandem with the return of church property confiscated in 1949. In 1992, a draft bill to return property to the Catholic Church failed in parliament. Ever since, the issue has been a source of dispute between the government and the Catholic Church, and today the Catholic Church continues to press for restitution.[17]

From the viewpoint of the church, the failure to secure economic independence is both practical and symbolic. Clerical salaries are small and well below the national average wage. Furthermore, salaries to bishops and priests, technically regarded as state employees, have remained the same while salaries to other state employees have increased. Important as these matters are, the issue of state financing is more than one of wages. The church's lack of funds limits its ability to pursue its religious activities. In this context, a crucial source of potential funding is the church property confiscated by the Communist regime. 'We would like to found schools and charitable institutions', explained Bishop Hrdlicka – 'the church wants to fulfil its mission and wants to have title at least to what belongs to the church'.[18] 'The church is completely free', argued Bishop Lobkowicz,

> yet there are some problems – the economic support. If a building needs to be repaired the church is required to pay for it as a foundation. The church in these instances finds it has no sources to undertake any large reparations. In the case of restitution I could sell one hectare of forest and then would have some money I could manage the property with. I could then do my own economy.[19]

Finally, restitution is important not only because of the possibilities it creates for increasing church revenue, but also because it would provide an independent source of income. The former regime's insistence on being the sole source of finance for the church was an undisguised strategy of control. And this very recent history has made the church wary of any arrangement where it is dependent on the state for funding. The restitutions are important, argues Cardinal Vlk, because 'in the past, the church has learned how dangerous it is to depend on the State, on the political power ... We want to be free. *So we have to find our own finances*'.[20]

The Failure of Church Economic Independence

The 1991 law on the position of churches failed to address the financial relationship between church and state. Ten years later, the commissions established to draft the replacement law Act Nr. 3/2002 met with a similar fate.[21] Not only does this failure contrast with the success of Poland, Slovakia, and Hungary in resolving these issues, but the failure also contrasts with the optimism expressed at the beginning of the democratic period that this matter would be swiftly resolved. Indeed, the atmosphere within the country's first post-Communist government was sufficiently positive for commentators to expect that 'by the end of 1992, prior to the implementation of tax reforms in the country, the issue of economic relations between the State and the churches will be settled'.[22]

In the light of a decade of failure to resolve the linked questions of economic independence and church restitutions, explanations have tended to emphasise the anti-Catholicism of the Czech public. This antipathy is argued to be the expression of either the historical anti-Catholicism engendered under the Austro-Hungarian Empire or the more recent history of anti-church policies under Communism. These views are prevalent among not only academics but also key protagonists in the dispute over restitution. For example, Jan Misovic argues that the lack of support for restitution is a consequence of the public's 'historical experience of Catholic activities'.[23] Cardinal Vlk explains, 'it is the heritage of the past ... Communism somehow remains in us and a certain anti-clericalism is still here even after six years',[24] and the Vice Chair of the Communist Party, commenting on the ex- Prime Minister's opposition to church restitution, remarks, 'Klaus blocked this [restitution] for many years ... because he is very sensible, *the majority of the population in the Czech Republic are against the property claims of the Catholic Church*'.[25]

The argument that church restitution has failed because 'the public' are against it should, however, be regarded with caution. Opinion polls carried out since 1991 show an average of 50 per cent or less opposed to church restitution, with this figure falling to 36 per cent by 1996.[26] Yet, importantly, the strength of opinion either in favour or against restitution is not represented in the polls. It is likely, however, that only a minority of the public have any strong opinions on restitution, for it is difficult to find evidence of much interest in the matter outside the rather narrow confines of the church or the parliamentary arena. Indeed, the lack of interest has encouraged a number of politically opposed journalists to agree on one issue – that the controversy over the restitution of church property 'has attracted scant public attention',[27] and that while 'the case about ownership ... is legally very difficult ... people are not going to talk about it in pubs (we mean voters)'.[28]

Furthermore, the suggested negative impact of Communism on support for the church may very well be double-edged. Communism could, in fact, be said to have strengthened the profile of the Catholic Church because it gave the church a much-needed opportunity to advance itself as 'defender of the nation'. Under the Habsburgs, forced Catholicisation proceeded hand-in-hand with Germanisation, and there has thus always been a feeling in the Czech lands that Catholicism, despite its being the majority religion, is also anti-national. Yet during Communism a number of key Catholic dissidents played an active role in the opposition. Frantisek Tomasek, Vaclav Maly, and Vaclav Benda are just some of the figures who became notable for the enormous respect they generated among believers and non-believers alike, allowing the reputable Radio Free Europe to remark that, after 1989, 'the Catholic Church could draw on a deep well of goodwill among Czechs and was in a strong position to re-establish itself immediately after the fall of Communism ... many people expected a reconstituted church to play a significant role in both social and political life'.[29] Today, key figures such as Vaclav Maly and Tomas Halik continue to inspire much public affection.[30]

But if church restitution has failed to ignite great passion within the public domain, this is not the case in the parliamentary arena. Since 1990 the issue has been the subject of heated debate among professional politicians and was one factor in the collapse of the coalition government in 1997.[31] As with perceptions of the public's attitude to restitution, the politicians' opposition is argued to be anti-Catholic. Bishop Maly's comment echoes that of many in the Bishops Conference:

In the minds of the politicians there are prejudices and worries that the church, if materially secure, would become a powerful institution, which would compete with the political parties ... but it is nonsense. Our church doesn't wish to renew the feudal state from the past – we are living at the end of the twentieth century and the only goal of the church is to have certain financial sources but not to be again a very powerful institution which is in competition with political parties.[32]

There are indeed grounds to support the contention that fears about Catholicism are behind the political failure to restitute property. For example, Jaromir Talir of KDU–CSL, explained: '[It] is the problem of the view of the Czech political parties on the Church. If you are talking to representatives of other political parties; CSSD and ODS, you can see that their opinion is that the Church should be poor and they should not own anything'.[33] And Miloslav Ransdorf the Vice Chair of the Communist Party, justifying the Communist opposition to restitution, explained: 'We are not against financing the activities of churches, we are against the creation of an ulterior economic basis for political clericalism in the Czech Republic'.[34] However, if deep-seated convictions of political parties are to explain the obstacles to church restitution, this argument sits uneasily with the readiness of political parties in parliament to change their position on the issue whenever narrow political gains are to be made. Throughout the period 1992–98 the only two parties that remained consistent on the issue of restitution were the Communists and the Christian Democratic Union–Czechoslovakian People's Party. (Neither of these two parties ever held the balance of power in any post-Communist government coalition). Prior to 1992 the smaller of the two Christian Democrats, Vaclav Benda's right-wing Christian Democrats (KDS), which began its political career with a firm commitment to restitution, modified its position substantially when it formed an electoral pact with Klaus' Conservative Civic Democratic Party (ODS), and throughout the government coalition held back from criticising the ODS' anti-church restitution line. The Civic Democratic Alliance (ODA) began with an anti-church restitution line and, after growing disillusionment in its partnership with Klaus, shifted its position to pro-restitution. Vaclav Klaus, the leader of ODS, led his party from an initial promise to restitute church property to belligerent refusal to discuss the matter. He subsequently agreed to restitute a small number of properties, later agreeing to restitute all property. Finally, Klaus proposed a decree that would bypass parliament to return church property but ultimately backed the Social Democrat policy to stop all church restitutions. The Social Democrats, for their part, were opposed to restitution. They modified their position on the eve of coming to power, stopped all restitutions when they came to power in autumn 1998 (on the basis that parliament was being bypassed in the decision-making), and then bypassed parliament themselves to return church property they did not want.

The constant shift in party attitudes towards the restitution issue cannot be regarded as reflecting a change in opinion on the virtues of restitution itself. Instead, the fluctuations in party position largely reflect the difficulties for post-Communist parties in building coherent party profiles. The majority of political parties in the Czech Republic are new parties with weak identities.[35] They have few roots in society and emerged at the elite level as a consequence of splits within parliament.[36] As a result, political parties in the Czech Republic face the challenge of building their constituencies from the top down, a process that is intensified by the fact that many of the parties are very similar. For example, Mateju and Vlachova's research into the role of political attitudes and values in electoral decisions concluded that 'both parties [ODS and ODA] are the virtual and ideological twins of the Czech political scene', and that the similarities are so strong 'that it is virtually impossible to model the choice between them'.[37] A similar potential for rivalry faces the Social Democrats and the Christian Democratic Union (KDU–CSL); 61 per cent of KDU–CSL supporters put themselves at the centre and 60 per cent of Social Democrat supporters also see themselves as being centrist.[38]

With the ODA and the ODS appealing to the same sectors of the electorate and the CSSD and KDU–CSL marked by a similar rivalry, it became necessary for these parties to establish themselves in society while, at the same time, distinguishing themselves from each other. The issue of church restitution offered the parties an opportunity to do this: an opportunity to build distinct publics. Although the public was not especially interested in church restitutions, the issue nevertheless gave the parties an opportunity to build their identities in opposition to each other. Church restitution was the 'political football' that allowed KDU–CSL to be characterised as the Vatican's representatives and the Social Democrats as Communist fanatics who wanted, as Klaus warned, 'to turn the clock back'. Indeed, Klaus recommended in his pro-restitution phase that all those who wanted to live in freedom should vote for ODS.[39]

In sum, a 'politics of demonisation' aptly describes much of political interaction in the Czech Republic. The lack of 'normal' political debate became a frequent subject of disapproval by both politicians and the public. The Czech sociologist Jiri Pehe captured the mood well in his comment that political culture would be best served 'if politicians started to focus on matter-of-fact discussion on various topics, if they stopped moving in an artificially created reality of myths which they themselves create and with which they expediently scare the society'.[40] In this context, the possibility of resolving the issue of church restitution through reasoned discussion was greatly reduced. When taken up at the level of the state, differences over the role of religion and the role of the church became assimilated to the more narrow concerns of parliamentarians. Ultimately, the line-up of political forces and their competing interests account for the church's slow progress in developing economic independence. Politics, not anti-Catholic attitudes, is the crucial and dynamic factor in explaining the church's continued reliance on the state.

RELIGIOUS AUTONOMY AND THE POLITICAL SPHERE

Although compromised by its failure to secure economic freedom, the church's position with respect to the major ideal-typical feature of civil society – independence from the state – can be judged to have improved significantly. But Eisenstadt reminds us that:

> It is not just the existence of multiple autonomous social sectors ... that is of crucial importance for the foundation and continuous functioning of democracies. Rather, it is the existence of institutional and ideological links between these sectors and the state.

One of the 'most important of these links', Eisenstadt maintains, has been 'the major institutionalised networks of political representation (legislatures and political parties)'.

In the Czech Republic, religious organisations have had little access to the political arena; their overriding experience has been one of exclusion from debates about their status, future, or financing. Although a commission was established to consider these issues, the commission, up until the election of the Social Democrats in 1998, either failed to meet, or made little progress when it did, mainly because of the lack of commitment on the part of the ODS representatives. Debates about the restitution of church property took place with little input from church officials. The result was a church increasingly distressed by the frequent exclusion from those decision-making processes that directly affected them. By early 1997, persistent expressions of concern from the church turned to more pointed disapproval, with the Cardinal publicly criticising Klaus' government for failing to engage in direct talks with the church on the restitution of lands and building seized by the Communists.[41] Certainly, since coming to power the Social Democrats have adopted a more inclusive style than the Klaus government, as is shown, at the least, in a greater commitment to the state–church commission. At the same time, the final version of Law 2002 was clearly an unwelcome surprise to the religious delegates on the commissions, raising questions about just how effective the new inclusive approach is.

The church's inability to have an impact on policy making either through direct linkages with the state or via the influence of political parties is perhaps most usefully examined in the context of a politics of exclusion experienced by virtually all civic organisations in the Czech Republic.[42] The success of this politics of exclusion is ultimately explained by reference to the structural legacies of the transition. As argued in the preceding pages, the prospects of a rational, coherent resolution to restitution were greatly reduced by the speed of the 'transition' and its impact on the parliamentary arena. This argument can be extended to explain the lack of access civic organisations have to the state, either directly or via the mediation of political parties. In the case of the newer political parties, the argument needs no revision to explain the paucity of links that parties have with social groups. The very speed with which Communism collapsed in Czechoslovakia, and the rapidity of the transition to a parliamentary democracy, did not give aspiring politicians enough time to develop constituencies within society. This readily accounts for the existence of parties like the ODS and the ODA, who have little contact with civic organisations and, in comparison with the Communists or KDU–CSL, a modest party membership.[43]

One problem with this description is that it fails to explain why those parties that are not 'new parties', for example, the Communist Party or KDU–CSL, nevertheless experience similar difficulties to the ODS and the ODA in consolidating their constituencies. But in the case of these older established parties the impact of the transition is relevant not so much for its impact on the parliamentary arena, but more for its impact on the Czech social structure. Here, constituencies in Czech society which were once regarded as stable have been thrown into disarray by the rapid change engendered by the events of 1989. Miloslav Ransdorf, the Vice Chair of the Communist Party, commenting on the weak links his party had with trade unions, remarked: 'It is not so simple because this period of socio-economic change was a time of huge social transformation. Can you imagine that 40 per cent of people in our country changed their jobs? ... So Czech social structure is not as in other countries of Eastern Europe ... not so settled.'[44]

Apart from the impact on electoral constituents, the de-structuration in society also, unsurprisingly, has its effects on Communist Party members, a process that has implications for the identity of the party itself. Almost as compensation for his party's failure to establish links with traditional worker groups, Ransdorf commented: 'But we try to spread our influence in all strata of population. We have also many, many entrepreneurs in our structure because many of our members and former members of the party have no chance to survive only to become entrepreneurs.'

In the case of a long established party like the Communist Party, it is likely that the effects of the speed of transition were first felt in the social sphere and then later in the political arena. Where the new parties began with uncertain identities and then went on to face the difficulties of establishing constituencies in a society suffering severe social dislocation, the scenario was the reverse for older parties. The older parties started with clear identities and a certain confidence as to their constituencies, a confidence that gradually became disrupted as the changes in society worked their way to the party level. On the whole, this worked against the quick and easy formation of links between social groups and political parties.

This interaction between a shifting social structure and the frenzied development of Parliament does much to explain the poor relationship the church has with political parties. Immediately after 1989, the most natural allies of the Catholic Church were the two Christian parties: the Christian Democratic Party (Vaclav Benda's CDP) and the Christian Democratic Union–Czechoslovak People's Party (Lux's KDU–CSL). The Christian Democratic Party was a breakaway party from Civic Forum and, as such, was one of the 'new' political aspirants. It failed to survive, as did many of the new groups on the political scene across Eastern Europe; a weak party with few roots in society, it merged with the ODS at the end of Klaus' first election term.

However, the KDU–CSL, also a Christian party, had little in common with its namesake, the Christian Democratic Union (CDP). Far from being a new organisation, the KDU–CSL has the distinction of being one of Czechoslovakia's oldest surviving political parties. Where other parties after 1989 had to re-evaluate the profile of their constituents, by all indicators the KDU–CSL was and is in a stronger position than other parties to maintain its traditional voter base. The supporters of the KDU–CSL, unlike the supporters of the Communists, are less likely to be forced by a revolutionised labour market to radically rethink their social identities. KDU party membership has remained reasonably stable, and membership at the parliamentary level was relatively untouched by the phenomenon of political tourism. Indeed, of all the party clubs in the Czech parliament, the KDU–CSL reveals itself to be the most stable, losing none of its parliamentary members in the lengthy period after the 1992 election which was characterised by endless splits and defections among parties. All told, the conditions described earlier as working against establishing linkages between parties and social constituencies were not relevant in the case of a party like the KDU–CSL.

Nevertheless, despite forecasts of a mutually beneficial relationship, which to an extent were fulfilled in the early years of the new democracy, the contemporary evidence is that both the KDU and the church are anxious to annul any perception of a close relationship between them. Jaromir Talir, KDU's ex-Minister of Culture commented: 'I have to say that this problem is difficult for our party. Our political rivals are trying to introduce our party as a party which does not have any other political programs, just this.' And Daniel Herman, spokesman for the Bishops Conference explained: 'You know this link [with KDU–CSL] is very very bad for us ... it is also based on experience ... that to co-operate only with one party will be counterproductive ... today we know that, but nine years ago, it was without any experience, any precedent.' Equally, for Talir, the KDU–CSL's efforts to represent the interests of the churches had brought certain disadvantages:

> When KDU pushes on this problem, its political rivals use this for its
> discreditation. In all elections all our rivals are saying to voters not to
> vote KDU–CSL, this is a party only for old people, for Catholics and
> they do not know anything else than to take care of the restitutions.[45]

Conditions were good for the KDU–CSL for making links with groups in civil society; it was not one of the many 'new parties' and nor was its constituents dramatically affected by the social upheaval wrought by the collapse of a command economy. The problem for the KDU–CSL lay not with its own party identity but with the lack of an identity for its competitors in parliament which were struggling to build coherent party profiles. And what ultimately made the creation of links between KDU and the church difficult was the energy devoted by other parties to portraying co-operation between the KDU and the church as a bad thing. In an attempt to forge their own identities by demonising the opposition, parties without a clear voter base concentrated on a 'we are not what you are' politics.

State–Church Links: Politics in a Vacuum

Political parties in the Czech Republic are a weak means for organisations to have an impact on political society. Yet this in itself does not preclude the possibility of an invitation from the state for organisations to participate more directly in the policy-making process, either through the creation of commissions or by representation on parliamentary committees.

Throughout the Klaus period, initiatives in this regard were not taken in the Czech Republic, but it is not possible to attribute this to a broad-based political opposition to organisations. Virtually all parties with the exception of the Civic Democratic Party (ODS) were keen to deepen democracy by encouraging the development and participation of interest groups. In fact, the anti-organisation stance was only ever strongly adopted by Klaus.

Klaus' views on politics are well known. He rejects civil society, arguing that 'we voted for something else. We voted for a democratic society whose bedrock is *individual* freedom ... The advocates of civil society think it necessary to increase the role of direct democracy. I disagree'.[46]

He has made the point clear elsewhere: 'My polemic is about a market without adjectives, a standard system of political parties, without a national front or civic movements.'[47] 'It is only these [parliamentary] institutions', Klaus argues, 'that can represent us, the citizens, because we elected them in democratic election.' He then adds somewhat rhetorically: 'Should the state ... allow people to sponsor non-profit-making organisations and be relieved from taxation and thus deprive the state of taxes that are truly beneficial for the majority?'[48] His goal was 'to stop deep-rooted government interference in the economy, to block popular redistributional practices, to dissolve dangerous lobbying, rent-seeking, protectionist organisations and pressure groups and so on'.[49]

His views are supported by Miroslava Nemcova, the former minister responsible for church affairs in the ODS-dominated governing coalition.

> According to my belief, civil society arises from the voluntary and free want of citizens, who ... with use of their own sources will try to somehow fulfil, organise and finance their goal. And this process starts by itself, without someone – the state – somehow instigating or putting in place this process. I think the civil society should come out from this, the free desire of citizens. *They should not strive for a part in state power.* State power arises from election, decisions of free citizens, who elect in a democracy, democratic representatives.[50]

Given the dominance of the ODS in the government from 1992 to 1997, Klaus' efforts at translating his particular model of society into reality have been remarkably successful. The ODS' power to block moves to widen access to government was unchallenged. Attempts by coalition or opposition groups to create opportunities for citizens or groups to air their concerns were persistently opposed by Klaus. Indeed, the coalition agreed on a number of occasions that the parties would negotiate on the church property issue, but the ODS' lack of commitment ensured that the State–Church Commission rarely met.

CONCLUSION

'Democracy', Dryzek and Holmes remind us, 'is not just something that arrives as a universal package in 1989, erasing the past.'[51] 'What democracy means in particular places depends to a considerable extent on the prevailing constellation of discourses, as well as the configuration of constitutional and material circumstances.'[52] In Eastern Europe, the often undifferentiated category of civil society has increasingly become a prism through which researchers analyse the development, growth, and institutions of autonomous action. As a political idea, civil society is subject to significantly different interpretations about the appropriate relationship between the citizen and the state. In the Czech Republic this space for opposing interpretations is guaranteed by a Constitution that dictates only that the state 'may not be bound ... by a particular religious faith'. An 'active' or 'passive' neutrality towards religious organisations is neither endorsed nor proscribed. As such, what state impartiality might mean in practice has become politically contested. In the case of church–state relations in the Czech Republic, success in applying the 'passive' approach is explained by political failure to make meaningful headway in the institutionalisation of a civil society; a failure that brought with it numerous attacks on many independent organisations, and not just the organisation of the Catholic Church.

This failure to strengthen Czech civil society is clearly located in the political programme of the Klaus administration and its post-Communist concerns to limit power to the parliament, and more particularly to the executive, where it had a dominant position. Yet Klaus' success in achieving his programme is more than simply ideological. The rapidity of the 'transition' disrupted the Czechoslovakian social structure. The resulting structural vacuum allowed the easy implementation of a radical ideology by a political entrepreneur who faced little opposition from parliamentary colleagues unable to find 'partners' in a post-Communist atomised society.

NOTES

1. The argument that only wholly democratic groups should be included in the definition of civil society makes the mistake of conflating questions about the institutional features of civil society with questions about the *potential* functions of its organisational members. Whether or not Catholic churches can contribute to the development or consolidation of democracy is a largely empirical question, and one that is not addressed here. Elsewhere I have argued that that in the case of the *Czech* Catholic Church, the elites of that organisation are firmly democratic and keen to contribute to the elaboration of democratic norms and institutions in the Czech Republic. J. O'Mahony, 'The Catholic Church and the Spirit of Democracy: Religious Elites in the Post-Communist Czech Republic', Political Studies Association Annual Conference, Aberdeen, 5–7 April 2000.
2. See e.g. R.A. Dahl, *Democracy and Its Critics* (London: Yale University Press 1989).

3. See the discussion on Arendt in A. Stewart, *Theories of Power and Domination* (London: Sage 2001).
4. S.N. Eisenstadt, 'Civil Society', in S.M. Lipset (ed.), *The Encyclopaedia of Democracy* (London: Routledge 1995), p.240.
5. Article 2 (1) General Provisions, Chapter One, Charter of Fundamental Rights and Basic Freedoms adopted under Article 3 of the Czech Constitution as a part of the constitutional order of the Czech Republic. 16 Dec. 1992. See the Czech parliament's website at www.psp.cz.
6. See S. Monsma and J. Soper, *The Challenge of Pluralism: Church and State in Five Democracies* (United States: Rowman & Littlefield 1997).
7. M. Hadjiisky, 'The Failure of the Participatory Democracy in the Czech Republic', *West European Politics* 24/3 (July 2001), pp.43–64. A similar distinction is drawn by M. Potucek, 'The Uneasy Birth of Czech Civil Society', *Voluntas: International Journal of Voluntary and Non-profit Organisations* 11/2 (2000), pp.107–22, and by R. Marada, 'Civil Society: Adventures of the Concept before and after 1989', *Czech Sociological Review* 5/1 (1997), pp.3–22. See also J.S. Dryzek and L. Holmes, 'The Real World of Civic Republicanism: Making Democracy Work in Poland and the Czech Republic', *Europe–Asia Studies* 52/6 (2000), pp.1043–68.
8. Hadjiisky, 'The Failure of the Participatory Democracy in the Czech Republic', p.45. In his article, Marada notes that there were distinct developmental stages in the articulation of a Czech participatory model; a pre-1989 phase, the 1989 to 1992 phase, and a third phase after 1994. Marada, 'Civil Society: Adventures of the Concept before and after 1989'.
9. Hadjiisky, 'The Failure of the Participatory Democracy in the Czech Republic', p.58.
10. Hadjiisky, 'The Failure of the Participatory Democracy in the Czech Republic', p.60. However, the Social Democrats (CSSD) emerged as the victors in the June 2002 elections with 70 seats against the ODS's 58. The CSSD are widely expected to enter an agreement with the coalition partners, Freedom Union–Democratic Union (US–DEU) and the Christian Democrats (KDU–CSL), whose combined total of 31 seats can give the CSSD control of parliament.
11. Indeed, as Hirst argues, this is increasingly the case in Western Europe, where civic organisations undertake an ever-expanding range of governing functions. P. Hirst, *From Statism to Pluralism* (London: UCL Press Ltd 1997). See also Monsma and Soper, who note in their research that 'the religious communities of all five countries considered in it are concerned with a wide range of public policy questions and are active in providing education, health care, and other social services'. *The Challenge of Pluralism*, p.9.
12. J. Cohen and A. Arato, *Civil Society and Political Theory* (Cambridge, MA: MIT 1992), p.6.
13. Slansky, quoted by L. Motycka, MP, in a speech proposing a draft bill to return property to the church. *Lidove Democracie*, 16 March 1992.
14. See P. Ramet (ed.), *Catholicism and Politics in Communist Societies* (USA: Duke University Press 1990); J. Cuhra, *Církevní Politika KSC a Státu v Letech 1969–1972* (Communist Policy towards the Churches in Czechoslovakia) (Praha 1999); E. Clark, 'Church–State Relations in the Czech Republic: Past Turmoil and Present Transformation', *Brigham Young University Law Review* 4 (1996), pp.1019–85.
15. See Articles 5, 6, and 9 of 'The Act on the freedom of religious faith and the position of churches and religious societies Nr. 308 of 4 July 1991'. The act can be viewed at http://spcp.prf.cuni.cz/aj/308-91en.htm.
16. These recent legal developments have proved unstable. The 2002 Law has sparked a new series of controversies. The most problematic aspect for the Catholic Church is that 'under this law churches are not allowed to establish philanthropic organizations and charities as an integral part of the church, but have to register them as separate civic enterprises'. Karel Nowak, President of the Seventh-day Adventist Church in the Czech Republic, cited at http://gbgm-umc.org/ mission_Programs/ecg/2.19/czech/latest_news.htm. It is unclear what the implications of this are for the traditional areas of church life, but there is sufficient ambiguity for the bill to have had substantial opposition. It was rejected by a majority of the Senate, President Havel attempted a veto of the bill, and on its final reading three of the four main opposition parties, the KDU–CSL, the Freedom Union, and the Communists voted against it. The Czech Ecumenical Council and the Catholic Church have lodged a joint appeal for a review of the legislation with the Constitutional Court. The churches and others

also oppose the Bill on the grounds that the registration system continues to discriminate against smaller religious groups. see 'Act Nr.3/2002 Coll on freedom of religious confession and the position of churches and religious societies and on the changes of some legal acts (Law on churches and religious societies' at http://spcp.prf.cuni.cz/aj/3-02en.htm.

17. The Communist state owned approximately 96% of real estate and property in Czechoslovakia. Three restitution laws were introduced between October 1991 and May 1991 returning businesses, industries, apartment buildings, houses, and land to their former owners. On the recommendation of Vaclav Klaus, the then Federation's Minister of Finance, church claims were removed from the draft legislation. Klaus announced his support for church restitutions in principle, but argued that the introduction of legislation for the return of church property should be done in conjunction with the ending of state funding to the churches. The general restitution laws passed so far contain blocking articles intended to prevent the state from selling to third parties properties, which the churches claim as their own.

18. Bishop Hrdlicka of Olomouc, interview with author, Nov. 1998.

19. Bishop Lobkowicz of Ostrava, interview with author, Nov. 1998.

20. Cardinal Miloslav Vlk, Cardinal of Prague, transcript of interview, Esras Film Archives: Dublin, June 1993.

21. This is in spite of the fact that one of the central intentions of the commissions was to address this issue. But eventually it was agreed to postpone the financial discussions to a later date because of the difficulties in coming to an agreement on an appropriate model of financing.

22. E.g. the optimistic approach of P. Martin 'The New Law on Freedom of Religion and the Churches', *Report on Eastern Europe* 36/17 (1991), 6 Sept. 1991.

23. J. Misovic, 'Czech Confidence in the Church in Comparison with Other Institutions', *Church–State Relations in Central and Eastern Europe* (Poland: Zaklad Wydawniczy, Nomos 1999), p.316.

24. Reuter News Service – Eastern Europe, 16 Aug. 1996

25. Miloslav Ransdorf, Vice Chair of the Communist Party, interview with author, Oct. 1998.

26. Polls by the Institute of Public Opinion Research August 1991 and February 1993. A poll carried out by the Czech Newspaper *Denni Telegraph* concluded that almost half of the respondents thought that all or some of the church's property should be returned to it. Another poll in 1996, again by the Institute of Public Opinion Research (IVVM), showed that a majority of respondents were in favour of restitution. Less than half were opposed to any church restitution: 21% supported partial restitution; 17% favoured restitution of all post-1948 seizures and another 7% favoured restitutions dating back to the First Republic.

27. Jan Oberman and Pavel Mates, beginning a commentary in one of the (generally pro-restitution) Radio Free Europe reports: 'Czech Republic debates return of church property', *RFE/RL Research Report*, 2/19, 7 May 1993, p.46.

28. Kauza Vik in the (generally anti-restitution) satirical journal *Nevidelny Pes* (Underground Dog), (30 July 1996).

29. S. Kettle, 'Church–State Standoff', *Transitions*, Radio Free Europe, 14 July 1995, p.22.

30. Despite support for key religious figures, general trends following the collapse of Communism show a declining interest in institutionalised Catholicism. In line with his general argument, Misovic attributes this decline to the church's pursuit of restitution. The recent census figures certainly support the argument of a decline showing a drop in the numbers of those claiming membership of the Catholic Church from 39% in early 1991 to just over 26% in March 2001. Dramatic as the drop is, the argument that it can be explained by reference to restitution is difficult to reconcile with the drop in support for other churches not involved in restitution claims. Indeed the recent census shows a slightly greater drop in support for those churches *not* involved in the restitution controversies. The figures are a drop in membership of 32.6% for the Catholic Church, 32.8% for the Evangelical Church of Czech Brethren, and 45.9% for the Hussite Church. Figures at the website of the Czech Statistical Office, www.czco.cz.

31. The fact that politicians may place far greater emphasis on an issue than the public is not unusual. Here, Jean Cohen and Andrew Arato's account of the elite model of democracy captures contemporary Czech political practice well. On the elite view, 'There is no pretense … that voters either set the political agenda or make political decisions; they neither generate issues nor choose policies. Rather, leaders (political parties) aggregate interests and decide which are to become politically salient. Moreover they select issues and structure public

opinion' (p.5) 'On this model societal interests cannot be represented. Neither public opinion nor raw individual interests find representation in the political system', p.608; J. Cohen and A. Arato, *Civil Society and Political Theory* (USA: MIT 1992). The break-up of Czechoslovakia in December 1992 is a case in point. The premiers of Slovakia and Czechia, Meciar and Klaus, refused to hold a referendum on the dissolution of the Czechoslovakian state amid clear calls for one and in the face of numerous polls showing majority preferences for an alternative solution. O. Krejci, *Kniha O Volbach* (Book about voting) (Praha: Victoria Publishing 1994), pp.271–2.

32. Bishop Vaclav Maly of Prague, Interview with author, Nov. 1998.
33. Jaromir Talir, ex-Minister of Culture, KDU–CSL, interview with author, Nov. 1998
34. Miloslav Ransdorf, Vice Chair of the Communist Party, interview with author, Oct. 1998.
35. See M. Klima, 'Consolidation and Stabilization of the Party System in the Czech Republic', *Political Studies* 46 (1998), p.498.
36. E.g., the ODA, the ODS, and Benda's KDS were successor parties to the broad-based Civic Forum.
37. P. Mateju and K. Vlachova, 'Values and Electoral Decisions in the Czech Republic', *Communist and Post Communist Studies* 31/3 (1998), p.264. See also P. Kopecky, 'Factionalism in Parliamentary Parties in the Czech Republic: A Concept and some Empirical Findings', *Democratisation* 2/1 (1995), pp.138–51. Kopecky's research shows no difference between the policies of Klaus' Civic Democratic Party and Kalvoda's Civic Democratic Alliance. (Interestingly in the analysis of what are the relevant considerations in voting decisions, church restitution or religion in general do not feature.)
38. Klima, 'Consolidation and Stabilization of the Party System in the Czech Republic', p.494, Table X.
39. Klaus, cited by Jiri Pehe, CTK (Czech News Agency), 7 May 1998.
40. Jiri Pehe, quotation from CTK (Czech News Agency), 7 May 1998.
41. *The Tablet*, 8 Feb. 1997.
42. See e.g. D. Novotny, *Une Dangerouse Meprise* (Paris: G. Wern 1996). Between 1992 and 1998, trade unions, media organisations, and environmental groups were the subject of numerous attacks by Klaus, the leader of the governing ODS party. This fact alone should guard against privileging the anti-Catholic factor.
43. The Communist Party is clearly not a new political aspirant. Where the strongest party, Klaus' Civic Democratic Party (ODS), had a membership of 22,000 in 1996, the Communist Party figure was over nine times that, with a declared membership of around 200,000; the highest of any party in the Czech Republic. The Christian and Democratic Union–Czechoslovak People's Party had an 80,000 membership figure, the Social Democrats 13,000, and the Civic Democratic Association 2,500. *Lidove Noviny*, 16 April 1996.
44. Miloslav Ransdorf, Vice Chair of the Communist Party, interview with author, Oct. 1998. 'In the year between May 1994 and May 1995, the proportion of Communist voters who described themselves as workers fell from 22.5 per cent to 15.9 per cent, and as employees from 27.5 per cent to 14.3 per cent, while those above the pension age rose from 28.0 per cent to a huge 59.1 per cent.' Figures from Rude Pravo, cited by Kettle, 'Church–State Standoff', p.73.
45. Jaromir Talir, ex-Minister for Culture, KDU–CSL, and Fr. Daniel Herman, Spokesman for the Czech Catholic Church, interviews with author, Nov. 1998.
46. V. Klaus in a discussion with President Havel aired on Czech Television on 25 May 1994. Reprinted in part in *Journal of Democracy* 7/1 (Jan. 1996), p.18 (emphasis added).
47. V. Klaus, 'Snahy o hledani treti cesty stale nekonci' (Attempts to fine the Third Way are ongoing), *Lidove Noviny*, 7 March 1994, p.1.
48. V. Klaus, 'Cim vice neziskovych organizaci, tim vice demockracie! (The more non-profitable organization the greater the democracy!), *Lidove Noviny*, 16 May 1994, p.5 – a criticism of what Klaus sees as the 'privileging' of the term 'non-profit'.
49. V. Klaus, 'Dismantling Socialism: A Preliminary Report', the 1991 John Bonython Lecture, The Regent of Sydney (Centre for Independent Studies, 25 July 1991), p.2.
50. Miroslava Nemcova, Shadow Minister of Culture ODS, interview with author, Nov. 1998.
51. Dryzek and Holmes, 'The Real World of Civic Republicanism', p.1044.
52. Ibid., p.1064.

The Policy Impact of Church–State Relations: Family Policy and Abortion in Britain, France, and Germany

MICHAEL MINKENBERG

The ongoing process of European integration has led to an historically unprecedented degree of harmonisation of political, legal, and economic matters across the EU member countries. The peak of this development for the time being has been the replacement of national currencies by a common European currency in most member countries in 2002. While this process has also reached part of the cultural arena, such as the mass media, it has made little progress in the field of religion and politics, and in particular regarding church–state relations. So far, only a few trends of convergence are detectable, such as the basic recognition of the principle of religious freedom in the laws of the community, beginning with the 1976 decision of the European Court of Justice.[1] But the member countries' church law has largely been ignored by the European Union. Thus, the patterns of church–state relations have remained rather diverse from country to country and contrast sharply with both the current level of economic standardisation and previous levels of ecclesiastical harmonisation especially in the days before the Protestant Reformation.

Nonetheless, the growing body of literature on church and state in Western Europe and beyond is full of efforts to systematise and categorise the multitude of patterns of church–state relations. Much of the literature relies on traditional distinctions between three basic types: the state church type which is characterised by a close relationship between state power and church existence on the one hand; the type of strict separation between state and church on the other; and a third type in between in which the idea of separation is modified by some overlap of state and church, thus resulting in the preservation of particular privileges of the main churches. Often Great Britain, or more specifically England (along with the Scandinavian countries), is presented as the prime case representing the first type of a state church, while France is quoted as the embodiment of the opposite type, the 'separationist' model; finally, the most prominent example for the third type is Germany.[2]

This study takes a closer look at these typologies, their underlying rationale, and their usefulness. More specifically, the purpose of this study is to examine varieties of state–church relations and assess their utility in terms of how and to what extent they shape political outcomes. Rather than addressing the question of the impact of secularisation or other historical forces and patterns on the relationship between church and state and treating it as a dependent variable,[3] the study attempts to comparatively analyse church–state relations in Western Europe as an independent variable. By doing so, it follows an institutionalist perspective which is 'enlightened' (von Beyme) in so far as it takes issue with older conceptualisations such as the view that institutions are only 'arenas' for the struggle of more 'primary' forces (such as class interests) or that they are the mere reflection of their social and political environment.[4] Instead, they are seen as relatively autonomous and coherent actors which not only create order and organise chaos but also provide symbols and thus 'interpretive coherence' to politics.[5] Accordingly, church–state relations represent an institutional arrangement which provides an 'opportunity structure' for religious interests in the political process and as such they determine to some extent whether churches, as political actors, operate as public institutions or as interest groups.

In this light, the study tests the proposition that patterns of church–state relations have an impact on public policy outputs. In particular, it addresses the question whether a clear-cut institutional separation of church and state leads to identifiable patterns of public policy in those areas where religious values and interests are clearly involved. This is done, first, by examining a variety of typologies of church–state relations in terms of their adequacy for and application to Western European democracies and in particular to the three largest countries, Britain, France, and Germany, which in conventional accounts represent the three basic types of church–state relations. The second step involves an analysis of relevant social policies, that is, family policy and abortion regimes.[6] The principal argument is that state–church relations matter with regard to policy outputs but mainly in conjunction with other variables. Taken alone, patterns of church–state relations as conceptualised in the 'inherited' typology show a limited relevance for policy outputs. The match can be improved by both using more developed typologies and adding cultural and political variables, such as distinctive traditions (like *laïcisme* in France) and confessional patterns, on the one hand, and distinct political contexts in which churches operate as public institutions (as in Britain and Germany) or as interest groups (as in France), on the other. Ultimately, these cultural and political contexts are embedded in processes of modernisation and secularisation which, as José Casanova observes, can enhance the public role and political impact of churches if they succeed in combining the religious message with a defence of modern values and liberal democracy and if they operate as society-oriented, rather than state-oriented, institutions.[7]

PATTERNS OF CHURCH–STATE RELATIONS: CONCEPTS AND EMPIRICAL FINDINGS

Conceptual efforts to categorise church–state relations are often based on constitutional criteria and begin with the basic difference between a close relationship between and a separation of church and state (see above). But constitutions alone are rather misleading and inaccurate guides to political reality. Even before the breakdown of state socialism in Eastern Europe, almost all of the world's constitutions explicitly proclaimed a guarantee of basic human rights, including religious freedom. Moreover, the constitutions of various countries of rather different regime type and cultural tradition, such as Germany, Colombia, Ireland, and the Islamic nations, contain an invocation of God, but it is questionable that they are all similarly authentic references.[8] Clearly, constitutions are one source for specifying church–state relationships, but even if they were accurate and authentic, the reality of the relationship lies deeper than constitutional statements and principles.

Current classifications of church–state relations in Western democracies must operate on the basis of the churches' historic decision (after 1945) to principally accept the idea of liberal democracy including the notion of human rights and religious freedom. In this light, one must distinguish two dimensions of the debate, one being normative, the other one empirical. Many texts more or less explicitly include the question of desirability of a strict separation and its implications for basic civil rights or democracy altogether. Here, the opinions differ significantly. After his historical overview of the relationship between church and state in 2000 years of European and Western history, Reinhard Zippelius concludes that the Jeffersonian model of a 'wall of separation' most adequately realises the prerequisites of religious freedom, whereas Christian Starck lauds the Basic Law's arrangement of partial establishment of the big churches and criticises the Constitutional Court's decision to draw a sharper distinction between state and church by not allowing the crucifix in public schools if parents, students, or teachers object.[9] In a similar vein, Stephen Monsma and J. Christopher Soper criticise the US Supreme Court's decisions on the separation of church and state as betraying the true nature of the First Amendment and conclude that Germany is a model case: 'Germany and the Netherlands have a far more expansive and, we contend, appropriate understanding of religious liberty than England, the United States or Australia.'[10]

It is important, as Monsma and Soper argue, to separate the issue of religious freedom from the church–state relationship rather than using it as an indicator. But their operationalisation of this relationship remains unclear. Their normative ideal of an appropriate relationship between state and church rests on their concept of a government's 'positive neutrality' in religious matters as exemplified for example in the German practice. Positive neutrality means that the state is not simply neutral towards religious communities but grants them certain privileges which are justified by a recognition of a positive role of religion in the country's public life. Thus, the authors use a yardstick which is in principle biased against any laicist arrangement such as in France, or, to a lesser degree, in Italy, Portugal, and Spain.[11] It is no accident that none of the Catholic countries were included in Monsma and Soper's analysis and that the French debate on *laïcité* and secularisation, not just in France, but in all Western societies, is largely ignored.[12] Moreover, by excluding Catholic countries from their analysis, the authors miss the opportunity to discuss the different dynamics of secularisation and laicisation as they have occurred in Protestant and in Catholic countries, and accompanying conflicts over issues such as religious freedom.[13]

For the present purposes, more empirically oriented efforts at operationalising the state–church relationship for comparative analysis need to be considered. However, the social and political sciences do not offer much in this respect. Many empirically oriented comparisons focus heavily on legal aspects. One such approach is suggested by Gerhard Robbers, who categorises state–church relations largely in constitutional and legal terms reflecting the degree of separation between church and state. He proposes three basic types: state church systems (Denmark, England, Greece, Sweden and Finland), a system of strict separation (France without Alsace and the Netherlands, but also Ireland) and a system of common tasks (Austria, Belgium, Germany, Italy, Portugal, Spain).[14] This is mirrored by Maurice Barbier, who uses as a yardstick the approximation to the French concept of *laïcité*, or constitutional separation of church and state, but with diverging results. He classifies Western European countries into the following cases: laicist (France); quasi-laicist (Italy, Spain, Portugal); semi-laicist (Belgium, Germany, Ireland, Luxembourg, the Netherlands); or non-laicist (Denmark, England, Greece).[15]

These concepts offer some insights, but they ignore some of the problems constitutional criteria raise (see above). In general, much of the existing body of literature is characterised by the fact that the various approaches are either built on a single dimension (like constitutional separation) or a small number of indicators, or they involve a broad variety of indicators but do not sufficiently distinguish between causes and effects in the church–state relationship, or the difference between the institutional arrangement itself and its political outcome. One such example is provided by Francis Messner, who uses as criteria the legal recognition of churches and denominations (or *législation cultuelle*) in the European Union and the consequence of such legislation for religious sects.[16] His index includes questions on whether there is religious instruction in public schools, freedom of religious organisation, religious care for military persons and prisoners, acceptance of religious marriage.[17] With this procedure, he arrives at four types of regimes: open universal regimes where there is no discrimination against small sects (France without Alsace, Ireland, the Netherlands); pluralistic regimes where there is a pluralism of churches and recognition with little discrimination (Alsace in France, Belgium, Luxembourg); hegemonic regimes with specially privileged churches and some discrimination (Austria, Germany, Italy, Spain); and closed regimes with only one official church (Denmark, Finland, Sweden as well as Greece, Portugal, the United Kingdom).

While Robbers' and Barbier's classifications are rather narrowly construed along constitutional criteria, Messner's operationalisation contains a variety of measures such as marriage laws or religious education in schools which for the purpose of policy analysis should be included in the dependent variable rather than the independent variable. In fact, very few approaches to conceptualise church–state relations overcome these shortcomings while at the same time attempting to cover the whole of Western democracies or, at least, Western Europe. A more robust operationalisation which involves political, economic, and juridical criteria but avoids mere historical or legalistic accounts and leaves room to distinguish between an institutional church–state relationship and its political outcomes is suggested by Mark Chaves and David E. Cann.[18] Their article is part of a larger ongoing debate in the US literature on how to understand and explain secularisation, which need not be discussed here.[19] However, their six-item index of church–state relations, measured by the degree of regulation or deregulation, seems useful because it avoids the problem of choosing a single dichotomy or continuum of 'established religion' vs. 'separation of state and church' which underlies others' typologies such as those of Gerhard Robbers and Roland Robertson.[20] In particular, the six items measure whether or not (a) there is a single, officially recognised state church; (b) there is official state recognition of some denominations but not others; (c) the state appoints or approves the appointment of church leaders; (d) the state directly pays church personnel salaries; (e) there is a system of ecclesiastical tax collection; (f) the state directly subsidises, beyond mere tax breaks, the operation, maintenance, or capital expenses of churches.[21] The result of this index is the classification of countries into categories which will be termed here as 'deregulation' or 'separation' (0 or 1 points: Ireland, the Netherlands, France), 'partial regulation' or 'partial establishment' (with 2 points: Austria, Spain, Portugal,[22] or 3 points: Belgium, Germany, Great Britain, Italy, and Switzerland – there is no case with 4 points); and 'full regulation' or 'full establishment' (5 or 6 points: Denmark, Finland, Norway, Sweden).[23]

An overview of these classifications of Western European countries by Robbers (separation scale), Barbier (laicism scale), Messner (openness

TABLE 1

SCALES OF CHURCH–STATE RELATIONS IN WESTERN EUROPE

Separation scale (Robbers)	strict separation F, IRE, NL,	common tasks A, B, D, I, P, SP	state church DK, GB, GR, SF, SW
Laicism scale (Barbier)	Laicist F	quasi-laicist I, P, SP	semi-laicist B, D, IRE, NL	non-laicist DK, GB, GR
Openness scale (Messner)	open universal F, IRE, NL	pluralistic B, LUX	hegemonic A, D, I, SP	closed DK, GB, GR, P, SF, SW
Regulation scale (Chaves/Cann)	Deregulation F, IRE, NL	partial regulation A, P, SP	(low/medium) B, CH, D, GB, I	full regulation DK, N, SF, SW

Abbreviations for Countries:

A:	Austria	GB:	Great Britain	N:	Norway
B:	Belgium	GR:	Greece	P:	Portugal
CH:	Switzerland	I:	Italy	SF:	Finland
D:	Germany	IRE:	Ireland	SP:	Spain
DK:	Denmark	LUX:	Luxembourg	SW:	Sweden
F:	France				

Sources: M. Barbier, La Laïcité (Paris: Éditions l'Harmatan 1995), pp.171–200; M. Chaves and D.E. Cann, 'Regulation, Pluralism, and Religious Market Structure', Rationality and Society 4/3 (July 1992), p.284; F. Messner, 'La législation cultuelle des pays de l'Union européenne face aux groupes sectaires', in F. Champion and M. Cohen (eds.) Sectes et Démocratie (Paris: Éditions du Seuil 1999), pp.331–58; G. Robbers, 'State and Church in the European Union', in idem (ed.), State and Church in the European Union (Baden-Baden: Nomos 1996), pp.324 ff.

scale) and Chaves and Cann (regulation scale) is summarised in Table 1. The distributions in Table 1 reveal a few interesting insights. First, there is a considerable divergence of classification depending on which criteria are used but in one point a consensus emerges. All authors agree that France should be put on the one end of the spectrum, and the Scandinavian countries on the other.[24] Thus, all state–church regimes in Western Europe can be situated somewhere between the French model and the Scandinavian model. Second, an significant overlap exists between Robbers', Messner's, and Chaves/Cann's scale in that, contrary to Barbier, but also to Monsma and Soper's argumentation, they group Ireland, along with the Netherlands, into the same group as France. It might seem surprising to find Ireland at the extreme end of these scales (not only along with laicist France and the pillarised Netherlands but also – according to Chaves and Cann – with the non-European cases Australia, Canada, New Zealand, and the United States). But this can be explained by the exclusion of the education system (which in Ireland has almost entirely been conceded to the church) from most of these scales and the fact that Catholicism has such a powerful presence in Ireland that the church is not directly established and endowed by the state.[25] Third, the distribution shows that, regardless of the scales used, there is a significant variation of church–state relationships *within* the group of Catholic countries such as Ireland on the one hand and Italy on the other, that is, 'although Catholic countries are uniformly non-pluralistic, they are not uniformly regulated'.[26] Fourth, the patterns as illustrated in Table 1 underline the importance of distinguishing modernisation, secularisation, and laicism as different, yet related trends.[27] If modernisation is understood as a functional differentiation of spheres of politics and society, a growing autonomy of subsystems, and individualisation, then clearly the Scandinavian group of countries is not (culturally) modernised because of the ongoing fusion of church and state. On the other hand, economic data indicate a high level of modernisation, and data on church-going or religious beliefs reveal an advanced state of secularisation.[28] Quite the opposite seems true for countries like Ireland and Spain (in Europe) and Canada and the United States (in North America) where church-going rates or subjective religiosity is comparatively high and the institutional separation of church and state rather advanced.

Finally, the grouping of Germany and Great Britain raises some interesting questions about the criteria to be used for classifying church–state relations. The European authors agree in putting Britain at the extreme end of their scales, along with the Scandinavian countries and Greece. From a narrow institutionalist viewpoint in general, and a French perspective in particular, this seems quite understandable because the overarching characteristic of the British case is the existence of two state churches and thus an arrangement of church–state relations which on the face of it is the polar opposite of French principles and practices. But one must also take into account the dynamism of change in the post-war decades, which, despite the persistence of the respective principles, has resulted in some convergence of church–state patterns in Britain, France, and Germany.

CHURCH–STATE RELATIONS IN BRITAIN, GERMANY, AND FRANCE: A CLOSER LOOK

It is a unique feature of the German Basic Law of 1949 (*Grundgesetz* or GG) that it contains those – and only those – articles of the 1919 Weimar Constitution (art. 136, 137, 138, 139, 141 of the *Weimarer Reichsverfassung* or WRV) which deal with the role of religion in public life (art. 140 GG). To these belong a no-establishment clause (art 137 WRV: 'there is no state church'), the constitutional protection of Sundays and religious holidays (art. 139 WRV), the autonomy and public-legal status of religious communities (art. 137 WRV), and the guarantee of religious freedom (art. 136 WRV). The latter is repeated in art. 4 of the Basic Law, which also contains an article prescribing religious education as a regular subject in the public school system (art. 7 GG). Moreover, based on art. 137 of the Weimar Constitution, the state collects a church tax from all members in the Catholic and Protestant churches and in Jewish congregations.[29] This brief enumeration of constitutional principles regulating the relationship between church and state in Germany already indicates the complex and comprehensively ordered nature of state–church relations in the Federal Republic. At the heart of this arrangement lies a principle which Monsma and Soper properly call 'positive neutrality': the state granting religious communities certain privileges justified by a recognition of their positive role in public life (see above). This is a partnership or 'limping separation' (*hinkende Trennung,* in the words of the German Constitutional Court[30]) linked to a 'public mandate' which has been underlined as rooted in German culture and thus indispensable as late as 1997 by the Council of the Evangelical Church.[31] The churches' privileged position has been reduced somewhat during the 1990s by the state of Brandenburg's decision to establish a new course on religion and morality in the mandatory curriculum of its public schools instead of the traditional religious courses as mandated by art. 7 (an issue still contested by the churches and the Christian

Democratic Union) and the Constitutional Court's decision in 1995 that the crucifix in the classroom of public schools, still widely displayed in many schools especially in southern Germany, violates the principle of separation of state and church and must be taken down if any students or teachers object.[32] But these are marginal modifications to the principled privileging of the major churches in the German political system.

In comparison, the state churches in Great Britain have undergone a more substantial decline. Nominally, the (Anglican) Church of England and the (Presbyterian) Church of Scotland are still 'established' and thus occupy a highly visible place in English and Scottish public life.[33] This includes the fact that the monarch is still the head of the Church of England and cannot be or marry a Catholic, that Church appointments are Crown appointments, that the Church of England carries out a variety of state functions (such as the coronation), and that the Archbishops of Canterbury and York, the Bishops of London, Durham, and Winchester, and the 21 most senior of the other diocesan bishops of the Church of England have seats in the House of Lords within the framework of the whole United Kingdom. But this is only a 'partial establishment' (Monsma/Soper). For example, the (Anglican) Church of Ireland was disestablished as early as 1871 (still affecting Northern Ireland today), the (Anglican) Church of Wales was disestablished in 1920, and, despite the comparatively strong formal and legal ties between the church and the state in England and Scotland, their political significance is rather limited. With more than 1,000 members in the unreformed House of Lords (that is, until 2000), the bishops were a very small numerical minority and where they have acted to constitute a majority, their political impact was constrained by the upper chamber's limited role in the legislative process. Moreover, church membership and church-going have reached a disproportionately low level in the European context.[34] Although there is no constitutionally entrenched principle of freedom of religious exercise, as in Germany or the United States, practice shows that all religious groups are free to associate, worship, publish, and promote their views so that, in the end, the continuing establishments cannot be said to represent any significant elements of monopoly. Whatever remains of the privileged position of the Church of England is rooted more in the general public's perception of the positive role of religion in British public life than in specific institutional arrangements guaranteeing political power to the church. Since this perception extends to religious communities and faiths other than the Church of England as well, and since they are increasingly included in public ceremonies, the British type of establishment today can be more properly termed 'ecumenical establishment'.[35]

In stark contrast to Germany and Britain, the French case stands out as an example of an unusual degree of consensus in the academic literature across the fields of legal scholarship and social sciences. But the simple principle of a strict separation, enunciated in the constitutions of the Fourth and Fifth Republic, which flatly state that 'la France est une république indivisible, laïque, démocratique et social' (art. 2 of the V. Republic's constitution), and spelled out in detail in the still valid 'separation law' of 1905,[36] overlooks the complexities of the French pattern of church–state relations and also some changes over the last decades. First of all, the strict separation as it exists in the United States is modified in France by the fact that the state owns all church buildings erected before 1905 and is responsible for their maintenance. Moreover, some church personnel such as chaplains in prisons, hospitals, and in the army receive their salary from the state, and, although public education is completely non-religious or laicist, the Catholic church runs a system of private schools which attracts about 15 per cent of the nation's students and, through contracts with the state, receives public money to finance their teachers. Finally, the special region of Alsace (Haut-Rhin, Bas-Rhin, Moselle) is exempted from these regulations because at the time of the passing of the separation law this region was part of the German empire. After German unification and the annexation of Alsace-Lorraine in 1871, the German emperor and the Holy See agreed not to change the religious laws in practice at the time which resulted from the Napoleonic concordat of 1801, and only a few modifications and amendments occurred. When the region returned to France in 1918, the politicians as well the population opted to continue the status quo, that is, the practice of 'establishment' by recognising certain religions (the Catholic, Lutheran, and Reformed churches, and the Jewish faith).[37] Accordingly, France does not receive 0 points in Chaves and Cann's index.

The French situation has grown more complex due to changes in the 1990s which produced a certain rapprochement of state and church in France. There is, for example, a growing recognition of the church's contribution to social life and welfare, including the private religious school system, and when the Pope visited France on an 'unofficial visit' (not as head of state of the Vatican but head of the Catholic church) in September 1996, a compromise was reached for his use of a military, that is, state-run, airport, but not without some controversy over whether this violated the principle of separation of state and church. Thus, experts argue for a 'nouveau pacte laïque' (Baubérot) or a 'laïcisation de la laïcité' (Willaime) in order to overcome the French tradition of a hostile anti-clericalism and the centuries-old 'guerre des deux Frances'.[38]

In sum, this more direct and detailed comparison between Britain, France, and Germany underlines that, in political terms which go beyond 'official' constitutional criteria, Britain and Germany are closer to each other than the usual distinction between 'state church' and 'partial establishment" suggests, and that even in the French case there is some movement towards the 'centre'. For this reason, the following analysis will employ the church–state index as suggested by Chaves and Cann and refer to the three categories as 'separation', 'partial establishment', and 'full establishment' which directly correspond to those of 'deregulation', 'partial regulation', and 'full regulation' as shown in Table 1.

FAMILY AND NATION: CHURCH–STATE RELATIONS AND PATTERNS OF PUBLIC POLICY IN WESTERN EUROPE

Very few comparative studies of public policy involve religion as a relevant factor, which is due, to some degree, to their focus on explaining public spending or welfare state arrangements. But there is more to policies than goods and services as measured in financial terms.[39] It is increasingly recognised that the importance of regulatory and symbolic, or, more generally, non-material policies, has grown over the last few decades as a result of various trends in Western nations such as urbanisation and post-industrialisation along with socio-cultural changes like the spread of mass education and 'value change'.[40] Thus, quality of life issues and related policies, such as education policy, abortion and other aspects of family policy, religious freedom, and immigration and naturalisation policies, have gained importance. In other words, in the context of these socio-cultural changes, personal concerns are increasingly public, and thus public policy, concerns.[41]

Most comparative public policy studies which deal with religion at all include religious variables either in terms of the predominant religious denomination (Protestant or Catholic) and/or the presence or absence of a Catholic or Christian-Democratic party in the party system.[42] For example, Francis Castles in his 'families of nations' concept explicitly models religion and cultural traditions as independent variables.[43] Criticising those approaches which look at churches solely as interest groups, he employs three religious variables: Christian Democratic incumbency, Catholicism (the percentage of the population baptised into a non-Protestant Christian faith, which gives Greece a high mark, Japan a very low one), and Catholic cultural impact, a summary measure of the former two.[44] The problem of this operationalisation is that it fuses various religious traditions as

'Catholic cultural impact', as in Germany, ignores the link between non-Christian Democratic conservative parties and the established churches, as in the UK, and does not take into account the issue of *laïcité* which decisively undercuts any Catholic cultural impact, as in France.

For these reasons, the party variable and the church/denomination variable are disentangled here so that they can be distinguished when discussing their impact on public policy. Clearly, churches can, like political parties, be independent actors in the policy process, and useful insights can be gained from studying their behaviour in the light of interest group theories.[45] On the other hand, unlike most other interest groups, churches in much of the Western world assume a special role in politics, which stems from their historical 'mission' and self-image. As Peter Katzenstein suggests, it is necessary to treat churches not as simple interest groups but as 'parapublic institutions'. This means they act like interest groups, but, as has been shown above, take on a heightened status because of their special public recognition, which links the private and public sectors firmly together; moreover, despite their special public recognition, they are active only on selected policy fields.[46] Finally, regarding Casanova's stress on the different roles of churches in modern society, the term 'parapublic institution' better captures the range from state-oriented to society-oriented behaviour of the churches than the concept of interest groups.

The policy areas included in the following analysis reflect those 'public policy concerns' which have acquired increasing salience in post-industrial societies and elicit particular activities by religiously concerned actors. They concern first the relationship between the individual und the family, often conceptualised as 'women's issues', such as a women-friendly family policy and abortion regimes on the one hand, and the relationship between (especially non-Christian) minority religions and the Western nation-state (with its Christian heritage). Concerning the first policy area, the data are taken from Harold Wilensky's rating of industrialised nations in terms of a 'women-friendly family policy'.[47] The ratings are based on three policy clusters with a five-point scale for each cluster: first, the existence and duration of parental and maternity leave; second, the availability of and the accessibility to public day-care facilities along with the existence of a government policy which strives to expand day-care; and, third, the flexibility of retirement systems.[48] With the help of these scales, Wilensky arrives at a three-fold typology of family policy, 'expansive' (very women-friendly), 'moderate' (partially women-friendly) and 'conservative' (indifferent to women's concerns) along which the various countries can be grouped. Arend Lijphart argues that the type of democracy matters for these policies, with consensus democracies scoring high on the women-friendly policy scale, whereas majoritarian democracies score rather low.[49] But France does not fit the classification because here we are dealing with a majoritarian democracy which, according to Wilensky's scale, implemented an expansive family policy. Moreover, the distributional pattern of types of democracy is not as clear as Lijphart suggests because he uses only one of the two dimensions which he applies to categorise democracies, the 'executives/parties' dimension, while ignoring the second, the 'federalism/unitary' dimension.[50] When applying both dimensions and regrouping the countries, the results are less clear. When the church–state dimension is added in, however, certain important linkages do emerge clearly (based here on the three-fold classification derived from Chaves and Cann's index).

Table 2 shows that the relationship between type of democracy and family policy is less strong than that between church–state relations and family policy. With the exception of France, a conservative family policy exists in all countries with a separation of church and state, whereas in countries where churches are fully established, again with one exception (Denmark), an expansive policy can be observed. The majority of countries with partial establishment exhibit a moderate policy. Since the majority of countries with a conservative policy are predominantly Protestant or mixed

TABLE 2

FAMILY POLICY AND CHURCH–STATE RELATIONS IN WESTERN EUROPE

	Expansive	Moderate	Conservative
Separation	France (M)		Ireland (M) The Netherlands (C)
Partial establishment	Belgium (C)	Austria (C) Italy Germany (C) Great Britain (M)	Switzerland (C)
Full establishment	Finland Norway Sweden	Denmark	

Notes: Categorisation of individual countries according to personal communication of the author with Arend Lijphart, 7 March 2000. No data available for Portugal and Spain. Consensus democracies are marked with a C, majoritarian democracies with an M according to Lijphart's two dimensions federalism-unitary and executives-parties. Catholic countries are underlined, predominantly Protestant countries are in italics.

Sources: A. Lijphart, Patterns of Democracy (New Haven, CT: Yale University Press 1999), p.248, and Table 1 above.

Catholic–Protestant, the pattern here cannot be explained with the confessional factor or a 'Catholic cultural impact' according to Castles' 'families of nations' concept. However, if religiosity (as measured, for example, in church-going rates) is added, a 'cultural impact' in conjunction with the 'institutional effect' of church–state relations becomes visible.

A similar pattern emerges in a related area, the world of abortion regimes. In fact, there are probably few issues in Western politics where churches take as definitive and public a stand as they do regarding abortion. For our purposes, they are classified regarding the role of the individual woman's decision to terminate her pregnancy.[51] Albin Eser distinguishes three types of abortion legislation along a continuum from a pole where we find priority of individual choice and to a pole where abortion is illegal and individual choice is replaced by various 'exceptions'. Thus the rather liberal 'period model' – unlimited individual choice within a legally defined period – is contrasted by the restrictive 'indication model' – where abortion is permitted only as an exception based on legal criteria and others' (usually physicians') judgement if these criteria are met. Somewhere in between is a 'distress model' – a woman can claim a situation of social or otherwise defined distress.[52] This model emphasises the priority of the unborn life but leaves the final decision up to the woman. Here, counselling is usually compulsory, there are waiting periods, and it is made clear that abortions are granted only exceptionally. Since the woman has to claim a situation of

TABLE 3

ABORTION REGIMES AND STATE–CHURCH RELATIONS IN WESTERN EUROPE

	Period model	Distress model	Indication model
Separation		France The Netherlands	(Ireland)
Partial establishment		Austria Belgium Italy Germany Great Britain	Portugal Spain Switzerland
Full establishment	Denmark Finland Norway Sweden		

Notes: Catholic countries are underlined, predominantly Protestant countries are in *italics*.

Source: M. Minkenberg, 'Religion and Public Policy: Institutional, Cultural, and Political Impact on the Shaping of Abortion Policies in Western Democracies', *Comparative Political Studies* 35/2 (March 2002), pp.233, 235 (Tables 3 and 4).

distress, even though the final decision is hers, the model can be classified as moderately liberal.

The distribution of Western European countries according to the classification in Table 3 reveals similar tendencies to those in Table 2. In all four Scandinavian countries – those cases with full establishment – and only there (as far as Western Europe is concerned), liberal abortion regimes exist. On the other hand, the restrictive indication model is concentrated in countries with partial or full separation, with Ireland, where the indication model exists only theoretically and abortion is practically non-existent, being the extreme outlier. Again, the churches' interests seem better served when they are not closely entangled with the state, when they assume, in Casanova's terms, less of a state-oriented and more of a society-oriented and yet 'de-privatised' role. Tables 2 and 3 also reveal effects by the interaction of institutional and confessional forces. In the Scandinavian countries where a Protestant heritage coexists with the continuation of established churches and a decline of religiosity (as measured, for example, in church-going rates), liberal policies have emerged. On the other hand, in those Catholic countries where, with the exception of France, the separation of state and church is most pronounced (Ireland, but also Portugal and Spain, see Table 1), more restrictive policies dominate.[53] Again, the 'Catholic cultural impact' is mediated through the political role of the churches, which, in turn, depends on their room for manoeuvre in the public realm. That is, other things being equal, a regime of church–state relations at the 'separationist' or 'non-establishment' end of the continuum provides a more favourable opportunity structure for the insertion of religious interests in the political process than does a privileged position of churches in countries with establishment.

FAMILY AND NATION IN BRITAIN, FRANCE, AND GERMANY: A CLOSER LOOK

The cultural factor shaping the church's influence on public policy is most tellingly illustrated when contrasting family policy in France to that in Ireland (see Table 2). In both countries, there exists an institutional separation of church and state and a Catholic legacy, although church-going rates differ widely.[54] In France, religiosity is exceptionally low, while in Ireland it is rather high. The French scenario, with strict separation, a 'culture' of *laïcité*, and a history of a cultural war between the 'two Frances' (Willaime), does not play into the hands of the interests of the Catholic Church. Given that the Catholic Church in France generally still adheres to more traditional values, including gender roles, than the average population while at the same time undergoing a process of internal differentiation, it is obvious that the church either could not or did not want to prevent a moderately innovative family policy.[55] In the face of a strong laicist tradition, the French Catholic Church's room for manoeuvre as an interest group seems constrained. The situation differs in the cases of Great Britain and Germany. Here, partial establishment and a moderate level of religiosity correlate with a moderately innovative family policy. During the 1980s, in both countries Conservative governments have engaged in 'moral crusades' which also included family issues, but the churches have rather stood on the sidelines.[56] In Britain, the Church of England occasionally criticised the 'socially divisive policies' of the Thatcher government, but significant elements of religious opinion also mobilised against an innovative Family Law Bill in 1995 without being able to prevent it.[57] The general impression from the British and German cases is that partial establishment somewhat inhibits a full political involvement of the churches on behalf of issues traditionally close to them – they tend to act less as interest groups than as institutions. By contrast, in countries where churches are disestablished, they have more room for manoeuvre in politics and thus have contributed more effectively to policy-making in this area.

This is also reflected in the regulation of the other policy issue under consideration, such as abortion. The compromise situation in Great Britain, which stems from the combination of a rather liberal practice and the contrasting principle that the legislation does not grant a woman the *right* to terminate her pregnancy, has provoked various attempts to reform the abortion regime since its enactment in the Abortion Act of 1967. In these attempts, a close partnership between the established churches in England and Scotland and the Tories has emerged, underlining that, at least with regard to abortion, the Church of England to an extent still operates as 'the Conservative Party at prayer'. However, the sharp public criticisms of the abortion ruling in the 1990s, for example by Cardinal Winning, Archbishop of Glasgow, and Cardinal Hume, Archbishop of Westminster, could not mask the fact that the main opposition derived from particular political alliances, such as the 'Prolife Alliance', rather than the churches themselves, or from within the House of Commons and that – except for staunch abortion critic Ian Paisley – opposition to abortion was phrased more in scientific than religious-moral terms.[58]

Quite surprisingly, despite the contrast in church–state relations, levels of religiosity and confessional composition, the French case shows up in the same category of abortion regimes as Great Britain and Germany – although it is slightly more liberal in its recognition of the individual right of the woman to choose an abortion.[59] Here abortion was liberalised in 1975 against opposition from conservative physicians, lawyer and women groups, and orthodox Catholic groups – the Catholic Church itself was rather absent from the debate.[60] Despite the takeover of government by the left in the 1980s, a further liberalisation was not accomplished, but the 1975 rule was reinforced and defended against a growing opposition, mainly from the political right. This included a new radical right party, the Front National, which entertains close links with ultra-Catholic groups that split from the Catholic Church on grounds of the latter's liberalism.[61] As in the British case, it was the opposition by 'technical experts' such as physicians and lawyers using scientific arguments which succeeded in opposing a more radical solution rather than the main churches which deployed religious and moral arguments.

In Germany, finally, opposition to a liberalisation of abortion by the main churches was more vociferous than in the other two cases, but the issue was settled in the Constitutional Court and not in parliament. The first attempt to reform the abortion law occurred in 1973 in the Bundestag and was introduced by the SPD-led coalition government. The parliamentary majority was overruled by the Constitutional Court's ruling at the behest of the Conservative opposition parties and supported by the Catholic Church. Contrary to the US Supreme Court's decision in *Roe v. Wade* in 1972, the German court ruling was based on the argument that according to the Basic Law the state is obliged to prioritise the protection of human life, including unborn life, over the right to self-determination by the woman.[62] By using this argument, the court referred to a passage in the German constitution which can be traced back to the German churches' prominent role in drafting part of the Basic Law as far as their interests were concerned in 1948/49.[63] The German abortion ruling prior to unification in 1989/90 reflected not so much any current input of the churches, based on their privileged position in the arrangement of a 'partial establishment', as the factors operating at the time of the drafting of the constitution which maintained their semi-established status and put future constraints on legislation such as the abortion law. This, however, could not prevent a further liberalisation after unification, when, due to the existence of a very liberal rule and practice in Eastern Germany (where church opposition was minimal at the time of the passing of the 1972 law under the tutelage of the ruling socialist party in the GDR), a compromise between the Western and Eastern abortion regimes was reached. As in 1975, the parliamentary solution of 1991 was overturned by the Constitutional Court with similar arguments. Thus, a new ruling was passed in 1992 which substituted the principle of indication in favour of a broad right of the woman to claim a distress situation (making it in practice a 'tamed period model').[64] But at the same time the law prescribes compulsory counselling by lay experts or church representatives. This gives the major churches a chance to be involved in abortion decisions, especially in areas where churches still dominate public life and alternative counselling facilities do not exist. The ruling put a particular stress on the Catholic Church in Germany, which, in line with the Vatican, officially rejected the new ruling, but at the same time did not want to lose the opportunity to counsel women and receive state funding for it. The resulting conflict between the Vatican and the Catholic Church in Germany was resolved in favour of a 'national' approach and a let-down of the Vatican by the German bishops.

Overall, despite a uniformly strong anti-abortion stance by all the major churches in the three countries, and against a backdrop of somewhat different confessional patterns and diverging church–state arrangements, Britain, France, and Germany exhibit similar, or at least similarly liberal or liberalising, approaches to the regulation of abortion. Church opposition to this development was sporadic, and mobilisation occurred on behalf of other, lay and expert, groups. The churches' reluctance to engage in a full-blown political battle, comparable to that of the German *Kulturkampf* in the late nineteenth century, is also demonstrated by the fact that in France and Germany (where comparable data are available) non-church anti-abortion groups staging protests in the period 1970–92 (44 in both France and Germany) clearly outnumbered those affiliated with the churches, although in Germany the number of church-related groups was somewhat higher than in France (28 in France, 33 in Germany).[65]

In sum, for religious interests in the French political process the institutional arrangement of laicism has created a favourable opportunity structure for the Catholic Church, but laicism, as a deeply rooted tradition, constrains its room for manoeuvre in politics and society significantly. In both cases of family policy and abortion legislation, the church was visible but not vociferous. The British–German comparison revealed, on the other hand, that it was the partial establishment of the major churches instead of a cultural tradition which inhibited a more active role of the churches. They tended to operate more like institutions than interest groups, with the German churches being privileged not just by their established status but also by the fact that in some areas of legislation which relate to existential issues such as abortion, their values had already entered the constitution in 1949. Thus, it was the Conservative parties and the Constitutional Court rather than the churches which were decisive in their opposition to a liberalisation of the abortion law.

CONCLUSIONS

This study has shown that the comparative analysis of church–state patterns in Western Europe can reveal important insights into wider political science concerns, particularly in the areas of public policy analysis and neo-institutionalism. The variety of church–state relations corresponds with a variety of other political factors, as was demonstrated with regard to certain fields of public policy. However, a simple structuring of the field of church–state relations with regard to the existence of an official state church on the one hand, or the relative prevalence of a strict separation of state and church on the other, must give way to more nuanced concepts. Our analysis has shown that a scale which is not oriented at the primarily formal or legal criteria of a state church or laicist system, but includes other, more economic and political, criteria seems best suited for such a comparative study, especially when treating church–state relations as an independent variable. The fact that both Germany and Great Britain end up in the same categories on the church–state index as well as on those of the chosen policy fields underscores the shortcomings of the conventional, legalist distinctions between countries with a state church and those without.

Moreover, the policy analysis demonstrated that established churches, whether partially or fully established, seem to have less policy impact in issues close to them and appear ready to make compromises on them. In other words, they behave more like institutions than interest groups. Thus, the widespread use of cultural – that is, confessional – variables in public policy analysis would benefit from the inclusion of an institutional component because the combination of both is more telling than the reference to a mere 'Catholic cultural impact'. As has been shown, churches as institutions or the patterns of church–state relations alone do not matter all that much, and secularisation as institutional differentiation has only a limited impact on policy outputs. But institutional differentiation does not lead to the weakening of religious inputs either. Churches which are free from the constraints of establishment may be more effective actors if they choose, in Casanova's words, to be 'de-privatised' and transform 'from a state-oriented to a society-oriented institution'.[66]

Here France is a special and particularly revealing case. It deviates from those cases of separation in southern Europe and in Ireland in that the French tradition of *laïcité* and the high levels of secularisation in terms of conventional measures of church-going and religiosity have resulted in a cultural paradigm which severely restricts the room for manoeuvre for the Catholic Church. It is only now that the traditional hostility towards the Catholic Church and religion in general is giving way to a new appraisal of the role of religion in French public life which may lead to a new social contract between the churches and the lay public. Similarly, the traditional privileging of the state churches or partially established churches in Great Britain and Germany, not least in the face of the growing importance of new religious communities and faiths, is in the process of being replaced by a new pattern of 'ecumenical establishment' which opens the door to a new plurality of privileges, and thus a more society-oriented approach by all religious communities.[67] In the end, it may not be the European Union, but the reality of post-industrial and multicultural societies and new issues stemming from them, which leads to a convergence of state–church relations in Western Europe.

NOTES

1. With the sentence by the European Court of Justice in the case *Prais vs. Council* (1976), the court recognised the protection of religious needs as community law and required all EU offices to avoid religious conflicts. At the EU level, religious freedom thus includes the protection of the private religious sphere of individuals from public interference, regardless of faith or denomination, as well as the responsibility of the EU and its bureaus to take organisational measures to provide adequate space for the exercise of religion. See G. Robbers, 'State and Church in the European Union', in idem (ed.), *State and Church in the European Union* (Baden-Baden: Nomos 1996), p.328.
2. See ibid., pp.326 ff., and J.P. Willaime, 'Les religions et l'unification Européenne', in G. Davie and D. Hervieu-Léger (eds.), *Identités religieuses en Europe* (Paris: La Découverte 1996), p.307.
3. See J. Madeley, 'A Framework for the Comparative Analysis of Church–State Relations in Europe, North, South, East and West', in this volume.
4. See K. von Beyme, *Die parlamentarische Demokratie. Entstehung und Funktionsweise 1789–1999* (Opladen/Wiesbaden: Westdeutscher Verlag 1999), p.56, and J.G. March and J.P. Olsen, 'The New Institutionalism: Organizational Factors in Political Life', *American Political Science Review* 78 (Sept. 1984), pp.735 ff.
5. March and Olsen, 'The New Institutionalism', p.740; see also B. Steunenberg and F. van Vught (eds.), *Political Institutions and Public Policy. Perspectives on European Decision Making* (Dordrecht: Kluwer 1997); R.K. Weaver and B. Rockman (eds.), *Do Institutions Matter? Government Capabilities in the United States and Abroad* (Washington, DC: The Brookings Institution 1993).
6. Here, regime refers to a 'complex of legal and organizational features' which are systematically interwoven in the relationship between state and society, see G. Esping-Anderson, *The Three Worlds of Welfare Capitalism* (Princeton, NJ: Princeton University Press 1990), p.2.
7. See J. Casanova, *Public Religions in the Modern World* (Chicago: University of Chicago Press, 1994).
8. See J. Markoff and D. Regan, 'Religion, the State and Political Legitimacy in the World's Constitutions', in T. Robbins and R. Robertson (eds.), *Church–State Relations*, pp.164–71; M. Minkenberg, 'Civil Religion and German Unification', *German Studies Review* 20 (Feb. 1997), pp.63–82.

9. R. Zippelius, *Staat und Kirche. Eine Geschichte von der Antike bis zur Gegenwart* (München: Beck 1997), p.164; C. Starck, 'Staat und Religion', *Juristen Zeitung* 55/1 (2000), p.7.
10. S. Monsma and J.C. Soper, *The Challenge of Pluralism. Church and State in Five Democracies* (Lanham, MD: Rowman & Littlefied 1997), p.202.
11. See e.g. M. Barbier, *La Laïcité* (Paris: Éditions l'Harmatan 1995), pp.188–200.
12. See D. Hervieu-Léger, *La religion en mouvement* (Paris, 1997); J.P. Willaime, 'Laïcité et religion en France', in G. Davie and D. Hervieu-Léger (eds.), *Identités religieuses en Europe*, pp.153–71; J. Zylberberg, 'Laïcité, connais pas: Allemagne, Canada, Etats-Unis, Royaume Uni', *Pouvoirs* 75 (1995), pp.37–71.
13. See F. Champion, 'Les rapports Eglise-Etat dans les pays européens de tradition protestante et de tradition catholique: essai d'analyse', *Social Compass* 40/4 (1993), pp.589–609.
14. Robbers, 'State and Church in the European Union', pp.324 ff.
15. Barbier, *La Laïcité*, pp.171–200; see also Zylberberg, 'Laïcité, connais pas'.
16. F. Messner, 'La legislation cultuelle des pays de l'Union européenne face aux groupes sectaires', in F. Champion and M. Cohen (eds.), *Sectes et Démocratie* (Paris: Éditions du Seuil 1999), pp.331–58.
17. Ibid., p.332.
18. M. Chaves and D.E. Cann, 'Regulation, Pluralism, and Religious Market Structure. Explaining Religion's Vitality', *Rationality and Society* 4/3 (July 1992), pp.272–90.
19. For an overview, see e.g. P.S. Gorski, 'Historicizing the Secularization Debate: Church, State and Society in Late Medieval and Early Modern Europe, ca. 1300–1700', *American Sociological Review* 65/1 (2000), pp.138–67.
20. R. Robertson, 'Church–State Relations in Comparative Perspective', p.158.
21. Chaves and Cann, 'Regulation, Pluralism, and Religious Market Structure', p.280.
22. Portugal which is missing in Chaves and Cann's classification is coded 2 according to their criteria based on V. Canas, 'State and Church in Portugal', in G. Robbers (ed.), *State and Church in the European Union* (Baden-Baden: Nomos 1996), pp.259–78.
23. See Figure 2 in Chaves and Cann, 'Regulation, Pluralism, and Religious Market Structure', p.284. Their analysis also includes non-European countries such as Australia, Canada, New Zealand, and the United States, which all score 0 points on their scale. These countries are not considered in this study, but see M. Minkenberg, 'Religion and Public Policy: Institutional, Cultural and Political Impact on the Shaping of Abortion Policies in Western Democracies', *Comparative Political Studies* 35/2 (March 2002), pp.221–47.
24. Barbier includes only Denmark in his analysis but by implication, Finland, Norway, and Sweden could be added to his group of 'non-laicist countries'.
25. Ireland's 1937 constitution contained a passage granting the Catholic Church special status (art. 44), but this remained very controversial throughout and was abolished following the 1972 referendum. The author is grateful to John Madeley for pointing out that in 1951 the church stopped a Labour government plan to create mother and child clinics which in turn led to the downfall of the government. See also Bill Kissane's contribution to this volume.
26. Chaves and Cann, 'Regulation, Pluralism, and Religious Market Structure', p.283.
27. See Champion, 'Les rapports Eglise-Etat'; D. Rucht, *Modernisierung und neue soziale Bewegungen* (Frankfurt/M: Campus 1994), p.54; J.P. Willaime, *Sociologie des religions* (Paris, 1995), pp.96 ff.
28. See R. Inglehart, *Modernization and Postmodernization* (Princeton, NJ: Princeton University Press 1997); and R. Inglehart and M. Minkenberg, 'Die Transformation religiöser Werte in entwickelten Industriegesellschaften', in I. Ostner, H.D. Meyer and M. Minkenberg (eds.), *Religion und Politik* (Opladen: Leske + Budrich 2000), pp.115–30.
29. See Monsma and Soper, *The Challenge of Pluralism*, pp.173–5.
30. Ibid., p.172.
31. See G. Robbers, 'State and Church in Germany', in idem (ed.), *State and Church in the European Union*, pp.64–6; Rat der Evangelischen Kirche in Deutschland, *Christentum und politische Kultur. Über das Verhältnis des demokratischen Rechtsstaates zum Christentum* (Hannover: Kirchenamt der EKD 1997).
32. For details see M. Minkenberg, 'Zivilreligion, Bürgerreligion, Staatsreligion: Anmerkungen

zur deutschen Debatte um das rechte Verhältnis von Religion und Politik', in H.D. Meyer, M. Minkenberg and I. Ostner (eds.), *Religion und Politik. Zwischen Universalismus und Partikularismus* (Opladen: Leske + Budrich 2000), pp.21–48. See also P. Caldwell, 'The Crucifix and German Constitutional Culture', *Cultural Anthropology* 11/2 (1996); and A. von Campenhausen, 'Zur Kruzifix-Entscheidung des Bundesverfassungsgerichts', *Archiv des öffentlichen Rechts* 121 (1996).

33. See K. Boyle and J. Sheen (eds.), *Freedom of Religion and Belief. A World Report* (London/New York: Routledge 1997), p.316; D. McClean, 'State and Church in the United Kingdom', in Robbers (ed.), *State and Church in the European Union*, pp.307–22.

34. See S. Bruce, *Religion in the Modern World. From Cathedrals to Cults* (Oxford: Oxford University Press 1999), pp.29–37; G. Davie, 'Croire sans appartenir: le cas britannique', in G. Davie and D. Hervieu-Léger (eds.), *Identités religieuses en Europe*, pp.175–94; G. Davie, *Religion in Modern Europe. A Memory Mutates* (Oxford: Oxford University Press 2000).

35. See Boyle and Sheen, *Freedom of Religion and Belief*, p.317; see also Monsma and Soper, *The Challenge of Pluralism*, pp.129–36; McClean, 'State and Church in the United Kingdom', pp.312–15.

36. See J.P. Willaime, 'Laïcité et religion en France', and B. Basdevant-Gaudenet, 'State and Church in France', in Robbers (ed.), *State and Church in the European Union*, pp.119–46.

37. See Boyle and Sheen, *Freedom of Religion and Belief*, p.295; see also Barbier, *La laïcité*; Messner, 'La legislation cultuelle des pays de l'Union européenne face aux groupes sectaires'.

38. See J.Baubérot, *Vers un nouveau pacte laïque?* (Paris: le Seuil 1990); J. Baubérot, 'La laïcité comme <<pacte laïque>>', paper at the VI. Congress of the French Association of Political Science (AFSP), Rennes, 28 Sept.–1 Oct. 1999; Willaime, 'Laïcité et religion en France'.

39. For the following, see Minkenberg, 'Religion and Public Policy', pp.223–7; see also B. Nelson, 'Public Policy and Administration: An Overview', in R.E. Goodin and H.D. Klingemann (eds.), *A New Handbook of Political Science* (Oxford: Oxford University Press 1998), pp.574–7.

40. See Inglehart, *Modernization and Postmodernization*; idem, *Culture Shift* (Princeton, NJ: Princeton University Press 1990).

41. See F. Castles, *Comparative Public Policy. Patterns of Post-War Transformation* (Cheltenham, 1998), p.248.

42. See Esping-Anderson, *The Three Worlds*, pp.26–9. See also K. van Kersbergen, *Social Capitalism. A Study of Christian Democracy and the Welfare State* (Boston: Routledge Kegan Paul 1995).

43. F. Castles (ed.), *Families of Nations. Patterns of Public Policies in Western Democracies* (Dartmouth: Aldershot 1993), and idem., *Comparative Public Policy*.

44. Castles, *Comparative Public Policy*, p.56.

45. See C. Warner, *Confessions of an Interest Group. The Catholic Church and Political Parties in Europe* (Princeton, NJ: Princeton University Press 2000); see also A. Gill, *Rendering unto Caesar. The Catholic Church and the State in Latin America* (Chicago/London: University of Chicago Press 1998).

46. See P.J. Katzenstein, *Policy and Politics in West Germany. The Growth of a Semi-Sovereign State* (Philadelphia, PA: Temple University Press 1987), pp.58–60. The term is Katzenstein's translation of the German word '*parastaatlich*', see M. Groser, 'Ökonomie parastaatlicher Institutionen', *Jahrbuch für Neue Politische Ökonomie* 2 (1983), pp.239–53.

47. See H. Wilensky, 'Common Problems, Divergent Policies. An Eighteen-Nation Study of Family Policy', in *Public Affairs Report* 31/3 (May 1990), pp.1–3; see also A. Lijphart, *Patterns of Democracy. Government Forms and Performance in Thirty-Six Countries* (New Haven, CT: Yale University Press 1999), pp.281 ff.

48. See Lijphart, *Patterns of Democracy*, p.282, n.3.

49. Ibid.

50. See ibid., p.312, and M. Schmidt, *Demokratietheorien* (Opladen: Leske + Budrich 2000), pp.340–44. Schmidt categorises Germany as a 'mixed type', which is surprising since in both of Lijphart's dimensions, Germany receives positive values.

51. For details see Minkenberg, 'Religion and Public Policy', and the appendix in M.

Minkenberg, 'Religion and Policy Effects. Church, State and Party Configurations in the Policy Making Process', paper for the ECPR 28th Joint Session of Workshops, Copenhagen (14–19 April 2000), Workshop 22, 'Church and State in Europe'.

52. A. Eser, *Schwangerschaftsabbruch: Auf dem verfassungsrechtlichen Prüfstand* (Baden-Baden 1994), pp.22 ff. These are my own translations of the German legal terms *Fristenmodell auf Selbstbestimmungsbasis, Indikationsmodell auf Drittbeurteilungsbasis,* and *Notlagenmodell auf Selbsteinschätzungsbasis.*

53. See also Minkenberg, 'Religion and Public Policy'.

54. For data, see Minkenberg, 'Religion and Public Policy', Table 6 (p.238).

55. See D. Hervieu-Léger, *Le pèlerin et le converti. La religion en mouvement* (Paris: Flammarion 1999), pp.201–7; Comité catholique français des religieux, *Vie religieuse, érémitisme, consecration des vierges, communautés nouvelles* (Paris: le Cerf 1993).

56. See M. Durham, *Moral Crusades. Family and Morality in the Thatcher Years* (New York: New York University Press 1991); P. Cowley (ed.), *Conscience and Parliament* (London: Frank Cass 1998); E. Grande, 'Neoconservatism without Neoconservatives?' The Renaissance and Transformation of Contemporary German Conservatism', in B. Girvin (ed.), *The Transformation of Contemporary Conservatism* (London: Sage 1988), pp.55–77.

57. See D. Kavanagh, *The Reordering of British Politics. Politics after Thatcher* (Oxford: Oxford University Press 1997), pp.130 ff.; Mosma and Soper, *The Challenge of Pluralism,* pp.129 ff.

58. See S. Millns and S. Sheldon, 'Abortion', in Cowley (ed.), *Conscience and Parliament,* pp.6–23. It is noteworthy that the elaborate treatment of the political role of the Church of England by Monsma and Soper does not include any reference to the abortion issue at all.

59. See also E. Gindulis, 'Die Bestimmungsfaktoren der Gesetzgebung über den Schwangerschaftsabbruch im OECD-Vergleich', *Zes-Arbeitspapier* 14/01 (Bremen: University of Bremen 2001), with a different coding of abortion regimes.

60. See Rucht, *Modernisierung und neue soziale Bewegungen,* pp.350–59; see also P. Ladrière, 'Religion, morale et politique: le débat sur l'avortement', *Revue française de sociologie* 23/3 (1982), pp.417–54.

61. See M. Minkenberg, *Die neue radikale Rechte im Vergleich. USA, Frankreich, Deutschland* (Opladen/Wiesbaden: Westdeutscher Verlag 1998), pp.269–8.

62. See Rucht, *Modernisierung und neue soziale Bewegungen,* pp.375 f

63. See K. von Beyme, *Das politische System der Bundesrepublik Deutschland* (Opladen/Wiesbaden: Westdeutscher Verlag 9th edn. 1999), pp.35–41.

64. Rucht, *Modernisierung und neue soziale Bewegungen,* p.390.

65. Ibid., p.396.

66. Casanova, *Public Religions in the Modern World,* p.220.

67. See T. Modood (ed.), *Church, State and Religious Minorities* (London: Policy Studies Institute 1997).

Conclusion:
Emerging Issues in the Study of
Church–State Relations

ZSOLT ENYEDI

The contributors to this volume have analysed recent developments in church and state relations in various European countries. They investigated particular dimensions of these relations, and pointed at new research directions in the field. On the basis of the analyses they have presented, one may identify eight major tasks lying ahead for political scientists who study the interpenetration of religion and politics in the European context. These tasks involve

1. the study of the dynamics of contemporary church–state relations;
2. the extension of existing theoretical frameworks to take account of East European developments;
3. the reassessment of the significance of denominational differences for the links between churches and state;
4. the scrutiny of the links between national identities and discrimination among churches;
5. the analysis of the impact of European integration, and of the development of global governance;
6. the conceptual clarification and operationalisation of the different dimensions of church and state relations;
7. systematic mapping of the strategic options of the churches in twenty-first century Europe; and, finally,
8. establishing the nature of the links between church–state regimes and the national political structures.

Some of these topics are age-old – but new developments or obsolete conceptual tools necessitate their revisiting – while others stem from recent political processes.

THE DYNAMICS OF CHURCH–STATE RELATIONS

Church and state relationships are, as is the case with other national institutional structures, the products both of historical traditions and of conscious, rationally planned, and democratically legitimised statecraft. But there are probably few areas where modern norms are as much in contradiction with inherited structures. The contradictions between the two principles do not necessarily lead to open political conflict, but the reform of old institutions and practices is today a topic of political discussion in virtually all European states. The reconfiguration of church–state relations typically happens through cautious and often tacit reinterpretation of the existing rules, but revolutionary changes do also occur, particularly in states undergoing political transformation.[1] There are some commonalities in the national and regional trends, but there is no common European model yet, although state support for church institutions, respect for the self-determination of religious communities and the extension of privileges to a growing circle of religious organisations seems to be the norm in most countries.[2] Secularisation, understood here as institutional differentiation and the dismantling of religious monopolies, is the leading trend, but it is far from being linear and monotonous.

There are converging tendencies not only across Europe but between Europe and the United States as well. Partly as a result of the policies pursued by the Bush administration, European-style state support for churches has attracted considerable interest. The irony is that while in the USA churches and politicians have begun to embrace the idea of closer co-operation between church and state, in Europe, the principle of separation finds growing support among religious sectors.

The European changes often have a common starting point, and this is the formal or informal establishment of one particular church. But even where the recent changes in church and state relations can be perceived as a move away from this starting point, the direction of the changes differ from country to country. While Ireland is ready to make concessions towards pluralism, but is less ready to embrace the spirit of classical liberalism, Greece is inclined to accept the predicaments of individual liberalism, but is reluctant to find room for genuine pluralism.[3]

As the individual contributions to this volume have shown, churches are still in very different positions in the European liberal democracies. In Greece, the Orthodox church is in the position of a quasi public authority vis-à-vis the other churches when it comes to decisions, for example about the construction of religious buildings.[4] As opposed to that, in the Czech Republic the majority church has had to struggle to have its voice heard in political discussions about the status and role of religion in the new post-Communist society.[5] To sum up, in spite of the common pressure towards less discrimination and more religious freedom, different starting points and different directions characterise church–state relations in Europe. Approaches that emphasise path-dependency may be particularly useful in explaining the variance.[6]

EASTERN EUROPE

The fall of the Berlin Wall signalled a new era in the study of church–state relations. Not only did a new region become accessible to researchers, but also new processes and configurations emerged as a result of the post-Communist transition. These processes and configurations refocused attention on questions of freedom of religion and religious equality. After regimes that oppressed and even, on occasion, attempted to suppress religion *tout court*, the new power holders throughout the region often came under pressure to establish a hierarchy of denominations based on historical traditions and on the 'appropriateness' of the present behaviour of the respective churches.

In terms of denominational composition, depth of religiosity and church–state relations, Eastern Europe confronts us with a bewildering complexity. Countries dominated by Catholic, Orthodox, Muslim, or Protestant churches, as well as confessionally mixed nations are found in the region.[7] Some of the most, and some of the least, religious countries of the continent are located here within close proximity to each other. Even the Communist past differs across the region, varying from a relatively high tolerance of church autonomy to exceptionally violent anti-religious and anti-church policies.

The patterns of political-ideological alliance differ too. While in the Catholic and mixed-confession countries there is generally a polarisation between Christian centre-right and anti-clerical left, in the Czech Republic the right is also dominated by secular, even anti-clerical forces. While nationalism, anti-Communism, and clericalism often form a single package, in the Orthodox countries anti-Communism is still not a self-evident part of this ideological pattern and the political space has not broken down into clerical and anti-clerical camps.

The churches in the region are both perpetrators and victims of the discriminatory state policies. After surviving the worst possible discrimination under Communism, they emerged as potentially influential political players, with considerable moral capital. Endowed with this initial advantage, but burdened with the consequences of long decades of suppression, the churches have had to make difficult choices. They had to commit themselves to particular institutional models, and to define their position *vis-à-vis* political actors, especially the political parties. The memory of the repressive anti-religious policies of the previous regime, the search for a new national identity, the need for the establishment of a new church–state model, and the ongoing crisis of political legitimacy often turned religion into a politically divisive factor.

Eastern Europe is a particularly promising area for the research of normative political approaches towards religious equality. While in long-standing democracies the inherited institutional relations between churches and the state are often accepted by the political actors without much critical reflection, in post-Communist countries any particular aspect of regulation must be argued for.[8] There is little space for inertia, even the maintenance of the status quo requires explicit justification. In the course of the political transition the logic of Communist dictatorship was replaced by the principles of democratic universalism and national sovereignty. But the national historical traditions are often at odds with the liberal egalitarian-universalistic principles. The constraining factors, the pre-Communist traditions, the interests of the actors involved, and the expectations of the international environment might point in different directions. The result is most often untidy compromise. But in the course of establishing a balance between these principles, a large number of practical and philosophical issues must be addressed, providing the observer with rich material for understanding the potential relationships between religion and politics.

DENOMINATIONAL DIFFERENCES

The inclusion of Eastern Europe into traditional typologies helps in clarifying the impact of confessional background as well. The impression that is gained from studies on European Union countries is that Catholic and Orthodox domination is not compatible with pluralism.[9] But in Eastern Europe the coexistence of majority Catholic and Orthodox churches with other significant denominations can be analysed in countries such as Hungary, the Czech Republic, Romania, or the Ukraine.

Confessional background is still one of the most powerful predictors of church and state relations. But denominational background must be studied *à la* Rokkan, in conjunction with historical alliances specific to the respective countries.[10] The different attitude of the Catholic Church in Poland and the Czech Republic and the fundamentally different relations between church and state in these countries are not understandable without taking into account the position of the church in the time of nation-formation.

In multiconfessional countries, the conflict potential of religious politics is higher, but it is also more likely that institutionalised practices of tolerance develop. Mono-confessional background, on the other hand, may lead to particularly severe clashes between clerical and anti-clerical forces (Catholicism) or to the development of inner pluralism within the ruling church (Lutheranism, Orthodoxy).[11] Comparing countries of different confessional backgrounds has the methodological benefit of reminding us that the power of churches cannot be measured with a single yardstick across denominations. Catholic churches, having a well-defined social teaching, pay close attention to public policy formation, especially on moral issues, while Orthodox churches focus on community-related issues, and tend to be less concerned with questions of individual morality.

But differences between individual countries even within the Orthodox world are obvious. While the Orthodox churches have generally been politically passive, functioning in symbiosis with sympathetic governments, this has not always been the case. Sometimes, as in Greece, the maintenance of close links with the state requires political mobilisation, and anti-governmental campaigns. The Romanian Orthodox clergy also has a political agenda. For example, it has pressurised the government for an elevated status in the constitution, the reservation of seats for the clergy in the upper chamber, and the maintenance of legal discrimination against homosexuals. Many of its demands are rejected by the government, and the church has even been ordered to return property to the Greek Catholics, a denomination whose legitimate existence is questioned by the Orthodox clergy.[12] Church–state relations are politicised, the stakes are high. But, in accordance with the Orthodox pattern, no open conflict has developed between the church and the state or the church and the various political parties, and no anti-clerical party has been formed.

NATIONAL IDENTITY

National identity, particularly on the peripheries of Europe, is often built around religious values and is linked to church–state regimes as well. Churches provide rituals, unity, and identity for community builders even in the modern world. Denominations differ in their readiness to combine with nationalism, but historical dynamics are as important as denominational differences. Churches with an international spirit can, over time, become national, and the reverse is also true.[13] Nationalism also deserves attention because it is intrinsically related to discrimination among churches. New religious movements are often regarded as 'anti-national', especially when they have a global centre outside the state.

The links between the nation and religion are often recognised, but the implications of these links for church–state relations must be more fully taken into account. These links mean that the logic of nationalism and national identity formation may have a direct impact on church–state relations and even on ecclesiastical structures. For example, ethnic, civic, diaspora, or imperial nationalisms may all require a different church structure as well. The tensions between Constantinople and Athens show that competing understandings of national interests may leave their mark on the power structures within the churches and shape the expectation towards the role of the state in regulating churches.[14]

EUROPEAN INTEGRATION AND GLOBAL GOVERNANCE

Domestic factors are less and less able to account for the dynamics of church and state relations. International NGOs, various European bodies, and the American government are all major players in shaping national patterns, particularly on issues related to discrimination among churches. In the last decade a large number of legislative drafts were prepared in countries like Georgia, Russia, Estonia, and Romania, aimed at restricting the rights of religious minorities. Yet these drafts were all, in the end, withdrawn, modified, or vetoed by the president, largely as a result of international pressure.

The process of globalisation, understood as the growth in economic, legal, cultural, and political interdependence, affects church–state relations in various ways. Accelerated immigration reduces religious homogeneity all over Europe, polarises opinions on the relationship between politics and religion, and leads to the appearance of religious organisations which do not easily fit into existing frameworks.[15] In Europe, the further integration and expansion of the European Union deserves most attention. The norms prevailing in the European Union have an especially great impact on those Eastern European countries that are asking for accession.

The practice of certain states like France and Belgium shows, at the same time, that blacklisting marginal denominations is not at all incompatible with EU membership. The activity of new religious movements is clearly a matter of concern for the European bodies. In 1996, the European Parliament warned member states to be cautious in granting legal status and tax exemption to these new organisations. The Assembly of the Council of Europe also discussed the issue of sects in 1999. The terminological uncertainties and the lack of a neutral language in these debates are telling. One rapporteur emphasised that 'present opinion tries to avoid all kind of ideological considerations and any argument or presupposition of a religious, theological or spiritual nature'. At the same time, he claimed that 'false teachers, dangerous sects and narrow-minded "religious" groups have always tried to pervert the natural sense of people for spiritual values', and warned that there is a new wave of such movements in Europe.[16] The Assembly discouraged nation states from adopting anti-sect legislation, warned against any discrimination of religious minorities, and committed itself to state neutrality. It also recommended the establishment of a European observatory institution to monitor 'groups of a religious, esoteric or spiritual nature'.[17]

The European Union's legal system is constantly challenged by the sharp differences between the member states' regulations on church and state matters, and it usually supports the status quo. As its decisions show, the European Court of Human Rights tolerates establishment, differential treatment of mainstream and peripheral churches, and the denial of 'church' status to certain religious groups. It has also found the banning of Refah, the Islamist Turkish party, acceptable, in spite of the fact that the party, which used to be the largest in the Turkish parliament, played by the rules of democratic competition. Even when state authorities are found to violate the rights of religious groups, the Court, as with its American counterpart, prefers to treat them not as freedom of religion, but as, for example, freedom of speech issues.

OPERATIONALISATION AND CONCEPTUAL CLARIFICATION

Concepts like neutrality, establishment, or erastianism are more at home in historical studies, legal theory, or political philosophy than in empirically oriented comparative politics. The various existing typologies provide us with many insights, but it is a further question whether these analytical concepts are empirically justified. In order to test the validity and reliability of these constructs, we need to break them down into components, and to see whether the various elements subsumed under a specific label hang together as well empirically. A preliminary analysis has distinguished seven major components of church–state relations: privileges attached to state recognition; threshold of state recognition; financial subsidies; discrimination; the general attitude of the state towards religion; church autonomy; and church influence over education.[18] Only after decomposing large concepts in this or in other alternative ways, and only after identifying the empirical indicators, may one hope to find answers to questions such as: Is the type and degree of privilege given to churches (tax exemptions, subsidies, access to public facilities) predictable from the size of the threshold that is required to pass in order to achieve church or recognised-denomination status? Is the amount of financial support given to churches systematically related to the degree of the autonomy of churches? Is there a linear correlation between degree of separation and the state's pro-religious orientation? Is there a positive relationship between the state support provided to religious welfare agencies and educational institutions? Is government support of religion associated with higher levels of control over churches?

A theoretically driven empirical investigation could also reveal whether there is a trade-off between the formal and informal privileging of churches, as the example of Ireland suggests, where formal establishment was unnecessary because of the tremendous informal power of the church. As Kissane shows, in such cases even state neutrality can become a technique for maintaining the social power of the church. The utility of representing dimensions of church and state relations in the form of ordinal scales is demonstrated by Minkenberg's chapter, which shows that church–state regimes are useful as independent variables not only for explaining religious vitality,[19] but for explaining public policy outputs as well.

Church–state regimes are independent variables also in the sense that they shape the self-image of the actors, and thereby determine their behaviour.[20] The way churches perceive their role is important since churches constitute complex organisational phenomena, which may appear in many guises. As stated elsewhere:

> Even within the restricted field of modern Europe, religious bodies (institutions, organisations, groups) have a protean capacity to present themselves vis-à-vis the state in a number of distinct guises, for example:

As providers of 'Truth' (cp. other worldviews and ideologies)
As more or less hierarchically organised bureaucracies
As voluntary associations (cp. stamp collectors or ramblers)
As interest or pressure groups (cp. labour unions)
As public corporations/public utilities (cp. post office or water works)
As institutions or sets of institutions (cp. university)
As states within the state (cp. the military).[21]

The multi-faceted nature of churches raises particularly interesting questions concerning the opposition between private and public. The insistence of churches on retaining or acquiring autonomy, or developing a political agenda, may be particularly contentious when they function as 'para-public' institutions.

A conceptual mapping of church–state relations must be sensitive to the paradoxical nature of these relations, meaning that while they involve two main types of actors, they affect three types of interests: the interests of states, churches, and of non-believers. The third group has often no institutional manifestation, although, in some countries and in some periods, liberal parties, humanist organisations, and various anti-clerical movements fulfil such a role. The complexity of the situation is further increased by the fact that clericalism and religiosity are different social phenomena, and therefore religious but not clerical and clerical but not religious groups may equally exist.

Most typologies of church–state relations, from as early as Weber's discussion of hierocracy and caesaropapism, concentrate on the question of which two institutional actors, church or state, has the upper hand. As the chapters of this volume have shown, the answer to this question is, in many cases, far from obvious. It is often difficult to detect which actor is using the other one.[22] States that were seen at some point as confessional have in retrospect become regarded as party states.[23]

Finally, a conceptual rethinking of church–state relations would need to reassess the validity of market analogies. Regulation, for example, is often regarded as the opposite of competition.[24] But fair competition presupposes a certain level of regulation, therefore the impact of state-determined thresholds on competition needs to be studied empirically

CHURCH STRATEGIES

Today churches are rarely dominant actors in their relationship with the state, but they are not passive subjects of state regulation either. Their political strategies in the context of the twenty-first century need to be systematically analysed.

Neutrality is a central concept in the analysis of church strategies. While states are expected to be religiously neutral, churches are expected to be politically impartial. Although it is rare for religious officials to be constrained in their political activity by law, direct partisan agitation is often seen as incompatible with democratic functioning. At the same time, protests on behalf of marginal groups such as immigrants, or opposition to extremist forces, for example, that of the French clergy's actions against Le Pen, are usually judged differently. Transitions from dictatorship to democracy also provide a context in which democrats expect churches to take a stand. And, indeed, the Southern and Eastern European political transitions have many examples of clergymen playing an instrumental role in the process of democratisation. Churches are part of civil society, and can promote civil virtues even when bound by a hierarchical organisation.[25]

But even churches which accept the basic principles of liberal democracy, like the Spanish Catholic church, may demand constitutional recognition of their primacy in certain cases, and even churches which acquiesce to the reality of church–state separation, like the Polish Catholic Church, may fight against its explicit inclusion in the Constitution.[26] The widespread demand of the churches for the recognition of their own particular role or of religious values contrasts sharply with the laicist demand for maintaining a 'naked public sphere'.

Anderson finds that

> the relationship of the churches to democratisation is shaped by their particular historical relationship with the political order, their perception (or mis-perception) of their political capital, and, in the Catholic case, of the broader attitude to political order, political influence and minority rights of the international institution at the point of transition.[27]

The contrast between Italy and Spain, the first a country where even in the 1990s the church was trying to maintain an organised form of united political Catholicism, and the second a country where the clergy has explicitly rejected the formation of a Christian party,[28] shows that different historical trajectories may undercut the relevance of denominational specificities.

The analysis of the dilemmas churches face over their choice of political strategy may show the untenability of the often invoked presupposition that the churches stand alone and united against the state. In reality, churches may politically be deeply divided and they can create alliances with other churches or with other political actors. The internal cohesion of churches, and their potential for coalition are important factors behind their eventual success in acquiring privileged status. Internal division is not always a drawback. As the Greek example shows, political decentralisation may actually help to maintain the influence of the church.[29]

The coalition possibilities available to mainstream and marginal churches may differ. The established churches, for example, may ally with the secular state against the marginal churches under the banner of anti-cultism. Alternatively, they may ally with the new religious movements against secular forces (including the state), in the form of a religious crusade against atheism, or they may fight both the state and the peripheral churches, in order to defend orthodoxy.

For the churches, it is often a rational strategy to strive for privileged access to the government, instead of engaging in outright competition.[30] But rent-seeking behaviour entails particular costs. Churches that acquire such a status, may find out that their position constrains them and it leads to sub-optimal impact over public policies.[31] In an anti-clerical environment, public ambitions may prove to be detrimental.

Abandoning neutrality towards political actors makes one vulnerable to the results of party competition. In cases where the victory of the friendly parties is uncertain, rational churches should opt for a more neutral strategy. A balanced strategy towards parties may secure privileges better than close association with one of the political actors.[32] A neutral strategy should be especially attractive when the potential ally is weak, as in the case of the Czech Republic.[33]

In spite of the high risks involved, churches often engage in political and partisan struggles. One likely explanation, often overlooked by rational choice approaches, is that churches have other goals than that of preserving their 'market position' or increasing their 'market share'. Often these other goals are strictly political. Clergymen are also political beings, with secular political preferences. The behaviour of the churches is likely to mirror in one way or another these preferences.

In the democratic era, the ability of churches to put pressure on the state depends to a large extent on how skilled they are in mobilising public opinion. As shown, even privileged churches such as the Orthodox church in Greece may need to mobilise the masses and engage in protest action.[34]

THE POLITICAL SYSTEM: PARTY POLITICS AND POLITICAL CULTURE

In modern politics, parties have a direct impact on the status of the churches and on church–state relations. Party politicians have a major say on the sort of church strategies that are acceptable, on what counts as a socially beneficial role, and on whether religious capital is a legitimate resource in every-day politics.[35] The party system, especially the pattern of competition, shapes the optimal strategies of the churches. For example, the transformation of the Italian centre-based party system into a pattern of bipolar competition radically altered the opportunity structure of the church.[36]

Such developments in the party sphere, along with the growing relevance of mass media campaigns and the de-ideologisation of party appeals, may change the weight of churches as potential allies. It is especially important for the options of the churches whether parties preserve their clerical or anti-clerical appeal. In addition, if parties have weak identities, their position on church–state issues may prove to be erratic.[37]

The political weight of churches may increase where governments are struggling with a lack of popular legitimacy.[38] In cartellised party systems churches may exert less leverage, while in the context of intensive competition churches may become much sought after partners or, on the other hand, be ostracised if they scare away voters. The configuration of party competition may determine how badly party leaders need external allies like churches.

The type of democratic regime also shapes the opportunity structure of the churches. While all the analysed countries may be subsumed under the label of liberal democracies, they differ in employing a participatory or a delegative principle. Varying amounts of assistance given to civic society organisations empower churches to different degrees.[39] The state's attitude towards private organisations (how easily the state delegates public functions to these organisations), the prevailing pattern of interest-integration and the degree of corporatism all shape the position of the churches as much as the fate of other institutions, like universities, chambers of commerce, trade unions, or parties.

Equally, it matters whether a regime is organised in elitist or populist ways. The wide use of referenda, for example, may compel churches to actively cultivate their social power, solidifying their position in various social institutions like associations, hospitals, schools, and so on.[40]

The analysis of church–state relations must be integrated into the analysis of democratisation and state-building. Government policies on religious and church matters are good indicators of the state's attitude towards equality, tolerance, pluralism, and freedom of religion, all important building blocks of well functioning democratic regimes. The support given to particular churches, and denied to others, shapes the resources of the social and political groups related to these churches, and thereby influences the outcome of future competitive struggles.

Finally, the outcome of conflicts relating to church and state matters are under the influence of more general patterns of conflict-resolution, such as pillarisation, consociationalism, or adversarial democracy. Practices developed centuries ago often provide a model for the accommodation of new churches as well.[41]

The simultaneous analysis of churches and governmental structures provides a useful complement to rational choice theories, identifying those structural constraints that prevent the elite from acting on the basis of a simple cost–benefit analysis.

CONCLUSIONS

The studies presented in this volume highlight the importance of the political context for the understanding of church–state relationships. The lesson is that specifically political science frameworks are needed for interpreting the dynamics of this field. The relevance of approaches using juridical, historical, economic, or philosophical perspectives is in no way denied. But by drawing analogies between churches and the other subjects of standard political science, like parties or corporations, or by contrasting types of church–state regimes and types of democracy, we may gain insights that the above-mentioned approaches cannot deliver. Both churches and the state are part of the political institutional setting that surrounds us, and therefore they should not be studied in isolation. The relationship between churches and states in Europe is in flux, and only by establishing the links with other sectors of the political system and by identifying the political interests involved are we likely to be able to account for the direction of the changes.

NOTES

1. G. Gustafsson's contribution above on the case of the recent church–state separation in Sweden indicates that large-scale changes also occur in the otherwise most stable corners of Western Europe.
2. G. Robbers, 'State and Church in the European Union', in idem (ed.), *State and Church in the European Union* (Baden-Baden: Nomos 1996), p.325.
3. See Kissane and Mavrogordatos, above.
4. See Mavrogordatos, above.
5. See O'Mahony, above.
6. See Madeley, 'European Liberal Democracy and the Principle of State Religious Neutrality', above.
7. See Madeley, 'A Framework for the Comparative Analysis of Church-State Relations in Europe', above.
8. See Enyedi, above.
9. See D. Martin, *A General Theory of Secularization* (Oxford: Blackwell 1978), pp.18–19.
10. See Madeley, 'Framework', above.
11. See ibid.
12. L. Stan and L. Turcescu, 'The Romanian Orthodox Church and Post-Communist Democratization', *Europe-Asia Studies* 52/8 (2000), pp.1467–88; and O. Gillet, *Religie si nationalism* (Bucuresti: Compania 2001).
13. See Mavrocordatos, above.
14. See ibid.
15. Robbers, 'State and Church in the European Union', pp.323–33.
16. Council of Europe, 20 April 1999, doc. 8379.
17. Recommendation on 'Illegal activities of sects' of the Parliamentary Assembly of the European Council, 1412/1999, accepted 1999 June 22.
18. Z. Enyedi *et al.*, 'The Structure and Dynamics of Church–State Relations in Europe', Plan of a collaborative research project.
19. L. Iannaccone, 'The Consequences of Religious Market Structure', *Rationality and Society*, 2 (1991), pp.156–77; L. Iannaccone, 'Introduction to the Economics of Religion', *Journal of Economic Literature*, 9 (1998), pp.1465–96; L. Iannaccone, R. Finke and R. Stark 'Deregulating Religion: The Economics of Church and State', *Economic Inquiry* 4 (1997), pp.350–64; R. Stark and L. Iannaccone 'A Supply-Side Reinterpretation of the "Secularization" of Europe', *Journal for the Scientific Study of Religion* 3 (1994), pp.230–52.
20. See Minkenberg, above.
21. See Z. Enyedi *et al.*, 'The Structure of Church–State Relations'. Unpublished paper outlining plans for a collaborative research project (Barcelona: ECPR Research Group Sessions, November 2000).
22. See Enyedi.
23. See Donovan.
24. M. Chaves and D.E. Cann, 'Regulation, Pluralism, and Religious Market Structure. Explaining Religion's Vitality', *Rationality and Society* 4/3 (1992), pp.272–90.
25. See O'Mahony, above.
26. See Anderson, above.
27. Ibid.
28. See Donovan and Anderson, above.
29. See Mavrogordatos, above.
30. A. Gill, 'Rendering unto Caesar? Religious Competition and Catholic Political Strategy in Latin America, 1962–79', *American Journal of Political Science* 2/403–25 (1994), p.406.
31. See Minkenberg, above.
32. A. Kilp, 'Religion Enters Politics: The Process of Politicization of Religious Issues in Four Post-Communist Countries' (MA Thesis, University of Tartu 2002).
33. See O'Mahony, above.

34. See Mavrogordatos, above.
35. See Enyedi, above.
36. See Donovan, above.
37. See O'Mahony, above.
38. See Enyedi, above.
39. See O'Mahony, above.
40. See Kissane, above.
41. S. Monsma and J.C. Soper, *The Challenge of Pluralism. Church and State in Five Democracies* (Lanham, MD: Rowman & Littlefield 1997), p.62.

Abstracts

European Liberal Democracy and the Principle of State Religious Neutrality, *by John T.S. Madeley*

Over the last 30 years political philosophers of a liberal persuasion have developed a doctrine which mandates the neutrality of the state in matters of religion, yet nowhere in Europe have its requirements been fully realised in practice. In a majority of the approximately 50 cases, the state is committed either *de jure* or *de facto* to the support of religious organisations and their aims. In some cases the justification takes the form of a commitment to a positive, or equal treatment, version of neutrality, while in others inherited patterns of discrimination have simply not been addressed. At a time of increasing religious pluralism everywhere, associated with both immigration and the development of new religious movements, state religious non-neutrality is more and more experienced as problematic.

A Framework for the Comparative Analysis of Church–State Relations in Europe, *by John T.S. Madeley*

Stein Rokkan's sequential model of state-, nation-, and cleavage-formation in Western Europe provides a useful starting-point for developing a framework for the comparative analysis of church–state relations in Europe as a whole. Such an exercise necessitates extending his conceptual map spatially so as to include Eastern Europe and temporally so as to take account of a 'critical juncture' long pre-dating the Reformation, namely, the division between Latin and Eastern Orthodox Christianity almost 1,000 years ago. An examination of current data on religious adherence reveals the continued existence of three historic mono-confessional blocs (Orthodox, Catholic and Lutheran) with two intervening multi-confessional belts of territory. In each of these it is hypothesized that quite distinctive patterns of church–state relations will be found as the different confessional traditions have reacted to the challenges and opportunities of both monopoly and minority settings.

Church–State Separation Swedish-style, *by Göran Gustafsson*

A more than 40-year-long process came to an end when relations between the Church of Sweden and the state were formally changed in the year 2000. Social Democrats and Liberals had taken the initiative in the 1950s. Several proposals for disestablishment were put forward in the 1970s, but none of them achieve political consensus. In addition, the representatives for all the political parties on the elected parochial church councils opposed every change, whereas the clergy often took a more positive view. Only in the 1990s did the political and the ecclesiastical systems finally agree a settlement that gave the Church of Sweden a greater degree of liberty. Even so, a Law for the Church of Sweden still defines the framework for the structures and work of the church.

The Illusion of State Neutrality in a Secularising Ireland, *by Bill Kissane*

Ireland is frequently cited as a case of church–state separation and state religious neutrality, but an examination of the 1937 constitution, and efforts to amend it, indicates that the Irish state has never been neutral when it comes to religion. On the other hand, if neutrality can be construed as the state regulating the affairs of different religious communities in an even-handed way, recent trends suggest that the Irish state is moving towards a position of 'religious neutrality', even if this falls far short of what liberals would demand. Indeed neutrality as practised in the Irish context precludes any separation of church and state and actually reinforces the position of the Catholic Church. As such there seems to be a weak relationship between the wider process of secularisation and Irish state policy.

Catholicism and Democratic Consolidation in Spain and Poland, *by John Anderson*

During the 'third wave' of democratisation, Catholic churches often played a key role in undermining the old authoritarian regimes. In the subsequent process of consolidation, however, these same organisations have often struggled to find a role. This article explores how the Spanish and Polish Catholic churches coped with the political changes following democratisation, focusing in particular on two issues. Firstly, their pursuit of constitutional and legal recognition in the new order and secondly, their interventions in the political arena and the difficulties they faced in lobbying whilst avoiding the charge of seeking privilege.

Orthodoxy and Nationalism in the Greek Case, *by George Th. Mavrogordatos*

The superiority and precedence of religion as a primordial line of national demarcation deserves a far more central place in theories of nationalism. This is demonstrated by the Greek case, which also illustrates the evolution of the Eastern Orthodox Church over the centuries, from ecumenism to nationalism. Both as a state church and as a national church, the Orthodox Church of Greece has a lot in common with Protestant state churches, and even with Catholicism in some countries. Like Ireland or Israel, however, the Greek case indicates that, as long as a particular religion continues to be identified with an 'endangered' nation, change in the direction of pluralism is even less probable than separation between church and state. Among Christian denominations, what may indeed be specific to Orthodoxy is a traumatic and defensive historical consciousness reaching into a far more distant past, but also fuelled by current insecurity.

The Italian State. No Longer Catholic, No Longer Christian, *by Mark Donovan*

Church–state relations in Italy have concerned the role of the Catholic Church in the failure of successive regimes to consolidate themselves and a triangular relationship involving the Christian Democrat (DC) party between 1943 and 1994. Despite a historic ambivalence about Christian Democracy, the church supported the party not least because of its concern about the challenge of the Communist Party. By the 1970s, the church was engaged in redefining its position vis-à-vis the state, leading to the renegotiation of the 1929 concordat in 1984. The demise of the DC in 1994 finally broke the myth of Catholic political unity.

The Catholic Church and Civil Society: Democratic Options in the Post-Communist Czech Republic, *by Joan O' Mahony*

In 1989, religious organisations in Czechoslovakia were liberated from 40 years of oppressive control under the Communist regime. Contrary to expectations, however, a decade of Czech democracy has failed to see the emergence of a stable relationship between the state and the Catholic Church. The cultural legacies of Communism, in particular a historic anti-Catholicism, are commonly held to be the causal factors. A different argument is developed here, namely, that opposing preferences for democracy, pursued within the structural consequences of the 'transition', have a greater impact on the present situation.

The Contested Politics of Positive Neutrality in Hungary, *by Zsolt Enyedi*

States treat churches differently even where legal frameworks stipulate neutrality. Next to demographic and historic factors, the differences between the statuses of the churches can best be explained by the dynamics of contemporary politics. The article shows that differences between the Hungarian churches in terms of their level of privilege are related to their interactions with political actors and to their own political actions. Hungarian churches are deeply politicised: they are deeply affected by political conflict and often become players in the political field. Although they are granted privileges by the state in return for the legitimacy they provide, the space for the provision of religious legitimacy is, itself, largely created by the politicians.

The Policy Impact of Church–State Relations: Family Policy and Abortion in Britain, France, and Germany, *by Michael Minkenberg*

This study tests the proposition that patterns of church–state relations have an impact on public policy outputs by examining family policy and abortion regimes in Britain, France, and Germany. Between them, these three large countries exemplify the three main types of church–state relations, as identified in conventional accounts. The study concludes that the different patterns of church–state relations thus identified provide only a limited match with policy outputs while other, more developed typologies improve the match, particularly when other cultural and political variables are factored in. The dynamics of influence are found to differ as between contexts where churches operate as public institutions (as in Britain and Germany) and where (as in the French case) they operate as interest groups.

Conclusion: Emerging Issues in the Study of Church–State Relations, by Zsolt Enyedi

A survey of the foregoing contributions suggests eight areas of investigation into church–state relations in Europe which remain ripe for further research. This conclusion lists and attempts to outline them in a way which does justice to the complexity of the structures and dynamics concerned as they continue to evolve particularly but not exclusively in those societies which are still currently undergoing processed of transition to full liberal democracy. It links them to some of the wider concerns which have occupied the attention of political scientists in recent years.

Notes on Contributors

John Anderson is Senior Lecturer and Chairman of the Department of International Relations at the University of St Andrews. His research interests lie in post-Soviet politics, in particular political change in Central Asia, and in religion and politics. His publications include *Religion, State and Politics in the Soviet Union and the Successor States* (1994) and *The Politics of Religion in Transitional Polities* (forthcoming).

Mark Donovan is a Senior Lecturer in the School of European Studies, Cardiff University. He is editor of *Modern Italy*. Recent publications include the two-volume reader *'Italy'* (1998); *Changing Party Systems in Western Europe* (1998, co-edited with D. Broughton); and *Writing National Histories. Western Europe since 1800* (1999, co-edited with S. Berger and K. Passmore).

Zsolt Enyedi is Assistant Professor at the Political Science Department of the Central European University. His research is focused on party politics, pillarisation, religion and politics and authoritarianism. His publications include *Politics in the Shadow of the Cross* (1998) and *Authoritarianism and Prejudice* (1999, co-edited with F. Erős).

Göran Gustafsson has just retired from a Chair in the Sociology of Religion at the Theological Faculty, Lund University, Sweden. His research interests include the relation between religion and politics and aspects of the secularisation process in Sweden. He has led several co-Nordic research programmes. Recent publications include *Folkkyrkor och religiös pluralism – den nordiska religiösa modellen (National Churches and Religious Pluralism – the Nordic Religious Model)* (2000, with Thorleif Pettersson).

Bill Kissane is a Lecturer in the Department of Government at the London School of Economics, where he took his Ph.D. in 1998 He is an expert on

Irish and comparative politics and is currently working on a study of the Irish Civil War. He recently published *Explaining Irish Democracy* (2002).

John T.S. Madeley is a Lecturer in the Department of Government at the London School of Economics. He writes on the government and politics of the Nordic countries and on religion and politics, particularly in Europe. He recently published the reader *Religion and Politics* in the Ashgate series: International Library of Politics and Comparative Government (2002).

George Th. Mavrogordatos is Professor of Political Science at the University of Athens. His books include *Stillborn Republic* (1983), for which he received the Woodrow Wilson Foundation Award of the American Political Science Association. Most recently, he has published (in Greek) a book entitled *Pressure Groups and Democracy*.

Michael Minkenberg is Professor of Political Science at the European University Viadrina, Frankfurt (Oder), Germany. His research interests are comparative right-wing radicalism and the relationship between religion and democracy. He is author of *Die neue radikale Rechte im Vergleich. USA, Frankreich, Deutschland* (1998).

Joan O' Mahony is a Ph.D. candidate in the Sociology Department at the London School of Economics. Her research interests are civil society and democratisation in Eastern Europe, and the role of civil society in regulating business risks.

Index

abortion *195–217*; Ireland 73, 81–6; Italy 99, 103; Poland 145, 149; Spain 140, 143; USA 6; and the Vatican 96, 149
Act of Settlement 3
Albania 15, 47, 128–9, 180
Anderson, B. 117
Anglicanism 14; and Catholicism 38, 81; Church of Ireland 81, 88; decline 203; in different parts of UK 32, 45, 47; national identity 118; political role 3–4, 210
anti-clericalism 25, 35, 139, 204, 226, 228–9; Eastern Europe 157, 161–2, 167, 220; and mono-confessionalism 37, 39, 102, 222
Arendt, H. 177
Armenia 34, 38, 119
Augsburg, Peace of 34, 43
Australia 134, 198, 201
Austria 26, 37, 44, 118, 198–9
Austro-Hungarian Empire 182

Baptism 51–3, 159
Barbier, M. 198–200
Barrett, D. 11–15
Barry, B. 18
Beaulieu, Edict of 33
Belgium 38, 118, 198–200, 224
bioethics 96, 112
blasphemy 87, 122
Bohemia 32, 43–4
Bosnia 17, 34, 118, 158
Bulgaria 14, 38, 127–8, 132, 151
Byzantine Empire 43, 124, 127, 131, 133

Calvinism: and Catholicism 38, 45, 118, 172; and the Holy Roman Empire 43; Hungary 158–9, 163–6, 168, 170, 172; mono-confessionalism 38; nationalism 119, 164, 166; United Protestant Church 46

Canada 201
Cann, D.E. 199, 201, 204, 207
Canterbury, Archbishop of 3, 19n. 11
Casanova, J. 2, 173, 197, 206, 209, 213
Castles, F. 205
Catholicism: and Calvinism 45; Czech Republic *177–94*; France 204, 209–11, 214; Germany 202, 212; as a global organisation 119; Greece 123, 128, 133, 159, 222; and the Holy Roman Empire 43–4; Hungary 158–9, 161, 163, 165–8, 170, 172; Ireland 14, 32, 73, 75–7, 130, 201; Italy *95–116*; Latin, use of 41; and Lutheranism 45, 51; mono-confessionalism 27–32, 36–9, 220–21; multi-confessionalism 33, 35, 220; and national interests 161; Netherlands 45; and the Orthodox Church 26, 40, 125, 133; Poland 2, 130, *144–56*, 222, 227; Scandinavia 37; schism 25; society, close relations with 42; Spain 137–44, 227; Sweden 51–2; Switzerland 45; Western Europe 25. *see also* papacy
censorship 76, 85, 149
Chadwick, H. 47
Chaves, M. 199, 201, 204, 207
Christodoulos, Archbishop 123–4, 130–31
Church of England, *see* Anglican Church
church–state separation, *see* separation of church and state
civil society 92, *177–94*
cleavages 41; religious 25, 44–5, 82, 125, 128, 157
Colombia 197
Communism: anti-Catholicism 182–3; anti-Communism 127, 137, 146, 152, 164; collapse 1, 23, 48, 104, 148, 158, 179, 187, 220–21; Czech Republic 179–80, 182–4, 187; Greece 127, 134; Hungary 159–160, 164; Italy 99, 101, 104, 109;

Poland 137, 144, 146, 148, 152, 154;
Spain 141
Concordats 1, 98, 103, 139, 141, 146–7
confessional state 9, 27, 31, 34, 51, 226;
constitutional aspects 100, 102, 111, 140;
and inclusiveness 36–7; and the Lateran
Pacts 100; legal apparatus 36; and
repression 42–3, 46. *see also*
establishment; mono-confessionalism;
multi-confessionalism
Congregation of the Faith 163
conscientious objectors 122, 160
consociationalism 44–5
Constantine, Emperor 10, 124
constitutions 13, 152, 197, 199, 205, 227;
Colombia 197; Czech Republic 178,
180; France 204; Germany 197, 202,
211; Greece 121; Hungary 161, 173;
Ireland 14, 74–83, 92, 197; Italy 111;
Poland 145–6, 151, 182, 227; Romania
222; Spain 140–42, 151, 227 Sweden 52;
USA 7, 14, 140
contraception 76, 81, 85
Counter-Reformation, *see* Reformation
Crouch, C. 2
cults, *see* new religious movements
Cyprus 2, 129
Czech Republic 15, 32, *177–94*, 219–22, 228

Davie, G. 23
de Valera, Eamon 80, 90, 92
Denmark 125, 198–200
divorce: legislation 76, 78–9, 81, 85, 103,
140–41; opposition to 82, 143;
referenda 73–4, 84, 87, 99, 102–4
Dryzek, J.S. 191

education: clerical control 75, 78; as measure
of church–state relations 225; minority
religious schools 89; religious education
and the syllabus 53,98, 103, 111–12,
145, 149, 170, 202; and religious
neutrality 75, 87–8, 91, 109, 162, 203;
the state and faith schools 1, 92, 96, 143,
162, 168, 180, 204
Eisenstadt, S.N. 177, 186
Elizabeth II, Queen 2
Enlightenment 47
equality, religious 153, 157, 167, 220, 230.
see also freedom, religious; toleration,
religious
Eser, A. 208
establishment 27, 37–8, 43, 134, 162, 195,
199, 201–3, 206, 209, 213, 219, 228;
'creeping' 149; disestablishment 17–18;
'formal' 123; France 204, 210, 214;

Germany 204, 211, 214; Greece 123; and
human rights 224; Hungary 169;
Ireland 77, 209, 225; Islam 123;
Orthodox 124, 127; 'partial' 203, 205,
207, 209–12, 214; Poland 149;
Russia 36; Scandinavia 209;
Spain 140–41; Sweden 51, 54–6, 62, 70;
United Kingdom 3–4, 32, 45, 47, 210,
212, 214. *see also* confessional state;
mono-confessionalism
Estonia 34, 223

fascism 98, 113
Finke, R. 37
Finland 14, 44, 49n. 17, 198–200
Flora, P. 26, 41
'folk church' 54, 61, 63
Formigoni, G. 99
France 1, 8, 37–8, 46, 129, *195–217*, 224,
227; Alsace-Lorraine 14, 199, 204;
Revolution 24, 41, 47
Franco, General 137, 139
Free Churches 53–4, 58
freedom, religious: and church–state
relations 123, 127, 198, 203, 230;
declining relevance of 157; European
Union 195; and human rights 147, 151,
167, 197, 223–4; and national
interests 142; political perspectives on
179; and post-Communism 1–2, 220;
public policy 205; and state neutrality
130, 173. *see also* equality, religious;
toleration, religious fundamentalism 82,
100, 107

Georgia 132, 223
Germany 8, 15, 17, 45, 119, *195–217*;
Brandenburg 202; Prussia 38, 46, 49n
29, 118; Saxony 46
Ghent, Pacification of 33
Glemp, Cardinal 144, 146, 148, 150, 152
Greece 117–36, 151, 198–9, 201, 205, 222,
228; liberalism and pluralism 219
Gregory V, Patriarch 126

Hadjiisky, M. 178
Hapsburgs 183
Hinduism 119
Holmes, L. 191
Holy Roman Empire 34, 43–5
homosexuality 77, 85, 222
Hoxha, Enver 47
human rights 2, 142, 147, 151, 197, 224;
European Convention on Human
Rights 3, 27, 120
Hume, Cardinal 210

Hungary 44, 157–76, 178, 182, 221
Huntington, S. 1
Hutterites 33

Iannacone, L.R. 37
immigration 18, 39, 58, 96, 205, 223
Industrial Revolution 24
Inquisition, Spanish 42
Iran 119
Ireland 73–94; church–state
    relations 198–201, 209, 213, 225;
    liberalism and pluralism 74, 219;
    nationalism and national identity 75, 77,
    117, 119, 130, 134; religious
    minorities 43; resistance to Anglicanism
    32, 38
Ireland, Northern, see United Kingdom
Islam 1, 14; Balkans 15, 34, 118, 128–9;
    Eastern Europe 220; Greece 121, 123,
    128–9, 131–2; and human rights 197;
    Hungary 159; Iran 119; Ireland 87; Italy
    103; Shiism 119; Spain 37, 42
Israel 134
Italy 1, 95–116, 198–200, 227

Japan 205
Jehovah's Witnesses 103, 122, 170
Jogaila of Lithuania, Grand Duke 10
Juan Carlos, King of Spain 140
Judaism 10, 14; anti-semitism 165;
    diaspora 132; France 204; Germany 202;
    Greece 123, 129, 132; Hungary 158,
    164; Israel 132; Italy 103; and national
    identity 119; in the Ottoman Empire 42;
    Spain 37; and the Vatican 165

Kalyvas, S.N. 95, 97
Kant, Immanuel 5, 56
Katzenstein, P. 206
Kepel, G. 2
Kosovo 15
Kymlicka, W. 5–6
Küng, H. 40

Lateran Pacts 97, 100
Latvia 34, 158
law: church law 78, 86, 147, 182; legal
    recognition of churches 199; penal law
    3, 32, 36, 46–7. see also constitutions
liberalism: and abortion 208–10; and anti-
    Communism 164; Catholic 100;
    differences between USA and Europe 8;
    Italian, collapse of 95; and nationalism
    99, 164, 166; and pluralism 74, 219; and
    religious education 111; and religious
    neutrality 5, 8, 18

Lijphart, A. 45, 206–7
Linz, J. 152
Lithuania 34
Locke, John 5
Lutheranism 14, 36, 39, 158–9, 163, 165–6,
    204, 222; and Catholicism 45, 51; and
    the Holy Roman Empire 43; mono-
    confessionalism 27–32, 36; multi-
    confessionalism 33, 35; and
    nationalism 119; United Protestant
    Church 46
Luxembourg 198–9

Macedonia 158
Mack, E. 6
Makarios, Archbishop 129
Martin, Cardinal González 141
Martin, D. 10, 23, 25
Marx, Karl 56
Mennonites 33
Messner, F. 199–201
Methodism 52–4, 160
Milan, Edict of 10
Mill, John Stuart 5
'millet' system 41–3, 124, 128
minority religions 89
Misovic, J. 182
modernisation 201
mono-confessionalism 26–42, 44, 222; and
    conservatism 37. see also confessional
    state; establishment monopoly,
    religious 37, 42, 46, 122, 140, 160, 219
Monsma, S. 7–8, 91, 197–8, 201–2
Montenegro 15
Moravia 33, 43
Mount Athos 131
multi-confessionalism 26, 32–5, 42–4, 48,
    158, 220, 222
multiculturalism 1, 18, 23, 39, 70, 96, 223;
    education 89
Mussolini, Benito 97, 113

Nantes, Edict of 37, 46
nationalism: and anti-Communism 220; and
    clericalism 220; and discrimination 223;
    Greece 117–36; Hungary 164, 166, 171;
    Ireland 75; Italy 99–100; Poland 144,
    151; Spain 139, 151
NATO 133
Nazarenes 160
Netherlands 8, 38, 44–5, 118–19, 130, 178,
    198, 200–201
neutrality, religious 17–18; and
    Catholicism 114, 148; Hungary 157–76;
    Ireland 73–94; and multi-confessionalism
    44, 48; normative principles of 4–8; and

politics 95, 107, 227–8; 'positive' 198,
202; usefulness of the concept 224–5.
see also separation of church and state
new religious movements 2, 18, 39, 142,
157–8, 171, 223–4, 228
New Zealand 201
Nonconformism 36, 39
Northern Ireland, *see* United Kingdom
Norway 23, 200

Orbán, Prime Minister
Orthodox Church 14, *117–36*, 219–22; and
Catholicism 26, 38–40, 103, 125, 133;
mono-confessionalism 27–32, 36, 38;
multi-confessionalism 35, 44; schism 25;
Ottoman Empire 26, 34, 38, 41–3, 118, 124,
127–8, 131, 133

Pace, E. 100
papacy 98–101, 105, 107, 119, 125, 131,
146–7, 151, 204, 212; caesar-papism 42;
John Paul II 104, 107, 114, 134, 141,
143–4, 150, 165; John XXIII 102; Paul
VI 104; Pius IX 97; Pius X 97; Pius
XII 100–101; Second Vatican Council
102–4, 113, 137, 139, 152, 157
Pehe, J. 185
Poland 38, 44, *144–56*, 227; mono-
confessionalism 32; nationalism and
national identity 117–19, 130; religious
decline 2; religious toleration 43, 47,
49n. 29; and the Ukraine 34
political parties, religious: and church–state
cleavages 44; constraints on 227; Czech
Republic 184–5, 188; Germany 45;
Greece 127; and human rights 224;
Hungary 163–4, 166, 168; Italy 95–8,
100, 102, 104–11, 113; Poland 147–8; in
public policy studies 205–6; Spain 142
Portugal 198–200, 209
Presbyterianism 47, 203
Protestantism 14, 26; and Catholicism 38, 45;
and conservatism 207; Eastern Europe
220; France 37; minorities 44; mono-
confessionalism 37, 41, 47; and national
interests 161; and nationalism 119, 130;
and the privatisation of religion 42;
Spain 37; state support for 46

Rawls, J. 5–6
Raz, J. 5
Reformation 24, 32–3, 41–2, 47, 125, 159,
195
Reformed Churches 166, 204
Rémond, R. 41
Robbers, G. 113, 198–201

Robertson, R. 200
Rokkan, S. 23, 25–6, 33–4, 41, 44, 221
Roman Empire 9–10, 24, 42
Romania 17, 38, 43, 47, 132, 165, 221–3
Russia: Bolshevism 47; Empire 26, 34, 42,
49n. 29; mono-confessionalism 38, 130,
132; religious revival 2; suppression of
religious freedoms 17, 151, 180, 223;
Tsarist control of Church 36, 46

Scandinavia 37, 39, 119, 130, 195, 201, 209
schism 11, 39; Great Schism of 1054 25, 124
Scientology 1
sects: and church 36; control of 147; legal
recognition 199, 224; and religious
toleration 2; suppression of 33, 43, 48,
122, 142
secularisation 1–2, 8, 54, 73, 138, 144, 157,
196–7, 199, 201, 219
secularism 38–9, 132, 154
separation of church and state: concepts 195,
197–9, 205, 213; and education 202–3;
Europe 219; and family policy 207;
France 204; Germany 203; Greece 120,
125–6; Hungary 167–8; Ireland 90, 92;
Italy 103; Poland 145–6; and public
policy 196; and religious political
interests 209; risks for church 125;
Spain 140; and state religious
orientation 42, 119, 225; Sweden 51–72;
USA 7, *see also* neutrality, religious
Serbia 15, 127, 130, 132, 134
Slovakia 178, 182
Smith, A.D. 117
Socialism 101–2, 105, 113, 143, 150, 166,
169
Soper, J.C. 7–8, 91, 197–8, 201–2
Soviet Union 15
Spain 42, 137–45, 147, 149, 198–9, 227
Stark, C. 197
state church, *see* establishment
state–church separation, *see* separation of
church and state
Stepan, A. 152
Sweden 17, 34, 51–72, 198–200
Switzerland 33, 44–5, 118, 200

Tarancón, Archbishop 137, 139–40, 142
toleration, religious 2, 53, 55, 76, 97, 121–2,
158–9, 230; and the confessional
state 38–9, 42–3; early experiments
in 33, 43, 47, 49n. 29; Holy Roman
Empire 44; Reformation period 47, *see
also* equality, religious; freedom,
religious
Turkey 129, 131, 133

Ukraine 221
Uniate Church 34
Unitarianism 159
United Kingdom 1–4, 45, 134, *195–217*;
    England 38, 45, 130, 198, 210; Northern
    Ireland 2, 45; Scotland 45, 47, 203, 210
USA 1, 6–8, 14, 37, 48, 140, 198, 201, 204,
    219

Vatican, *see* papacy
Vlk, Cardinal 182
von Beyme, K. 196

Walzer, M. 48
Weber, Max 226
welfare state 112–13
Westphalia, Peace of 32, 34, 36
Wilensky, H. 206–7
Willaime, J.P. 209

Yugoslavia 2, 15, 32, 34, 133

Zippelius, R. 197